A POETICS OF PLOT FOR THE TWENTY-FIRST CENTURY

THEORY AND INTERPRETATION OF NARRATIVE
James Phelan, Peter J. Rabinowitz, and Katra Byram, Series Editors

A POETICS OF PLOT FOR THE TWENTY-FIRST CENTURY

THEORIZING UNRULY NARRATIVES

BRIAN RICHARDSON

THE OHIO STATE UNIVERSITY PRESS
COLUMBUS

Copyright © 2019 by The Ohio State University.
All rights reserved.

Library of Congress Cataloging-in-Publication Data is available online at catalog.loc.gov.

Cover design by Laurence J. Nozik
Text design by Juliet Williams
Type set in Adobe Minion Pro

To Claudine, for everything

CONTENTS

Preface		ix
Acknowledgments		xiii
INTRODUCTION	Mimetic and Antimimetic Narrative Dynamics	1
CHAPTER 1	Narrative, the Nonnarrative, and the Unnarratable	13
CHAPTER 2	Modeling Narrative Beginnings	37
CHAPTER 3	Narrative Middles I: Plot, Probability, and Tellability	59
CHAPTER 4	Narrative Middles II: Non-Plot-Based Narrative Progressions	83
CHAPTER 5	The Varieties of Narrative Time	99
CHAPTER 6	Adventures of the Book: Fabricating Fabula and Syuzhet	127
CHAPTER 7	Narrative Endings: Fixed, Unfixed, Illusory, and Unnatural	149
CONCLUSION	Narrative Theory and the Poetics of Story and Plot	169
Works Cited		175
Index		191

PREFACE

STATED MOST SIMPLY, this book is intended to offer a comprehensive account of story and plot that is able to include the achievements and challenges of postmodern and other experimental poetics. Most existing accounts of story and plot do a good job of accounting for more realistic kinds of narrative progression, but they are often unable to manage the many innovative treatments of emplotment, endings, temporality, and story construction that have been developed by contemporary authors. In addition to these more familiar aspects of narrative theory, this book also takes up the intimately related but comparatively understudied topics of narrative beginnings, narrative sequencing, and non-plot-based narrative progressions. Examining these aspects of recent works often allows us to excavate similar practices that occurred earlier in the history of narrative fiction and drama—stretching back to the ancient Greeks—as what seem to be distinctively postmodern narrative strategies often turn out to be recent manifestations of narrative constructions with a much older pedigree.

The primary purpose of this book is thus to examine, extend, and supplement existing narrative theory to enable it to do justice to the profusion of postmodern and avant-garde texts that currently elude many existing formulations. In most chapters, I will begin with a brief discussion of recent critical accounts, after which I will often make the case for one position or another. After discussing some salient examples, I will outline how existing theoretical formulations can be modified to better model a greater range of texts, both pre- and postmodern. Depending on the subject, some chapters will be concerned primarily with postmodern examples; others, with relatively few.

Each chapter will have a slightly different relation to the existing body of narrative theory. The first chapter, on narrative, confines itself largely to existing conceptions, which I feel are mostly adequate, and argues in favor of one of the well-established definitions of narrative. I do try to extend this conception in a few ways and propose the category of the "quasi narrative," but for the most part I am satisfied with most items in the existing narratological toolbox for this subject. The chapter on non-plot-based forms of narrative sequencing, however, covers important material that narrative theory has not incorporated. Thus I am required to assemble a set of new concepts, categories, and terms; the chapter is much more in dialogue with the work of particular critics and specialized literary historians than it is with narrative theorists. Other chapters have still other relations to current narratological accounts: my work on beginnings refers to the very few studies of the subject that we have, while my discussion of endings draws on and attempts to extend the work of D. A. Miller and J. Hillis Miller and argues against theorists like Peter Brooks and Tzvetan Todorov. At the same time, I include discussions of several kinds of unnatural closure that have largely been neglected in narratological circles.

As is perhaps only appropriate for a volume on this subject, I have designed the book so that it can be read in different sequences: I have made the chapters largely independent so that each can be read in isolation from the others; readers are thus free to determine the order of their encounter with the text. Since some works by a few authors (Beckett, Robbe-Grillet, Ana Castillo) present interesting questions in several areas—beginnings, sequencing, time, and endings—they are mentioned in several chapters. I hope that any repeated statements of distinctive features of the texts will not excessively annoy a linear reader who moves from the first page to the last, even as this framework strives to give the hopscotching reader more possibilities for different kinds of engagement.

It will no doubt be useful for me to situate this book in relation to my other work in narrative theory. My first book, *Unlikely Stories: Causality and the Nature of Modern Narrative*, is primarily about fictional worlds; its emphasis is on characters' interpretations of the kind of universe they inhabit and the laws—supernatural, naturalistic, chance, or metafictional—that govern its causal setting. My next monograph, *Unnatural Voices*, explored and analyzed a large range of unusual and impossible narrators and acts of narration. This present book moves on to the stories themselves, how they are fabricated and how they unfold, and thus presents another base or pillar in an interconnected account of fictional worlds, narration, and story. In the jointly authored volume *Narrative Theory: Core Concepts and Current Debates,* David Herman, James Phelan and Peter Rabinowitz (together), Robyn Warhol, and I each provide a condensed overview of our positions on several subjects: authors and narrators, story and temporality, narrative space, characters, readers and reception, and narrative and aesthetic value. I have also put together a volume that elucidates the general theory and outlines the history of what I call antimimetic or unnatural narratives: *Unnatural Narrative: History, Theory, and Practice.* My future work will engage with the theory of character.

ACKNOWLEDGMENTS

I HAVE WORKED on this book over many years, and several people have provided valuable assistance over that time. Those who have been particularly helpful in reading pages and discussing ideas include Porter Abbott, Lars Bernaerts, Shang Biwu, Bohumil Fořt, Melba Cuddy-Keane, David Herman, Luc Herman, Emma Kafalenos, Suzanne Keen, Brian McHale, Sylvie Patron, Ellen Peel, John Pier, Gerald Prince, David Richter, Catherine Romagnolo, Philippe Roussin, Eyal Segal, Dan Shen, Roy Sommer, Leona Toker, Bart Vervaeck, Robyn Warhol, and Katherine Weese. Special thanks go out to unnatural narrative theorists and fellow travelers Jan Alber, Stefan Iversen, Maria Mäkela, and Henrik Skov Nielsen, who have done so much to help me clarify and extend my thinking on these matters. I wish to offer particular thanks to Jim Phelan and Peter Rabinowitz, who have provided long hours of engaged, helpful, and often frankly brilliant editing, and whose comments, suggestions, and concerns have clearly made this a superior book. I thank the Freiburg Institute for Advanced Study (FRIAS), University of Freiburg, Germany, for a fellowship that allowed me to work on this book during the spring of 2017. The research leading to the completion of this book was also funded by the People Programme (Marie Curie Actions) of the European Union's Seventh Framework Programme. I am very grateful for a RASA grant from the University of Maryland's College of Arts and Humanities which also helped enable me to finish the volume. I deeply thank my department chairs, Kent Cartwright, William Cohen, and Amanda Bailey, for their support of my work in general and of this project in particular. I particularly wish to thank Monika Fludernik, who helped me in a number of ways before and during my stay in Freiburg.

Parts of this book have previously appeared in other publications. Most of chapter 2 is reproduced from *Narrative Beginnings: Theories and Practices*, edited by Brian E. Richardson by permission of the University of Nebraska Press. Copyright 2008 by the Board of Regents of the University of Nebraska. Earlier versions of several sections of chapter 3 appeared first in an article titled "Story, Plot, and Narrative Progression" in *Teaching Narrative Theory*, edited by David Herman, Brian McHale, and James Phelan pp. 109–22, published by the Modern Language Association in 2010; it is reprinted by permission of copyright owner, the Modern Language Association of America. An earlier version of chapter 4 was published in *A Companion to Narrative Theory*, edited by James Phelan and Peter Rabinowitz (Blackwell, 2005). Parts of chapters 5 and 6 incorporate material that appeared in "Beyond Story and Discourse: Narrative Time in Postmodern and Non-Mimetic Fiction," in *Narrative Dynamics: Essays on Time, Plot, Closure, and Frames*, edited by Brian Richardson, The Ohio State University Press, 2002, pp. 47–63. Chapter 6 also includes most of my essay, "Unusual and Unnatural Narrative Sequences," from *Narrative Sequence in Contemporary Narratology*, edited by Raphaël Baroni and Françoise Revaz, The Ohio State University Press, 2016. Chapter 7 includes some pages from my essay "Unnatural Endings in Fiction and Drama," which first appeared in *The Edinburgh Companion to Narrative Theories*, edited by Zara Dinen and Robyn Warhol, Edinburgh University Press, 2018, pp. 332–45. Lastly, chapters 1, 6, and 7 contain several paragraphs that originally appeared in "Unnatural Stories and Sequences" in *A Poetics of Unnatural Narrative*, edited by Jan Alber, Henrik Skov Nielsen, and Brian Richardson, The Ohio State University Press, 2013, pp. 26–48. I gratefully thank the publishers for permission to reprint this material.

INTRODUCTION

Mimetic and Antimimetic Narrative Dynamics

SINCE THE 1950s, innovative authors have produced some of the most compelling acts of story construction in the history of literature. These works move far beyond the realist parameters of nineteenth- and early twentieth-century novelists and take narrative into entirely new regions. The writers of these fictions are not interested in telling traditional stories in conventional ways. Whereas Balzac could take pride in being thought of as the secretary of society, many later novelists would refuse to reproduce the world around them in the manner of realism, preferring instead to reconfigure or invert basic relations between events or to even create realms and forms that had never before existed.

A brief listing of some of these texts can provide a sense of the ways in which narratives are being made new. Among the most compelling recent works are Martin Amis's *Time's Arrow* (1991), which moves backward in time, second by second; Paul Auster's *4 3 2 1* (2017), which tells the story of the same life in four different variations; David Markson's *This Is Not a Novel* (2001), a work that challenges the very idea of narrative; Ian McEwan's *Atonement* (2001), which partially negates and reconfigures its story at the end of the novel; and Kate Atkinson's *Life after Life* (2014), which traces the life (lives?) of a woman who dies several times during the course of the narrative, only to have each death negated and the story move forward. David Mitchell's *Cloud Atlas* (2004) has six nested, minimally connected narratives presented first in a chronological and then an antichronological order; Jennifer Egan's *A Visit from the Goon Squad* (2011) assembles a cluster of related stories and partly concludes in a PowerPoint presentation; and there is Ali Smith's 2014 diptych novel, *How to Be Both*, a narrative in two parts, separated by several centuries, that nevertheless interact upon each other—published in two different formats, each one placing a different half of the novel first. Other works push the physical book to greater extremes: Mark Z. Danielewski's *Only Revolutions* (2006) has two front covers and can be read in either direction. Each side of the volume is narrated by a different character, and each page contains the other text in an upside-down version at the bottom of the page. Chris Ware's *Building Stories* (2013) is still more unusual: it comes in a large box and contains fourteen differently sized, formatted, and bound items, including books, pamphlets, newspapers, comic strips, various scraps, and other physical writings that the reader is encouraged to assemble.

These are only some of the most prominent examples of what might be called the *new narrative order*. It is also important to observe that digital fictions further add to the richness of the world of narrative, providing new kinds of beginnings, sequencings, and endings. These texts challenge and extend existing practices of fiction making as new kinds of emplotment, sequencing, embedding, ending, and narrative itself, are employed. These and similar works are provoking some major questions: How do we theorize impossible narrative temporalities? What is the meaning of story after its attenuation in postmodern texts? How are narratives developed if traditional plotting is abandoned? We also wonder how to theorize variable sequencing, works that straddle the boundary of narrative, or a story line that has been erased. As we inquire how we can model endings when there are multiple, contradictory conclusions, we will have to take a hard look at claims like those of Peter Brooks that the ending determines all that comes before it. Similarly, the simple conception of fabula (*histoire*) and syuzhet (*récit*) and the attendant concept of temporal order as articulated by Gérard Genette, though extremely widespread in the field, need to be adjusted or reformulated. Narrative theory has not yet fully taken up the challenges of postmodernism, often restricting itself to more conventional, realistic examples and simpler, more sweeping, and increasingly inadequate formulations. In this volume I try to indicate what a more ample and inclusive poetics might look like.

Theoretical Model

Two terms need to be presented and defined here: *mimetic* and *antimimetic*. By *mimetic* I mean fictional representations that resemble nonfictional ones.

We can think of a mimetic representation as a generous conception of realism. It treats characters as if they were people, and the events they engage in as essentially similar to the kinds of events we might encounter in our lived experience. Space and time in such fiction are recognizable extensions of the spatial and temporal parameters of our world. The canon of probability that governs the universe is assumed to be largely the same in mimetic fictional worlds. But there is another tradition, or rather a countertradition, of antimimetic works that elude, defy, or parody the conventions painstakingly upheld by the mimetic authors, and this tradition is highly visible in postmodern narratives. Represented events that are antimimetic (or *unnatural*, a term that I will use synonymously with *antimimetic*) do not copy or extend but rather violate some of the laws of everyday existence; these events cannot happen in real life.[1] Antimimetic writers do not wish to repeat conventional forms of representation but rather develop new methods and techniques. They transform the patterns found in the world in order to create new narrative possibilities. In the real world, time flows forward and the past is unalterable. Antimimetic authors may run time backward and reverse the order of cause and effect; they may change the past or include incompatible versions of it; they may fabricate contradictory temporal sequences as time flows differently for different characters; and they may form temporal loops. Such authors may create impossible spaces and feature characters with too few or too many characteristics for them to be humanlike. The one thing they don't do is follow any fixed, well-established orderings. This principle is probably best expressed in a spirited exchange involving Jean-Luc Godard. "Surely," a frustrated critic once implored, Godard would agree that a film "must have a beginning, a middle, and an end?" The filmmaker responded, "Yes, but not necessarily in that order" (cited in Sterritt 20).

A central axiom of antimimetic poetics is what I have called the *Loki Principle*, which states that whenever a literary convention becomes powerful or ubiquitous, someone will come along and violate that convention. Thus, the neoclassical doctrine of the "unity of time" (itself a simplistic mimetic demand), advocated by many and put into regular practice by Ben Jonson and others, was routinely flouted by Shakespeare, whose only plays that adhered to this pseudo-Aristotelian rule were his first and his last. In between, he would not only bring out Father Time in *The Winter's Tale* to explain (to the horror

---

1. For the most part, I will use the less ambiguous term *antimimetic* to depict events and scenes that violate real-world parameters; readers who are primarily interested in plot, time, endings, and narrative will not need to venture into any larger, metacritical debates over the philosophy of narratology that concepts of the unnatural have provoked. Readers of my earlier work, however, will readily recognize the continuity this volume shares with my more explicit studies of unnatural narrative.

of temporal puritans) that fifteen years of story time had just passed; he would also create temporal contradictions in a number of his plays.

As is no doubt becoming evident by the examples set forth in this introduction, every convention can be violated. Such transgressions are present in many anticonventional works of literature and have been for millennia. Antimimetic works require an extended poetics, a counterpoise to the mimetic principles it draws on, strays from, and parodies. In the rest of this book, I will attempt to do justice to both traditions, which in turn leads to a larger, more inclusive, postmimetic concept of narrative: one that includes both the mimetic aspects of narrative and their negation. It is a dialectical conception that eschews any simple through line, not unlike the ancient symbol Ouroboros which shows a serpent biting its own tail.

It will be noted that I use many conventional terms like *plot, fabula, narrative,* and so forth, without calling for an entire reconceptualization of each. I do so because I consider my positions to be complementary to rather than replacements of most existing narratological concepts. We need the traditional concept of fabula, but we also need to extend its application in multiple new ways to account for contradictory, variable, multiple, and self-negating fabulas. The standard conception of fabula (or *histoire* in its French incarnation) is the chronological story we are able to derive from reading or hearing the discourse of a work, as opposed to the syuzhet, which is the text itself as it is presented to us. Such a definition derives from nonfiction and mimetic fiction that aims to reproduce the orders of nonfiction, but it is entirely inadequate to encompass the kinds of antimimetic constructs we find in playful kinds of fiction. As Luc Herman and Bart Vervaeck have explained, "If it is impossible to reconstruct story events and to order them into a clear chronology, order in narrative texts cannot be assessed by using the structuralist method" (64). We need to stretch existing concepts to accommodate the texts they should be covering, and we are best served with a broader conception of fabula (and plot and other terms) to encompass both mimetic and antimimetic practices.

I will not be offering any single model of a narrative that runs throughout this study, the way *À la recherché du temps perdu* runs through Genette's *Discours du récit.* I believe that fictional narratives are highly protean and variable and need to be studied aspect by aspect. Some texts do transcend traditional mimetic practices in a number of complementary ways; for example, Ana Castillo's *The Mixquiahuala Letters* presents challenges to existing notions of beginnings, fabula, syuzhet, narrative sequence, and endings. Other texts work differently. Many that have a theoretically fascinating ending may have an utterly ordinary beginning; in fact, the ordinary beginning may have been selected to better foreground the unusual ending. Similarly, a fairly ordinary fabula may be presented in an extraordinary syuzhet, and vice versa. As the rest of this book will exemplify, I try to resist the temptation to produce a general theory of narrative dynamics that takes us firmly from beginning through the main aspects of the middle to the definitive ending, with appropriate nods to fabula construction, temporality, and syuzhet arrangement. I do so because many or most fictional narratives simply aren't like that; it is not helpful to consider every novel a more or less failed attempt to be *Tom Jones* or *Emma*. Many components of narrative can be reasonably autonomous; I try to respect this autonomy, do justice to the heterogeneity of narrative practices, and appreciate both inorganic and unnatural forms.

Historical Background

The explosion of twenty-first-century works that remake narrative in basic ways is by no means unprecedented; it is in fact a kind of second flowering of the extraordinary period from the mid-1950s to the mid-1970s that also produced a rich array of experiments in narrative. These include the contradictory fictions of Alain Robbe-Grillet, Anna Kavan, and Robert Coover; William Burroughs's "cut-up" constructions; John Fowles's *The French Lieutenant's Woman* with its different endings; B. S. Johnson's "novel in a box," *The Unfortunates*; and, most important, the writings of Samuel Beckett. This period witnessed a proliferation of experimental works from numerous poetics, including the *nouveau roman*, the *tel quel roman*, magical realism, *écriture féminine*, surfiction, and early postmodernism. Still earlier we find numerous intriguing transformations of story, text, and time in Nabokov, Queneau, Borges, and Blanchot; and before them there were the radical constructions that many of the modernists produced in the late 1920s and '30s, such as Woolf's *The Waves* or Joyce's *Finnegans Wake*. These works themselves followed a range of different avant-garde experiments (e.g., Gertrude Stein: expressionism, surrealism, and metadrama) in the 1910s and '20s. There is in fact a powerful, rich, varied, and continuous tradition of innovative narrative construction extending back over a century.

Narrative theory also experienced a renaissance in the study of story and plot from the mid-1960s to the end of 1980s; these tended to follow one of four largely independent tracks. First, a number of structuralist or structuralist-inspired narratologists, building on and greatly extending the work of Vladimir Propp, developed the concept of the plot grammar that was intended to articulate the basic trajectories and possible transformations of any narrative. Different models were produced by Claude Bremond, A. J. Greimas, Roland

Barthes, Gerald Prince, and Thomas Pavel; later adaptations of these models were made by Marie-Laure Ryan (*Possible* 124–47), David Herman (*Story* 85–114), and Emma Kafalenos (*Narrative*).

Second, an entirely antithetical approach to narrative construction was produced in response to a new wave of highly innovative novels, many associated with the *nouveau roman* and related experiments; these include the theoretical works of Jean Ricardou (*Pour une théorie du nouveau roman*, 1971), Ann Jefferson (*The Nouveau Roman and the Poetics of Fiction*, 1984), David Hayman (*Re-Forming the Narrative: Toward a Mechanics of Modernist Fiction*, 1987), Dina Sherzer (*Representation in Contemporary French Fiction*, 1987), and Leonard Orr (*Problems and Poetics of the Nonaristotelian Novel*, 1991). Interestingly, Roland Barthes, who had produced one of the more compelling story grammars, abandoned that model precisely so that he could better conceptualize the new kind of writing he would call *texts* (*Image* 54–64).

In addition, at a slightly more local level, a number of important studies of narrative endings began to appear, as did a few works dealing with beginnings and exposition; these infused new energy into the study of narrative construction, the most prominent of these being Edward Said's *Beginnings* (1975); Meir Sternberg's *Expositional Modes and Temporal Order in Fiction* (1971); Frank Kermode's *The Sense of an Ending* (1967); and David Richter's *Fable's End* (1974). These would soon be joined by important work on endings by Marianna Torgovnick, D. A. Miller, Armine Kotin Mortimer, Barbara Korte, and Rachel Blau DuPlessis. In many cases, the study of beginnings and endings has led directly and unsurprisingly to ideological concerns—it is at these points that ideology most transparently affects the organization of a narrative.

Third, ideological concerns, frameworks, and practices were added to the understanding of narrative, as feminist and queer studies made significant contributions to the understanding of the politics of plot by exploring narrative trajectories that have excluded women; the role of gendered masterplots; implicitly and explicitly female kinds of sequencing; and the possible effects of linearity and fixed closure. In addition to DuPlessis, these scholars include Hélène Cixous, Teresa de Lauretis, Nancy K. Miller, Mieke Bal, Susan Winnett, Ross Chambers, Robyn Warhol, Sally Robinson, Judith Roof, Susan S. Lanser, Susan Stanford Friedman, and Alison Case. Soon after, postcolonial and US ethnic narrative studies would extend this kind of approach still further and into new directions.

Finally, the 1980s also produced two ambitious, important, and influential works on story and plot in narrative theory, works which I will be in dialogue with during the course of this study: Peter Brooks's *Reading for the Plot* (1984) and James Phelan's *Reading People, Reading Plots: Character, Pro-*

gression, and the Interpretation of Narrative (1989). J. Hillis Miller's important though rather underappreciated volume, *Reading Narrative* (1998), also deserves special mention here for its ingenious deconstruction of traditional concepts of narrative beginnings, middles, and endings. Recently, four works have appeared that are pushing our knowledge deeper: Caroline Levine's *The Serious Pleasures of Suspense: Victorian Realism and Narrative Doubt* (2003), which stressed the role of skepticism in suspense; Raphael Baroni's *La tension narrative* (2007), which uses cognitive and rhetorical models to analyze narrative tension produced by curiosity and suspense; Hilary P. Dannenberg's *Coincidence and Counterfactuality: Plotting Space and Time in Narrative Fiction* (2008), which explores multiple fictional worlds as well as extreme play with coincidence; and Patrick Colm Hogan's *Affective Narratology: The Emotional Structure of Stories* (2011), which judiciously draws on recent work in cognitive studies. The anthologies *Narrative Beginnings* (Richardson, 2009), *Narrative Middles* (Caroline Levine and Mario Ortiz-Robles, 2011), and *Narrative Sequence in Contemporary Narratology* (Raphael Baroni and Françoise Revaz, 2016) also contain important new work in these fields. There has probably never been a more rewarding time to study story and plot, in all of their many aspects, forms, and locations.

Residual Problems

Despite this flurry of theoretical activity, some significant problems remain in the study of story and plot. The primary one is the continued insistence of what I will call the "classic" account of plot, one which postulates a distinct beginning and valorizes a series of events that form a reasonably firm causal chain, little of which material is extraneous or adventitious; these events progress to heightened drama that may be resolved in the ending. This conception, in one form or another, stretches from Aristotle to the neo-Aristotelians of the sixteenth to nineteenth centuries, is reaffirmed by E. M. Forster in his well-known remarks on story and plot, appears again very prominently in the work of Peter Brooks, and is currently being reintroduced by many cognitive narratologists. The problem, as I will argue in the course of this study, is that while such a conception is valuable for discussing many narratives, it is too limited to be a foundational model; there are far too many other important kinds of narratives that fail to conform to this pattern—as we have already seen, many of them are deliberately designed to elude, resist, or transcend it. Our theories of story and plot need to be as supple as the material they are intended to circumscribe.

A related problem is the common assumption that beginnings and endings can be easily cordoned off and effectively delineated—in fact, such delimitation is generally presupposed by and may be essential for the "classic" model of story and plot. Here too I will argue for a more dialectical approach to these subjects and to narrative itself. We will see how arbitrary or even illusory the idea of firmly fixed beginnings and endings can be. At a more general level, I will operate on the assumption that it is fundamentally misleading to suggest that fictional narratives can be comfortably contained within ready formulas or basic patterns. One of the functions of literature is precisely to modify or tamper with fixed, predictable orders, so narrative theory needs to be particularly alert to this practice and its often unexpected consequences.

Multilinear narratives also present numerous challenges to traditional accounts as well as opportunities for a more flexible theoretical approach. It is clear that including narratives with more than one beginning, several kinds of possible sequencing, forking paths in the story, incompatible or denarrated events, and multiple endings will greatly enrich and enhance our theoretical accounts. Attending to these can also help us reinterpret seemingly more ordinary or conventional texts.

Methodology

Some words on questions of methodology will no doubt be useful to articulate at this point. My work is inductive; I try to assemble the most important, relevant, and interesting narratives I encounter. I then go on to model this material as effectively as possible, identifying shared features and noting salient differences. My method thus contrasts significantly with that of theorists who begin with an ideal conception or with a single, paradigmatic text, analyze it thoroughly, and then go on to try to extend these findings to other texts.[2] This "paradigmatic" method is necessarily limited by the form it valorizes or the example it has selected for this end and will generally fail to be of much value for texts that are appreciably different. A narratologist may choose to theorize novels like *Tom Jones* or *Á la recherche du temps perdu* and works that are similar to the paradigm text; however, this seems to me to be an unnecessary self-limitation, one that runs counter to the protean nature of literature itself. While studying some subjects, it is an excellent practice to seek paradigmatic cases, invariant structures, and universal laws. Literature, however, whether

---

2. In the next chapter, I will also indicate the flaws of the prototype account of narrative, a somewhat similar theoretical move.

high or low, both follows rules and violates them; adheres to generic forms and formulates new ones; and repeats the old patterns and creates unprecedented ones. It is a system, or rather a cluster of systems, that is constantly self-modifying. The temptation and the demise of story grammars after the late 1970s may be due precisely to the kinds of limitations present in the strict models I refer to here. I try instead to follow out both the systematic and the antisystematic aspects of narrative. Surely, the purpose of a theory of plot is, at a minimum, to conceptually circumscribe the culture's most important plots, including the seemingly deviant ones.

I will also add that this work is primarily one of descriptive poetics; it attempts to identify and model narrative elements, orders, and swerves within works of fiction. Thus, I mention but do not explore in detail questions of the effects of reading and the act of reception. For related reasons, I do not write much in this book on ideological issues. At times, however, I will allow myself to stray into areas of ideological analysis and reader response as a particular subject, such as beginnings or endings, may seem to require. I will note here that I do take up issues of both reception and ideology in a number of my articles published elsewhere; many of them are included in the works cited.

The Design of This Study

In the first chapter, I will ask the basic question of what a narrative is. I will survey existing concepts and definitions of narrative and note their strengths and weaknesses, looking in particular at those best suited to engage with postmodern practices and challenges. I will use Beckett's "Ping," Robbe-Grillet's "The Secret Room," and David Shields's "Life Story" as liminal examples that show how authors explore and help establish the boundaries of narrativity, and I will pay particular attention to David Markson's daring text, *This Is Not a Novel*. Having determined what a *narrative* is, I go on to examine what a *single* narrative consists of by analyzing works with multiple narrative strands, some of which may appear to constitute two or more narratives that are provocatively presented as a single one. The analysis will move from simpler cases like *King Lear* to more difficult ones like Beckett's *Molloy* to extremes like Faulkner's *The Wild Palms*. I investigate texts that try to extend or go beyond the idea of a single story, providing instead suggestive parallel narratives (Caryl Phillips's *Crossing the River* and T. Coraghessan Boyle's "The Extinction Tales").

The rest of this chapter examines the largest questions involving narrative and analyzes the difference between narrative and nonnarrative genres such as description, lists, and portraits. I note ways in which nonnarrative kinds of writing can seep into or generate narratives and note the "gravitational pull" that narrative seems to possess. By charting the boundaries of narrative, we are better able to understand the effects of transgressing those boundaries. I go on to discuss the status of nonnarrative elements (such as descriptions) in narratives, consider the unnarrated (sometimes the most important aspects of a story are left untold), and explore the unnarratable (what cannot be told in a given narrative, like the sex lives of Jane Austen's characters, or especially traumatic or cruel events).

George Eliot states that "man cannot do without the make-believe of a beginning" (1), and chapter 2 examines narrative beginnings, discloses how arbitrary or unstable they can be, and notes the playful strategies that authors of modernist, postmodern, and hypertext fictions have employed to dislodge or disrupt this seemingly essential feature. I examine beginnings in the story, in the text, and in what Genette calls the *paratext*. My major examples are the hidden beginnings of Joyce's "The Dead" and the self-negating beginnings of Beckett's *Molloy*.

Chapter 3 examines the theory of plot, what Brooks calls "the dynamic shaping force of the narrative discourse" (13). I discuss the role of plot in mimetic works and mimetic theories, particularly the classic kind of emplotment outlined by Aristotle, Forster, Brooks, and others. Next, I go on to investigate works that problematize these models, that is, those texts that minimize, attenuate, parody, or refuse to be governed by their logic, such as, respectively, picaresque tales, modernist novels, postmodern narratives, and avant-garde experiments. In addition to tightly plotted and episodically conjoined events, I discuss fragmented and "forking-path" progressions found in many experimental novels and hyperfiction, and explore connections in carnivalesque narratives. I will examine just how plotting works in a contradictory novel by tracing out its dynamics in Kate Atkinson's *Life after Life*. I then offer an account of "tellability," or what makes a story worth telling, and examine how tellability changes over time and differs for divergent audiences, noting in particular modernists' resistance to conventional tellability and its larger implications. Dorothy Richardson stated, "Plot nowadays, save the cosmic plot, is inexcusable. Lollipops for children" (139); I will speculate on why many modernists refused to provide a compelling plot and why so many postmodernists parody it.

In chapter 4, I explore what I call *non-plot-based narrative progressions* and determine how certain texts sequence their material once they have supplemented or abandoned the generating principle of the traditional plot. Here

I locate a number of ordering patterns, including musical structures, alphabetical arrangements, verbal generators, metaphors made literal, collage compositions, and designs based on geometrical and other forms (triad, circle, hourglass shape, and others), noting the ways in which such orderings complement, parallel, or frustrate traditional kinds of emplotment. Here, I use Joyce's *Ulysses* as my main example.

In chapter 5 I offer an account of narrative temporality that attempts to encompass several postmodern practices. I argue that a theory of narrative time is most useful if it contains six aspects: the time of the story, the sequence in which it is presented, the time of the telling, the time of its reception, the frequency of representations of the same events, and the correspondence or noncorrespondence with historical events that occur at the same time as the fictional ones. I then investigate the increasing number of antimimetic works that violate physically or logically possible temporality. Such practices include circular narratives, the last sentence of which is also the work's first sentence; narratives that move backward temporally and causally; narratives with multiple contradictory story lines; and those with systematically conflated temporalities. I try to demonstrate the consequences and utility of this approach with an analysis of the complex fabricated temporalities of Virginia Woolf's *To the Lighthouse*.

Next, in chapter 6, I take up one of the most foundational concepts of narrative theory: the distinction between the story and the sequence in which it is told, a relation usually referred to as *fabula* (*histoire*) and *syuzhet* (*récit*). Postmodern and other antimimetic narratives require an expansive conception of story, one that includes the multiple, impossible stories of experimental texts. The text or syuzhet can also be variable, as in B. S. Johnson's *The Unfortunates*, an unbound novel whose chapters may be physically arranged and rearranged by the reader. Most hyperfictions also have variable syuzhets. The reader of Ana Castillo's *The Mixquiahuala Letters* is similarly asked to choose one of three possible reading sequences, each of which produces a different story with a different ending. There are works with erased stories, novels that can be read in multiple ways, books physically bound together in two formats, and even a narrative written on a deck of playing cards; this chapter attempts to survey each major type.

In chapter 7, I move on to the question of endings, discussing earlier conceptions of the function of endings and asking how works with experimental progressions arrive at closure. I also examine what additional variations are produced by postmodern texts and the status of endings that have been chosen by the reader. I pay attention to disparities between the ending of the story and the cessation of the text, and discuss serial and historical narratives that are not exactly intended to have an ending. I note the curious status of performed narratives in which the enactment can problematize the story. I also discuss some much-debated questions concerning the aesthetics and the ideological valences of strategies of closure. The conclusion summarizes my theses and underscores the importance of engaging with many postmodern, contemporary, and digital narratives.

CHAPTER 1

Narrative, the Nonnarrative, and the Unnarratable

NARRATIVE THEORISTS have always sought an effective definition of narrative. It is especially important to do so now for two reasons. First, the "narrative turn" has affected numerous other disciplines, such as philosophy, history, anthropology, law, medicine, and even theology; each approach necessarily looks to narrative theory to provide the definitions that constitute the others' starting points. Not only do we need to define our area of study, but others require us to do so for theirs. Second, a considerable number of recent experimental works test or seek to transcend the very boundaries of narrative, and it is essential to know what these are in order to realize just what is being challenged and to determine how far the transgression extends. Formulating an adequate definition has historically proven to be somewhat difficult. As we will see, many of the proffered definitions are perfectly adequate for garden-variety narratives, but they run into trouble when we begin to approach unusual, minimal, or borderline narratives.

In this chapter, I will critically summarize some of the most influential definitions of narrative that have appeared. Then I will look at a number of unusual texts that attempt to extend, challenge, or defy the concept of narrative. These texts include a provocative piece by Gertrude Stein, an austere one by Samuel Beckett, a contradictory one by Alain Robbe-Grillet, a devious collection of actual bumper stickers assembled by David Shields called "Life Story," and finally, David Markson's defiant work, *This Is Not a Novel*. I will examine these works to see whether they live up (or down?) to the challenge posed by Markson's title and will go on to evaluate the different definitions of narrative in the light of these experimental works. I will then look at some unusual texts by William Faulkner, T. Coraghessan Boyle, and Caryl Phillips that provoke the question of the limits of a single narrative. I will go on to discuss texts like descriptions, lists, self-help manuals, and recipes, which normally are nonnarrative but, since they are representations of possible persons, places, and events, can easily glide toward and nestle within the boundaries of narrative. Finally, we will look at what is invariably left out of a narrative: the unnarrated, the disnarrated, and the unnarratable.

Narrative and Narration

A clarification to begin with: some narratologists contend that a narrative can only be a story that is narrated and has a narrator. Epic, fiction, biography, and history qualify, but not drama, film, opera, or ballet. This limited view of narrative seems problematic on many counts: the narrated and the nonnarrated genres can be much closer together than such formulations suggest or allow. For example, think of novels that are almost exclusively presented in dialogues, or plays and films that have a narrator whose story is then enacted in the represented events (e.g., Tennessee Williams's *The Glass Menagerie* and Bertolt Brecht's *Der Kaukasische Kreidekreis*; Billy Wilder's *Sunset Boulevard* and Woody Allen's *Annie Hall*; see Richardson, "Voice and Narration"; Kozloff). Furthermore, some theorists argue that plays and films do have narrators and that they are the figures responsible for the settings, stage directions, camera angles, and other aspects of the scripted performance (Jahn). It also seems strange if not silly to discuss the events of the narrative of Othello in Cinthio's prose narrative (Shakespeare's source), in a comic-book version, or even in a possible novelization of the play but not in the enacted versions of the story in other genres like tragedy, opera, and ballet (though, of course, one may speak of aspects of its narration in the narrated versions). Finally, narrated stories are a subcategory of stories; even if one chooses to limit one's theories to those that are told by a narrator, there still remain hundreds of thousands of stories that are not told by a narrator. These stories also require theoretical analysis when the subject is anything other than narration or an aspect of narration.

Nor is it necessary to invent a new category of "supernarrative" to cover them all. When discussing different aspects of the poetics of narrative, Aristotle was equally at home with epic and dramatic narratives. Most theorists of character and many of plot range effortlessly from fiction to drama and film;

they do not limit their discussions of characters and endings merely to those that occur in narrated genres. I see no need or utility for such a delimitation (except when discussing narration and narrators). For the reasons indicated here, I feel it is essential that we theorize all narratives. An increasing number of theorists now agree with Roland Barthes's enumeration of narrative's "almost infinite diversity of forms" in a justly famous observation: "Narrative is present in myth, legend, fable, tale, novella, epic, history, tragedy, drama, comedy, mime, painting (think of Carpaccio's *Saint Ursula*), stained glass windows, cinema, comics, news item, conversation" (*Image 79*; see Abbott, *Cambridge* 1–2). To this list we may add hyperfiction, graphic novels, online collective narratives, fanfiction, blogs, PowerPoint narratives, some types of computer games, the Twitter story (e.g., Jennifer Egan's 2012 "Black Box"), and Xu Bing's *Book from the Ground,* a narrative that is composed entirely of emojis and icons (see Konstantinou).[1]

Definitions

Some theorists, such as Thomas B. Leitch (86), claim that narrative is a mode of reception rather than a feature of a text; whatever we read *as* a narrative thus *is* a narrative. Sternberg similarly states that "since a narrative is a construct of our minds, any sign or collection of signs is a narrative if it produces in us suspense, curiosity, or surprise" ("Reconceptualizing" 48).[2] Many nonnarrative signs, however, can readily produce these emotions, especially surprise or curiosity—for example, an unusual recipe, a fallacious syllogism, peculiar listings in a phone book, the unexpected box score of a basketball game, or the excessive bill at an expensive bar. Narrating is an intentional act and is indicated as such by many recognizable discursive features. Another, larger, problem with the reception account is that some texts lend themselves to being read as narratives much more than others do; an anecdote or an animal fable invites a reading as a narrative much more so than does a mathematical theorem, a chemical formula, or a computer program. If one accepts this account, then one next needs to ascertain what it is about some texts that rewards a narrative reading and what it is that works against or precludes such a reading in others.

Commenting on this reception-type of account as proposed by Monika Fludernik (*Towards*) and William Nelles, Pekka Tammi argues that such an

---

1. See Ryan, *Avatars*, pp. 181–203, on computer games as narratives.

2. Earlier, Sternberg had offered a slightly more restrictive definition in "Telling in Time II," p. 529, but it is still subject to the same objections.

approach begs the question: if narratives are simply defined as "what readers pursue and what narratologists study, we should next start defining 'narrativity.' . . . What is it, more precisely, that we impose on texts? Whether one wished it or not, we are once more led back—in a circular route—to ponder the *features* already isolated in previous definitions" (24).[3] Reading a text as a narrative does not make it one, any more than viewing a group of stars as a bear makes it a bear. By the same token, calling or reading a phone book as a poem, a dialogue, or a prayer does not make it into any of these discourse forms. We can try to read a law, a syllogism, a geographical description, or even stray marks in the sand as a narrative, and we may derive something of some value in doing so; but the fact remains that doing so doesn't thereby transform these other text types into narratives.[4] Finally, it may be observed that if reading a text as a narrative makes it a narrative, then every text is a narrative.

Gérard Genette offers one of the most casual definitions of narrative; for him, any linguistic production that relates at least a single event, such as, "I walk," is a narrative since it implies a transformation or change of state—in this example, from that before walking began (*Narrative* 30). He states, "As soon as there is an action or an event, even a single one, there is a story because there is a transformation" (19). The main problem with Genette's conception is that it is far too inclusive to be of much use; numerous descriptions ("night falls" or even "the sun is shining") thus become narratives, since they imply a transition from an earlier state to a later one. The important distinction between description and narration, which Genette did so much to clarify, can become lost in this formulation. I argue that we will still need to differentiate between an event that functions like a description, such as "night falls," even though it does imply a narrative, and a causally related series of statements that clearly *constitute* a narrative ("The button was pushed; the explosion quickly followed"). It seems evident that we need a more restrictive definition if it is to be useful.

James Phelan's rhetorical theory of narrative offers the following commonsensical definition: narrative is "somebody telling somebody else on some occasion and for some purpose(s) that something happened" (*Experiencing* 3).

---

3. Fludernik explains her account in *Towards a 'Natural' Narratology*, pp. 26–30; she distinguishes it from Sternberg's on pp. 321–23.

4. I am not asserting that there may not be useful cases when one might productively read a syllogism, a law, or a phone book as a narrative, or use this type of material to construct a narrative. My point is simply that reading a nonnarrative discourse as a narrative does not ipso facto make it a narrative, any more than reading *King Lear* as a standard comedy makes it a comedy, despite its admitted comic aspects at various points in the play.

This account is perfectly adequate for most ordinary narratives, and, to be fair, this is essentially the purpose of the definition. As Phelan has recently written, "I have never argued that this definition was the best among the many that narrative theorists have proposed, because I don't believe that there is a Platonic ideal of narrative that can be invoked as to the standard by which to measure the adequacy of any definition." He wants instead to provide "a rough general sense of what narrative is" ("Authors" 1). In this, he is no doubt considerably successful. Nevertheless, I suggest that when we encounter narratives that test the boundaries of narrativity, we will need an account that specifies exactly what the "something" that is told needs to be; in the end, the question is not about an ideal definition, but about the most accurate one.

Among the current definitions of narrative, a widespread position is that which insists on the representations of events in time. Gerald Prince has defined narrative as "the representation of *at least two* real or fictive events in a time sequence, neither of which presupposes or entails the other" (*Narratology* 4); he has recently rephrased this definition to read: "An object is a narrative if it is taken to be the logically consistent representation of at least two asynchronous events that do not presuppose or imply each other" ("Narrativehood" 19). This general position is affirmed by several other theorists, including Mieke Bal (5) and Shlomith Rimmon-Kenan (2). But there are a number of problems with this kind of definition. Take the following statement: "In ancient times, Theseus slew the minotaur; yesterday, the mail came late." I don't think anyone would claim this is a narrative, despite its having satisfied the criterion of temporal sequence. The same is true of stories in a newspaper, as Wallace Martin has observed (73); there may be several in a time sequence, but they do not constitute a single narrative (though of course they can if they do, in fact, form parts of a single story, as in a time of war). Interestingly, Ford Madox Ford made this very complaint about the newspapers of his day: "With the coming of the Modern Newspaper, the Book has been deposed from its intimate position in the hearts of men. You cannot in London read a book from day to day, because you must know the news, in order to be a fit companion for your fellow Londoner. Connected thinking has become nearly impossible, because it is nearly impossible to find any general idea that will connect into one train of thought: 'Home Rule for Egypt,' 'A Batch of Stabbing Cases,' and 'Infant Motorists.' It is hardly worthwhile to trace the evolution of this process" (134–35). Once again, mere temporal sequence proves inadequate to define a narrative.

The issues involved can be further clarified by looking at genres which, unlike fiction, may or may not have narratives. David Bordwell and Kristin Thompson provide a telling test case of a series of cinematic images: "A man tosses and turns, unable to sleep. A mirror breaks. A telephone rings" (55). Alone, this is a nonnarrative sequence. But if there are, in fact, connections that would weave these images together into a related sequence of events, then we have a narrative. Bordwell and Thompson offer just such a possible connection: the man can't sleep because he's had a fight with his boss, and in the morning he is still so angry that he smashes the mirror while shaving; next, his telephone rings and he learns that his boss has called to apologize. In this example, causal ties are necessary to produce the work's narrative status; without them, it is merely a suggestive, nonnarrative montage sequence.[5]

This "causal" position originates with Boris Tomashevsky, who explained that a fabula "requires not only indications of time, but also indications of cause" (66). A growing number of theorists have gravitated toward a position that includes some form of causal connection, including Dorrit Cohn, who defines narrative as "a series of statements that deal with a causally related sequence of events that concern human (or human-like) beings" (12). Susan Onega and José Angel García Landa also affirm this stance (3). In his study of the subject, Göran Rossholm concludes that causal connections are necessary for narrativity, and Noël Carroll has defended a relatively narrow version of this position. It should be stressed that these theorists do not insist on a tightly woven causal chain linking all the events, but rather affirm that they participate in the same general causal matrix. As Carroll specifies, "Most narratives are not strings of causal entailments; instead, the earlier events in a sequence of events underdetermine later events" ("On the Narrative Connection" 26).

One narratologist directly confronts the problems inherent in a temporal definition, though in a way that ultimately works to validate the causal position. Shlomith Rimmon-Kenan admits that "there would indeed be something very odd about the following bit of story: 'Little Red Riding-Hood strays into the forest and then Pip aids the runaway convict.' But if we accept this as the possible paraphrase of *some* text," she continues, "then the temporal conjunction requires us to imagine some world where these events can co-exist" (19). This kind of reasoning begs the question it is attempting to demonstrate: without any causal connection, this is not a single narrative; however, if we supply a shared storyworld in which these events can interact, then we would

---

5. Noël Carroll offers an additional example: "'The Tartar hordes swept over Russia; Socrates swallowed hemlock; Noël Carroll got his first computer; Jackie Chan made his most successful movie; and dinosaurs became extinct.' I suspect that almost everyone will agree that this is not a narrative" ("Narrative Connection" 22–23). He goes on to explain that "it is about disconnected subjects" and thus fails to possess narrative connection and thus be a narrative (23).

have a story. This reasoning seems to prove instead the necessity of causal connection.[6]

A possible counterexample to the causal theory of narrative has recently appeared in the form of Ali Smith's novel, *How to Be Both* (2014). The work has two distinct story lines: one is about a fifteenth-century Italian painter, Francesco del Cossa; and the other is the narrative of a young woman in twenty-first-century England. The two lives are almost entirely independent, though several points of connection emerge. The young woman, called George, sees del Cossa's paintings in Ferrara with her mother; after her mother is dead, she seeks out del Cossa's work in London and learns what she can about his life. In the other narrative, what seems to be the spirit of the painter observes the young woman in a gallery where his paintings are hung. It is clear that there are a few causal connections between the two stories, but the question that arises is whether these connections are enough. The answer is no; these are two distinct narratives even though they are not unconnected. If, on the other hand, the two are more tightly conjoined, as would be the case if George were to actually write the life story of del Cossa as she briefly imagines doing (323–25), and if this were, in fact, the book's other story, then we would have a single narrative.[7] We may therefore go on to modify the position to state that there must be substantial rather than minimal causal connections among the events for them to constitute a single narrative.

Recently, the notion of a "prototypical narrative" has been advocated by Marie-Laure Ryan ("Narrative") and several cognitive-oriented theorists to take the place of a standard definition.[8] They develop the idea that humans share a basic idea of what a prototypical narrative is. I argue that the concept is problematic for several reasons. Not all concepts have a single prototype, and

---

6. For Wolf Schmid, "The minimal condition of narrativity is that at least one change of state be represented." He also insists that "the minimal definition of narrativity should be formulated in such a way that it does not require the presence of an additional (e.g. causal) connection between the states" (4). It seems to me that a change of state in an entity would imply some sort of connection, so the two events are part of the same causal matrix.

7. See, however, Eva von Contzen's reading of this text which aligns it with medieval concepts of story and progression.

8. See Matti Hyvärinen for a lucid account of the development and implications of the concept of the prototypical narrative. Somewhat comparable positions have been developed by Bal and by Schmid, for whom the predominant mode or function is what ultimately determines a text's narrative status. For Bal, Eliot's *The Waste Land*, despite its numerous narrative components, is usually not considered a narrative poem since it "displays other, more salient characteristics, such as poetic ones; Eliot's poem remains first a poem, and its narrative features are of but secondary importance" (10). Schmid argues that "whether a text is descriptive or narrative in nature depends not on the quantity of the static or dynamic elements in it, but on the function which they have in the overall context of the work" (5).

prototypes can vary across cultures. For example, the prototypical tree might be a tall pointed fir, a round leafy maple, or a languid palm tree, depending on the audience's experiences. The notion of a prototypical instance is misleading for more complex concepts: knowing what a prototypical concept of a tree is does not assist in but could rather get in the way of establishing a scientific account of what a tree is. Prototype theory accounts for how groups of people categorize some (but by no means all) concepts; it does not claim to say much if anything about the meaning of those concepts. Even if we could determine what a prototypical example of a narrative or a tree might be, it would still not help us *define* what either is.

Most problematic is that prototypes suggest gradations of resemblance, but as Porter Abbott has clearly shown in a discussion which I will return to shortly, narrative itself is an either/or feature: a work is or is not a narrative—except in very rare cases that presuppose this opposition ("What"). Thus it can be quite misleading to say that a text is minimally narrative. Finally, there may also be a problem at the center of the prototype idea, since a very high degree of all the standard components of narrativity, as in melodrama, can act as an unintended parody and thus reduce or deflate the very narrativity it was presumably intended to produce. The same of course is true of postmodern works like Coover's "The Babysitter," works that deliberately exaggerate their narrativity. That is, there may a black hole at the center of this conception.

Insofar as advocates of this notion attempt to replace a definition of narrative with an account of a prototypical one, it commits the logical error of conflating two separate concepts. A text may or may not be a narrative; if it is a narrative, it will have more or fewer features of what is felt to be a typical or prototypical narrative, but it needs to be recognized that these are two different kinds of operation that do not overlap.[9] The question "Is *Finnegans Wake* more or less a narrative than *The Perils of Pauline*?" seems to me a misguided one: both are narratives, although *Pauline* certainly has more tellability. To deny that narratives with minimal tellability are in fact narratives is to commit a category fallacy.[10] Replacing the definition of narrative with a prototypical account is also unfortunate insofar as it hypostatizes certain early twenty-

---

9. Just this conflation leads Roy Sommer to claim that Beckett's *The Unnamable* is "certainly not" a narrative, despite its having a narrator who narrates a number of events ("Unnatural" 409).

10. See Prince's "Narrativehood" for a clarification of these and related concepts that are sometimes confused.

first-century Western notions about narrative and thereby denies a conceptual space in which to debate this fundamental and most important issue.[11]

Before moving on, I will address some reservations expressed by Pekka Tammi concerning the kinds of definitions I am assessing here. Tammi objects to narratologists' interest in and emphasis on all narratives, both of which direct us away from distinctively *literary* narratives that may differ radically from ordinary, standard, or otherwise unremarkable narratives. He states that literary narratology should move "away from general model building and standard definitions" and focus instead on "the subversive and strange, previously untheorized or insufficiently theorized cases: the glorious exceptions to rules that classical definitions have been altogether too sweeping to recognize" (29). My response is that Tammi is offering a false set of alternatives. As I hope to demonstrate in the next pages, one needs an accurate definition of narrative in order to determine how and how far "subversive and strange" works transgress or transcend our concept of narrative. Tammi is entirely right in wanting to move beyond definitions that are too narrow or restrictive, but this simply means that we need to have better, more accurate definitions, not that we need to abandon the effort altogether. Two unconnected issues are here conflated: more work does need to be done on distinctively literary narratives, but this does not preclude our working to establish a definition of all narratives—in fact, it may actually presuppose it.

Quasi-Narrative Texts

Let us, then, examine some radical challenges of traditional kinds of story and look at some works that probe the boundaries of narrative itself. These pieces ask whether a given assemblage of words constitutes a narrative, whether it constitutes a different kind of text—or whether it hovers somewhere at the very border of narrativity. A number of unusual and unnatural texts navigate just this limit, so many, in fact, that we want a term to designate them. I'll call them *quasi narratives,* thereby leaving open the question of whether they are on one side or the other of this boundary. It strikes me that the most intriguing aspect of these works is their play on the borderline rather than which side they finally occupy.

---

11. In *The Cambridge Introduction to Narrative*, Porter Abbott seems to be content with a notion of narrative that works in two ways: a compact one with fixed terms, and a looser one for various forms of interruption and subversion (14–15). I believe instead that a single capacious definition should perform both tasks. There will be gray areas and borderline cases in addition to texts that test the very boundaries of narrative, however we may delineate them.

In some form, such challenges stretch back to Gertrude Stein. Her text "What Happened: A Play" tests the very idea of representation, and even of coherent discourse itself. Legend has it that Stein wrote this text after she attended a party in 1913, at which point she resolved to depict those events—but with a difference: the work would "tell what could be told if one did not tell anything" (*Lectures* 118). This method would provide "the essence of what happened" (119). The work discourses about several scenes, descriptions, possible events, and numerous kinds of artistic representation: "a series of photographs and also [. . .] a treacherous piece of sculpture" (*Geography* 206). Modes of mechanical and pictorial representation, especially those associated with cameras (shutter, shoot) mingle with natural images and reflections (shade, windows, memories); many of the objects depicted are those frequently found in still lifes (blossoms, oranges, apples, a slice). Throughout, there is play with what "is original and has a source"; the verbal drama with the word *slice* may just culminate in an oblique reference to a "slice of life": "an occasion, a slice and a substitute a single hurry and a circumstance that shows that" (207). Mark C. Robinson concludes that "what happens in *What Happened* is looking itself, a living process, the act of perceiving made as visible as the thing perceived" (14). In the end, we get not a narrative but a tantalizing set of protonarrative fragments that point toward the play with the boundaries of narrative that will appear later in the twentieth century and into the twenty-first.

Samuel Beckett's story "Ping" presents a series of descriptions that are repeated and slightly varied throughout the text. The text also lacks active verbs; it does, however, contain the single-syllable word *ping*, which appears at irregular intervals. The reader is challenged by numerous interpretive questions, the central one being whether the text is a narrative or not. That is, does the text display a group of descriptions, or do those images constitute a narrative? In other words, can one derive a fabula from these images? The space of the storyworld is a confined, white enclosure: "White walls one yard by two white ceiling one square yard never seen" (193). The central figure is human or humanoid: "bare white body fixed one yard legs joined like sewn" (193). The body is immobile in a semigeometrical position: "hands hanging palms front white feet heels together right angle" (193). The only nonwhite entity seems to the figure's eyes: "Only the eyes only just light blue almost white" (193).

As these descriptions recur, the reader, like the narratologist, looks for signs of life or movement; without some transformation, there can be no story. As James Phelan correctly observes, "If there is no change in character or situation, we begin to leave the realm of narrative" (*Living* 161). Beckett teasingly offers a few scraps of possible, if minimal, transformation. The light is sometimes described as "light grey almost white" (193); this could mean that the light source changes or merely that the original depiction is being slightly modified. There seems to be a sound: "Murmur only just almost never one second perhaps not alone" (193). This is our first indication of any passage of time; the murmur would presumably be coming from the supine figure. Another possible source of movement, if not exactly action, is suggested by the sentence that follows the one I have just quoted: "Given rose only just bare white body fixed one yard white on white invisible" (193). What does "given rose" refer to? The possible options would seem to be a hint of color on the body or the past tense of the verb to rise, or it might simply refer to the murmur rising from the figure, even though we are informed that the mouth is a "white seam like sewn invisible" (194).

There is the irregularly occurring word *ping*, which may be a repeated mechanical sound in the storyworld or simply an aspect of the work's strange discourse. Often, *ping* seems to alter the course of things: "white fixed front ping murmur ping silence" (194), as if the word is determining the movement of the text, as the murmur appears and then is replaced by silence. Elsewhere, the blue eyes seem to turn black, and a possible fleeting memory may appear as the *ping* syllable recurs with greater frequency: "Ping perhaps not alone one second with image same time a little less dim eye black and white half closed long lashes imploring that much memory almost never" (195). It is not immediately clear what the phrase (if it is a single phrase) "imploring that much memory" means (the figure has enough memory to enable him to implore?); the two terms *imploring* and *memory* do suggest a temporal passage, if only a brief, painful one. This reading seems confirmed by the text's last sentence: "Head haught eyes white fixed front old ping last murmur one second perhaps not alone eye unlustrous black and white half closed long lashes imploring ping silence ping over" (196). This text plays at the edges of narrative, suggesting the most minimal possible narrative of a largely immobile figure in pain, with memories, murmuring, imploring; at the end of the text, we may conclude that it does in fact just cross over the boundary into narrative.

Alain Robbe-Grillet challenges narrativity from the opposite end of the spectrum. If Beckett's text has too few events, Robbe-Grillet's has too many contradictory ones. His story "La Chambre secrète" ("The Secret Room," 1962), presents several depictions of what superficially appears to be the same scene at different times. These images usually depict a large spiral staircase, a bound woman, and a fleeing man. Sometimes they appear to be a series of actions, scrambled in time; at other times they suggest that the text displays several visual images, presumably paintings, which either can form a narrative or may merely be variations on a theme. Both interpretations are right and wrong: characters are described as moving, which indicates the presence of a narrative, even though other images are depicted as painted. The reader is invited to construct from the pieces of the text a narrative of a gothic murder and the escape of the killer. However, because of contradictions, the fabula will not stay fixed. A narrative emerges only if a reader sorts through the contradictory events and, adding the narrativity, actively turns them into a story. The governing (or generating) figure of this odd text is the spiral, which is manifested in numerous spatial patterns as well as in the work's curvilinear temporality. It becomes clear that the text is not a realistic representation of a series of events that could occur in the world, but rather a uniquely fictional creation that can exist only as literature.

Some texts play with but may not quite attain narrative status; that is, the assemblages fail to cohere into an identifiable story. This is the case in David Shields's unusual piece, suggestively titled "Life Story," which is a collection of actual American bumper stickers arranged in thematic clusters along a vaguely temporal trajectory. It begins:

First things first.

You're only young once, but you can be immature forever. I may grow old, but I'll never grow up. Too fast to live, too young to die. Life's a beach.

Not all men are fools; some are single. 100% Single. I'm not playing hard to get; I am hard to get. I love being exactly who I am.

Heaven doesn't want me and Hell's afraid I'll take over. I'm the person your mother warned you about. Ex-girlfriend in trunk. Don't laugh; your girlfriend might be in here. (15)

The text goes on to assemble a number of other clusters concerning activities, personal predilections, and sexual identifiers. The latter include a number of insistently erotic ones: "Girls wanted, all positions, will train. Playgirl on board. Party girl on board. Sexy blonde on board. Not all dumbs are blonde." Additional philosophical statements about the nature of human existence appear later in the text: "Love sucks and then you die. Gravity's a lie; life sucks. Life's a bitch; you marry one, then you die. Life's a bitch and so am I. Beyond bitch" (15). Culturally coded female voices emerge with greater frequency, some crass, others cynical: "So many men, so little time. Expensive but worth it. If you're rich, I'm single. Richer is better. Shopaholic on board.

Born to shop. I'd rather be shopping at Nordstrom. Born to be pampered. A woman's place is the mall. When the going gets tough, the tough go shopping. Consume and die. He who dies with the most toys wins. She who dies with the most jewels wins. Die, yuppie scum" (16). The entire cycle of family life is represented, from "Baby on board" to "My kid beat up your honor student" to references to aging: "I may be growing old, but I refuse to grow up. Get even: live long enough to become a problem to your kids. We're out spending our children's inheritance." The text ends, naturally, with images of demise and death: "Of all the things I've lost, I miss my mind the most. I brake for unicorns. Choose death" (17).

Nearly all the definitions of narrative we have examined so far will be of little help with this text. The reception-oriented, the Genettean, the temporal, and possibly the rhetorical definitions will unproblematically accept this text as a narrative; each appears unable to take up its implicit challenge to the concept of narrative. The same is largely true of the examples of Beckett and Robbe-Grillet, though we may note that Prince's second formulation is explicitly designed to exclude Robbe-Grillet, and Phelan's rhetorical criterion holds well concerning "Ping": there, the fundamental narratological question is whether something has, in fact, occurred. For the advocates of prototypicality, most of the examples have what they would call *minimal narrativity* and thus indifferently occupy the outer reaches of possible narrative.

The account based on causal relations, however, proves particularly useful here. It includes both the example from Beckett (barely) and that from Robbe-Grillet. We may well ask whether the latter's contradictions should ipso facto dissolve its narrative status? Many playful narratives include some minor or not-so-minor contradictions, such as *The French Lieutenant's Woman*, and no one doubts that this novel is a narrative. In addition, if narrative is a representation of a causally connected series of events of some magnitude, then it is apparent that Shields's collection does not qualify as a narrative. The subject seems too scattered, too contradictory; the narrative too unconnected, often because it is too specific in identifying antithetical predilections and its incompatible target audiences. Significantly, this text has been reprinted under the title "Life Stories" as if to acknowledge its heterogeneity. I see it ultimately as a pseudonarrative, a collection that mimics but does not comprise a genuine narrative, however minimal.

Something rather different seems to be happening to narrativity in David Markson's provocatively titled book, *This Is Not a Novel* (2001). This unusual text consists primarily of a series of epigrams, most commonly stating the way that writers, artists, and other public figures died. Thus, we get entries like:

"Alexander Pope died of dropsy." (8)

"John Milton died of gout." (8)

"Thomas Mann died of phlebitis." (9)

And so on. There are a few surprises: "Antonio Gaudi died after being hit by a streetcar in Barcelona" (61), but, on the whole, the causes of deaths are rarely exotic or unlikely, although there does seem to be a rather high proportion of tuberculosis and surprisingly few from cirrhosis of the liver. In between the announcements of causes of death, there are a number of literary and artistic anecdotes, observations, quotations, and critical disparagements, such as:

"Leonardo is a bore, according to Renoir."

"My cook knows more about counterpoint, said Handel the first time he heard Gluck." [. . .]

"Flaubert died of what was then called apoplexy, i.e., presumably a stroke."

"If its length is not considered a merit it has no other, said Edmund Waller of *Paradise Lost*." (35)

As is probably already evident, certain names recur, and a few basic patterns continue to appear. We cannot help following these out to see whether any minimal narrative emerges from them. For the most part, narrative fails to coalesce, even though many narrative elements are present: that Alexander Pope faced hostility; that many negative things are said about major creators; and that all authors die, and they die in different ways. Of greatest interest to us are the self-reflexive statements about novel writing attributed to the author, or at least a character called "Writer." Writer is said to be weary of making up stories, tired of inventing characters. He affirms the goal of Flaubert's *livre sur rien*: "A novel with no intimation of story whatsoever, Writer would like to contrive. / And with no characters. None" (2). Such a text would have "no *setting*. / With no so-called furniture. / Ergo meaning finally without *descriptions*" (5).[12] The text would have no social themes or depictions "of

---

12. Markson situates this practice still further back; his novel's epigraph is Swift's statement, "I am now trying an Experiment very frequent among Modern Authors, which is to *write upon nothing*."

contemporary manners and/or morals" (7). "A novel entirely without symbols" (8), Writer continues. "Ultimately, a work of art without even a subject" (9). At the same time, Writer would like this work to have a beginning, a middle, and an end, and even a note of sadness at the close (4).

The narrator frequently comments on the exact status of his work, stating that "this is a novel if Writer" says so (18). But is it enough to call something a novel in order for it to be a novel? This question was largely settled in the realm of art criticism a century ago after an ordinary urinal was exhibited by Marcel Duchamp as the "readymade" sculpture *Fountain* in 1917. Picasso did something similar with a bicycle seat and handlebar (*Head of a Bull*, 1943). This position has been articulated theoretically by aesthetician George Dickey in his institutional theory of art.

But all definitions of the novel or narrative require something more. The narrator offers several alternate descriptions of his opus, some exaggerated, some revealing, as the text unfolds. He claims that it is "even an epic poem, if Writer says so" (21); "Also even a sequence of cantos awaiting numbering, if Writer says so" (23); "even a mural of sorts" (36); "an autobiography" (53); "a heap of riddles" (70); most extravagantly, "a polyphonic opera of a kind" (73); most indisputably, "a disquisition on the maladies of the life of art" (86); more imaginatively, "an ersatz prose alternative to *The Waste Land* " (101); and rather improbably, "even a classic tragedy" (171).

Though insisting there are no characters, the narrator nevertheless acknowledges "Obviously Writer exists. / Not being a character but the author, here. / Writer is *writing*, for heaven's sake" (13). Even as Writer continues to deny that there are characters in his text, he gradually takes on more distinctive features, becoming a personality in his own right. He has his bodily pains and his own likes and dislikes; he realizes that "all this preoccupation" with art, death, and failure implies "that Writer is turning older" (147). He dreams about winning a MacArthur Foundation award; talks to himself; mocks Harold Bloom for speed-reading the classics; and constantly displays his sense of the unfairness of the poverty, misery, ill-health, and critical neglect of artists and writers.

This work, both in its contents and in its very title, challenges our notion of narrative. Does it exemplify its title, or is it instead a different kind of novel, the way Diderot's "Ceci n'est pas une conte" [This Is Not a Story] is actually a story, albeit a somewhat unusual one. By situating itself on the fault line of narrativity, it can therefore serve as an excellent test case for rival theories of narrative. This text spells trouble for those who prefer the temporal definition of narrative, since the three statements "Trifles, Catullus waved away his verses as"; "Ben Shahn was once an assistant to Diego Rivera"; and "Raymond

Carver died of lung cancer"—all appearing on the same page (65)—are clearly representations of three events in a time sequence. But they equally clearly do not by themselves constitute a narrative, any more than any three randomly selected representations of events do. The temporal definition will entirely elide the challenge this work provokes. For Genette, these would constitute three distinct narratives; indeed, the entire work would contain some two thousand separate narratives. But his formulation gives us no help in determining whether they can form one narrative. The reception-based definition is singularly clear: it is a narrative if you read it as one, but this is equally unhelpful in answering the question that the text provokes.

Here again, we find the rhetorical position "somebody telling somebody else on some occasion and for some purpose(s), that something happened" (Phelan, *Experiencing* 3) helpful, since the key question, What constitutes that elusive "something"?, is in this case central to the work's status as a narrative: the figure called Writer is telling readers several things, but do they form a single, related set of events, however oblique their connection may be?

I suggest once more that the most useful definition will be one that is less strict, less tightly bound to traditional practices, and less dependent on a realistic or humanistic paradigm. My own preferred formulation is the following: *narrative is a representation of a causally related series of events*. This definition would include verbal as well as nonverbal narratives (in painting, ballet, mime, etc.); "causally related" would be understood as "generally connected" in a substantial manner or part of the same general causal matrix—a much looser, more oblique, and more indefinite relation than direct entailment. It is further assumed that numerous nonnarrative elements may comfortably reside within a larger narrative framework and that human or humanlike characters are not required. Consider this account: "About 11,000 years ago, the Wisconsin glaciations ended. The ice sheet that covered the northern half of the United States receded, carving out the Great Lakes and creating many current geological features of the North American landscape." It seems clear to me that the text is a narrative, that is, the story of the movement of the glacier, despite its lack of humans, agency, teleology, closure, or allegory. Finally, the narratives we are dealing with in this study require an unnatural extension of this concept: we note that the causal definition does not discriminate against works that have one or more contradictions in the narrated events—a situation more common than is typically assumed, as we will see in chapter 5. Likewise, we do not require the events to be connected by human or natural agents; verbal generators, for example, can cause the successive events to ensue, as we will see in chapter 4.

On the last five pages of Markson's text we encounter these lines: "Writer's silent heart attack" (186); "Writer's right-lung lobectomy and resected ribs" (188); and "Writer's cancer" (190). It appears that Writer has been and may well be mortally ill. Though no timeline is given, the magnitude of these ailments suggests that death is probably not too far off. This gives the scattered lines a possible frame: the reader would seem to be invited to construe the preceding text as the thoughts or jottings of a man who has been very ill and is approaching death. In such an interpretation, in which the reader puts the narrative into the text in a much more active manner than one normally produces narrativity, there is a causally related sequence of events of a certain magnitude, as the lines about the deaths and sufferings of artists become plausible events in the consciousness of Writer. The book thereby becomes a narrative, even a novel, despite its title. It also has "an end, and even a note of sadness at the close" (4).

Defining a Single Narrative

Having established what a narrative is, we now may explore what a *single* narrative is; that is, at what point do divergent story lines break off and constitute independent narratives? As soon as an author decides to add a subplot to the main narrative, the question arises concerning how tightly it should be connected to the main plot or, conversely, how waywardly it may be allowed to roam. Many authors cannot resist the temptation to push narrative connection to its limit—and beyond. We may arrange these in a spectrum that moves from a single narrative to multiple ones. *King Lear* (1605) builds on two largely unconnected main plots that are, however, fused firmly together by the end of the play. The different stories about related characters at different times of their lives in Jennifer Egan's *A Visit from the Goon Squad* (2010) are sufficiently and substantially connected to form a single narrative, albeit a loose one. In Italo Calvino's *If on a winter's night a traveler* (1979), the frame tale is enough to (almost literally) bind together the otherwise unconnected chapters it surrounds; it rests comfortably at the edge of the boundary of a single narrative. Samuel Beckett's *Molloy* (1953) is situated precisely on the border separating a single story and two narratives; it seems, in fact, designed to produce this dilemma concerning its status and identity (see Richardson, "Causality"). I suggest that David Mitchell's *The Cloud Atlas* (2004) is ultimately composed of six separate novellas rather than constituting a single novel; the connections between the different stories (shared birthmark, awareness of the earlier narratives, hints that they are reincarnations of each other) are too slight to establish a substantial connection among them, a situation that was also the case of Ali Smith's *How to Be Both*. The same may be said of Joyce's *Dubliners* (1914): it remains primarily a set of distinct stories, despite claims occasionally made for the book to be considered a novel. Traveling further along this path, we reach William Faulkner's *The Wild Palms [If I Forget Thee, Jerusalem]* (1939), two separate narratives presented as alternating chapters in a single bound book (but also published separately; "Old Man" has frequently appeared alone). Here the connection is, as is often the case with such texts, thematic: a couple travels to preserve their love in one story, while in the counterstory an individual travels to flee love. Despite the thematic connection, there is no single narrative due to the absence of any causal relation embracing both stories.

This principle is tested by T. Coraghessan Boyle, who challenges the boundaries of (a single) narrative from the position of thematic connection. His text "The Extinction Tales" (1977) recounts the stories of several actual or attempted extinctions: the Stephen Island wren, the passenger pigeon, European Jewry, the smallpox virus, the Syrian wild ass, the aboriginal people of Tasmania, the dodo, and others. Near the end, the narrator describes the impending death of the solar system; in the last paragraph, he recounts a visit to his father's grave on a winter night. The power of the juxtapositions impels us to try to connect the multiple stories into a single larger, even cosmic, tale, perhaps of humanity's repeated destruction of other species and peoples. But it is not a simple story or an invariant one: the extinction may be intentional or accidental. Most are to be lamented or cause horror (genocides), but some are good for humans and promote life (the eradication of the virus that causes smallpox). The question of the work's narrativity comes down to whether all these instances can be viewed as an aspect of a single, larger story—say, that of the ultimate destruction of all living things—or whether, at the opposite end of the cosmic scale, the narrator's contemplation of his father's tombstone can somehow contain or encompass the various extinction tales. My own sense is that the final passages frame multiple distinct narratives rather than conclude a single story.

As indicated by Boyle's related stories, the question of the identity of a narrative's actual subject or subjects is of considerable significance in determining the status of that narrative. We see this more prominently in Caryl Phillips's work *Crossing the River* (1993), a text that likewise challenges the definition of narrative. Composed of a preface and four sections that are set in three continents over two and a half centuries, these narratives of the African diaspora are independent when treated as the stories of unrelated individuals; the parts are instead connected merely thematically—with the exception of a distant African narrative voice that appears in the beginning and at the end of the text. But the book, through its genre identification as "a novel," insists on its status as a single narrative and thereby invites us to read it as a united, if extremely episodic, story of the African experience around the Atlantic. The ancient African narrator says he has sold three of his children into slavery; the three stories represent all of slavery's children. Each of the three central characters has a history that is similar or analogous to the others' in significant ways. Still, there is no reason to assume that Martha, the freed slave who dies in Denver on her way to California to look for her child, is a close relative or direct descendant of the characters presented in an earlier time frame. But in an important sense she is a later avatar of them, emblematic of the familial quests and dislocations that haunt them all.

To place this work in its context, we may note that there are several African American dramas that similarly chronicle a century or more of the group's historical experience by focusing on multiple different, unrelated individuals who are connected not by blood but by history (see Richardson, "Genre, Transgression"). These include Langston Hughes's "Don't You Want to Be Free?" (1938) and Amiri Baraka's "Slave Ship" (1967). Baraka's story starts on a slave ship in the Atlantic; moves on to a nineteenth-century slave plantation; and ends in the 1960s. Other postcolonial authors situate their narratives within an even longer temporal period. Ayi Kwei Armah's novel *Two Thousand Seasons,* as its title announces, covers the history of black Africans for a thousand years. Perhaps the longest is presented in Qurratulain Hyder's *River of Fire* (1959), which traces out the lives of similar and similarly named individuals in India who all face analogous problems during a period that lasts more than two thousand years. These works, too, stretch or straddle the boundaries of narrative.

It might also be noted that there is also an equal and opposite postmodern strategy for destabilizing the narrative line: the repetition of a single story with certain variations that eventually produce a very different story. Clarice Lispector begins her tale "The Fifth Story" with the following words: "This story could be called 'The Statues.' Another possible title would be 'The Killing.' Or even 'How to Kill Cockroaches.' . . . Although they constitute one story, they could become a thousand and one, were I to be granted a thousand and one nights" (75). In this work, a series of ever more detailed, varied, and allegorical accounts of the same basic narrative situation produces a cluster of ever-changing stories, the fifth of which is titled "Leibnitz and the Transcendence of Love in Polynesia." Here, no story ever stays the same; every new version is a partially new narrative.

What Is Not Narrative?

Having clarified the concept of narrative, we need now to establish its extent. As David Herman has affirmed, the status of being a narrative "is a binary predicate: something either is or is not a story" (*Story* 90). Porter Abbott similarly observes that once a text's status as a narrative is established, "you can't turn a narrative into non-narrative" no matter how much nonnarrative material it may contain. In the case of *Moby Dick,* despite the numerous nonnarrative elements—the descriptions, the philosophical asides, the encyclopedia entries, the quotations from whaling manuals, and so forth—the work is just as much a narrative as if there had been none of these ("What" 270). Likewise, legal documents or philosophical treatises may contain a large number of narratives, but they do not change their fundamental status as nonnarrative texts. Once we determine the essentially narrative nature of the text, the work's basic narrativity is established, as the examples of borderline cases I have discussed in this chapter bear out, I believe. Generally speaking, once we establish that "Ping" or *This Is Not a Novel* is a narrative, there is a "click" that, to employ Abbott's metaphor, is like a switch being thrown; the work is and remains a narrative.[13] Once we perceive that *Moby Dick* is a narrative, no amount of nonnarrative material can undo its narrative status.

These issues are important because narrative is frequently defined in relation to other texts or discourse types that share some features with it but ultimately are different. Abbott writes, "Without an event or an action, you may have a 'description,' an 'exposition,' an 'argument,' or a 'lyric,' some combination of these or something else altogether, but you won't have a narrative" (*Cambridge* 13). Herman similarly contrasts genuine narratives with "an exchange of greetings, a recipe for salad dressing, or a railway timetable" (*Basic* 2). Phelan distinguishes narrative from lyric and portraiture (*Living* 161–63), and Wolf Schmid asserts that "descriptive texts are the opposite of texts which are narrative. . . . Descriptive texts represent states: they describe conditions, draw pictures or portraits, portray social milieus, or categorize natural or social phenomena"; he clarifies that "they represent a single moment in time and a singular state of affairs" (5).

Generally speaking, these narratologists are essentially correct; some of these other discursive types, however, have occasionally strayed into the realm of narrative, especially lyric poetry, which frequently includes compelling micronarratives and gestures toward a larger narrative framework. Creative writers love a challenge, and, as the Loki Principle indicates, transgressing

---

13. An exception to this rule would be the case of a text that begins with a short, illustrative narrative and then goes on to become a nonnarrative text like a law article, critical study, or psychological analysis; in this case, the narrative "click" is dissolved.

the boundaries of one text type into another often proves to be irresistible. As I will discuss more extensively in chapter 6, a number of texts take nonnarrative forms and then, by adding narrative elements, transform into fullfledged narratives. John Updike uses the format of arithmetical test questions to relate a narrative in his short story "Problems" (1979), and several authors use the self-help manual form, including Pam Houston ("How to Talk to a Hunter") and Lorrie Moore (many of the stories in *Self-Help*). Other authors have turned recipes into stories, like Harry Mathews's "Country Cooking from Central France: Roast Boned Rolled Stuffed Shoulder of Lamb (Farcie Double)"; many others have transgressed the boundaries between lists and narratives, as I have discussed in a paper on the subject ("Modern"). One reason that narratives in the form of recipes or self-help books are so entertaining is that we can observe them moving from the nonnarrative realm into that of narrative proper. Ruth Ronen has noted the ways that descriptions become narrative acts in many modern texts; Robbe-Grillet is especially ingenious in ways in which he collapses the two categories, as we can see from "The Secret Room" and the painting *The Defeat of Reichenfels* which comes alive at the beginning of *Dans le labyrinthe*. In all these cases, we may see the Loki Principle in action, as these creative artists cannot resist transgressing the fixed boundaries of standard discursive forms.

We need to also note seminarrative genres like annals and chronicles (see Hayden White), and the portrait and the sketch. These normally exist on the boundary between clearly narrative forms like a story and typically nonnarrative form like a list or a description. They are often defined as nonnarrative genres; in his study of the subject, Amanpal Garcha observes that "the sketch, by its origin, history, and form, is [. . .] opposed to plottedness" and notes that its stasis stands "against narrative movement" (40). In many instances, however, we see a limited set of connections between a few events. Even Kafka's text "A Little Woman," which Todorov adduces as an example of the nontemporal and nonnarrative genre of the portrait (42), is filled with narrative elements, such as the question of how the woman came to hate and vow revenge against the narrator. Many of these can best be seen as minimally narrative forms, almost, as Ryan says of annals and chronicles, "plotless forms of narrative" ("Cheap" 69).

Events, Eventfulness, and Non-Events

Narratives are composed of events; events are their fundamental unit. Porter Abbott, however, has ingeniously established that an event is not a stable, theoretical primitive, but rather something always able to be differently configured: "There has been much theorizing about such problematic issues as what constitutes an event, how events may be classified, and whether some kinds of events do or do not qualify as narrative events. But one problem that has rarely come up is the fact that all events can be decompressed. That is, any event can be opened up to reveal events within it[,] . . . and so on interminably" ("Law" 4). Readers will always constitute events, and will often constitute them differently. In his important work on the subject, Wolf Schmid attempts to delimit the concept of event. Building on studies by Yuri Lotman and others, he identifies an event as a deviation from normative regularity. He further differentiates events from mere changes of state: "Every event is a change of state, but not every change of state is an event" (9). These distinctions can be useful when discussing modernist authors' fascination with seemingly trivial events (or changes); nevertheless, it needs to be observed that Abbott's objections to the concept of the event also apply to Schmid's construction. Finally, we note that Peter Hühn has gone on to develop the concept of the non-event, that is, an anticipated event that does not occur (e.g., Godot's failure to arrive). This is a frequent trope of modern fiction; we may even say that never before have so many events failed to occur.

The Unnarrated, the Disnarrated, the Denarrated

All narratives necessarily leave aspects of the story unnarrated, and what is not narrated can be of great importance—more important, at times, than some of what is narrated. As D. A. Miller noted, "Every discourse is uttered against a background of all the things that it chooses, for one reason or another, not to say. Three subjects that Jane Austen's novels do not treat, for instance, are the Napoleonic wars, the sex lives of the characters, and the labor of the tenants who farm their estates. The first of these is only an unincluded subject of discourse; the second in an unincluded and also forbidden topic; the third is unincluded and perhaps (there are more than sexual taboos) forbidden as well" (4).

Gerald Prince has offered the category of the disnarrated to cover "all the events that *do not* happen but, nonetheless, are referred to (in a negative or hypothetical mode) by the narrative text" ("Disnarrated" 2). Concerning the nature and content of the disnarrated, Prince notes "The level at which it functions, the relative frequency with which it appears, and the relative amount of space it occupies can be a useful tool for characterizing narrative manners, schools, movements, and even entire periods" (6); he observes that it is in decline in contemporary literature. He further notes that "one narrator's unnarratable can very well be another's narratable" and refers to the example of Beckett (2); *Waiting for Godot* has been humorously described as the play in which nothing happens, twice. Philippe Carrard has shown that historical narratives contain numerous disnarrations, such as, "Had Hitler then gone on to attack Moscow, the war would have changed. Instead . . ." ("What If"). Alethea Black, in "You, On a Good Day" (2012), has written an extended story, the first half of which is entirely composed of disnarrated statements: "You do not come home, you do not drink a bottle of wine, and feel that you could easily drink another. You do not smoke the pack of cigarettes you promised yourself you wouldn't smoke but nonetheless failed to throw away" (7–8).

Building on the work of both D. A. Miller and Gerald Prince, Robyn Warhol has produced an excellent guide to this important but potentially nebulous territory. She offers four categories of the unnarratable, which, according to a given narrative, (1) needn't be told (the subnarratable) because it is too trivial; (2) can't be told because it transcends narrative articulation (the supranarratable), such as representations of major traumas; (3) shouldn't be told (the antinarratable) due to cultural prohibitions; and (4) wouldn't be told (the paranarratable) due to genre conventions; for example, the heroine of a romantic comedy cannot accidentally kill her new husband on their wedding night ("Neonarrative" 222).

Warhol observes that both copulation and excretion were antinarratable in Victorian fiction, "so that when James Joyce places Leopold Bloom on a toilet in *Ulysses,* he is perhaps making his most radical break with Victorian limits of unnarratability by changing the boundaries of the unnarratable" (224). Joyce includes many other previously unnarratable events in his epic of the human body, including urination, nose-picking, masturbation, and menstruation. He delves deep into the previously antinarratable as he is occupying large swaths of the subnarratable. Warhol's categories are especially useful to describe the change in what was narratable as performed by modernist writers.

Elsewhere, Warhol (like Prince) is careful not to overextend her claims; she wisely clarifies that she is generally discussing each concept "*according to a given narrative*" (222). These terms can become slippery as soon as one ventures beyond the confines of a single text. What is subnarratable for many traditional male writers, like sewing, arranging flowers, or cooking, may be highly narratable for women, as Virginia Woolf and many others have shown. The supranarratable may be still more variable: some writers excel at narrating extreme experiences that others find untellable. The antinarratable is quite vexing. The question will always be: antinarratable to whom? Though Jane Austen could not narrate the sex lives of her characters, others could and did in sexual fiction, from Cleland's *Fanny Hill* to Victorian pornographers. It could be written and secretly published, but not legally disseminated. And what do we do with books like *Ulysses* or *Lolita* which were banned and generally unable to be read in the US and the UK for many years, even though they obviously could be written? There may be a legal as well as an ideological component to the antinarratable—as is certainly true for writers working under conditions of censorship. Nevertheless, these are very useful categories that deserve to be explored more fully.

Extending these observations, we may rethink some basic aspects of modern and contemporary narrative practice. Concerning the antinarratable, the changes are obvious: there is very little—no matter how sexually explicit, intimately private, graphically violent, vulgar, disgusting, cruel, or obscene—that does not routinely appear in widely circulated narratives, especially on the internet. As to the subnarratable, the transformations have also been sweeping. Whether it is Joyce following the ramblings of a couple of Dubliners on a June day, or Woolf describing the events leading up to a dinner party, or Musil's opening chapter in *Der Man ohne Eigenschaften,* "From Which, Remarkably Enough, Nothing Follows," as the English translation of its title states, it is clear that many modernists are consciously attempting to radically extend the realm of the narratable, and to take the conventionally unnarratable and make it worthy of a story, even as they chip away further at the limitations imposed by the antinarratable. The work of Beckett and many *nouveau romanciers* go much further in both of these directions, as does Nicholson Baker, whose novel *The Mezzanine* will be discussed in chapter 3.

CHAPTER 2

Modeling Narrative Beginnings

BEGINNINGS ARE a foundational element of every narrative, fictional or nonfictional, public or private, official or subversive. Generally speaking, this subject has been rather neglected and is only recently becoming known. Currently, there are only a handful of studies that address this surprisingly rich and elusive subject, but other works are now starting to give beginnings the historical, theoretical, and ideological analysis that the subject requires. This critical and theoretical neglect is particularly surprising given the power that beginnings possess for the act of reading. Many readers remember for years salient beginning sentences such as the following: "It is a truth universally acknowledged, that a single man in possession of a good fortune must be in want of a wife"; "Call me Ishmael"; "All happy families resemble one another, but each unhappy family is unhappy in its own way"; "Longtemps, je me suis couché de bonne heure"; "Mrs. Dalloway said she would buy the flowers herself"; "A screaming came across the sky." Such a list (which could be extended considerably) indicates the conceptual and emotional power concentrated in resonant opening lines of works that move us—or even those that no longer move us. For example, although Camus is rapidly falling out of the canon, the first words of *L'Étranger* continue to reverberate: "Aujourd'hui, maman est morte."

Two key moments in the history of literature continue to resonate among narrative beginnings. One is Tristram Shandy's unfortunate conception, birth, and christening, which doom him to be out of order for the rest of his life. This beginning is accompanied by the nonchronological presentation of the rest of the story, including an array of temporally anterior episodes that threaten to undermine the possibility of establishing a fixed beginning point in the story, or *fabula*. This regressive narration is in turn paralleled by the unconventional placement of normally prefatory paratextual material throughout the text (most notoriously, the situating of the author's preface in the middle of the third volume). Sterne's practice would rapidly become an irresistible model for subsequent authors who played with chronology and beginnings, from Denis Diderot and Lord Byron to Salman Rushdie and Alasdair Gray.

The second key moment is the famous pause before the first stroke of Lily Briscoe's paintbrush in *To the Lighthouse* (1927):

> She took her hand and raised her brush. For a moment it stayed trembling in a painful but exciting ecstasy in the air. Where to begin?—that was the question; at what point to make the first mark? One line placed on the canvas committed her to innumerable risks, to frequent and irrevocable decisions. All that in idea seemed simple became in practice immediately complex; [. . . .] Still the risk must be run; the mark made. With a curious physical sensation, as if she were urged forward and at the same time must hold herself back, she made her first quick decisive stroke. (157–58)

Woolf here articulates key psychological and compositional implications of beginning an artwork; intriguingly, they do not match up at all with Woolf's own inspired beginning of *To the Lighthouse*—she wrote the first twenty-two pages "straight off in less than a fortnight" (Lee 471)—but they correspond better with the difficult beginning of her previous novel, *Mrs. Dalloway* (1925), which required several drafts. This passage also encapsulates some of the issues that would later be debated by narrative theorists, including the question of how much a work's beginning determines what follows it.

A brief glance at some of the varieties of beginnings that have been deployed in narrative will help frame the discussion that follows. Postmodern texts frequently foreground the first passages of the narrative, often in a paradoxical or parodic manner. The first words of Raymond Federman's *Double or Nothing* (1971) appear in a section whose heading reads, "This Is Not the Beginning." There are many examples we might draw from Beckett, such as "Birth was the death of him" (*Fizzle* 4), which contest the ordinary function of the beginning, as I will be discussing later in this chapter. In Flann O'Brien's early proto-postmodern text, *At Swim-Two-Birds* (1939), the narrator states: "One beginning and one ending was a thing I did not agree with. A good book may have three openings entirely dissimilar and inter-related only in the prescience of the author" (9), and this novel, in fact, has four beginnings, as Brian McHale has discussed (*Postmodernist* 109). Daniel Handler's *Watch Your Mouth* (2000) similarly has four beginnings in homage to "Beethoven, whose only opera clears its throat with not one but four possible overtures" (5).

Nabokov's *Ada* (1969) begins allusively and parodically: "'All happy families are more or less dissimilar; all unhappy ones are more or less alike,' says a great Russian writer in the beginning of a famous novel (*Anna Arkadievitch Karenina*, transfigured into English by R. G. Stonelower, Mount Tabor Ltd., 1880). That pronouncement has little if any relation to the story to be unfolded now" (3). Alasdair Gray redeploys a number of Shandean strategies in *Lanarck* (1981): the novel begins with Book Three, and it is followed, one hundred pages later, by the Prologue and Book One. In *Midnight's Children* (1981), Salman Rushdie is constantly interrogating beginnings—national, individual, and novelistic—and the novel contains numerous false beginnings as well. At the beginning of the eleventh chapter the narrator, Saleem Sinai, pretentiously refers to Valmiki's dictation of the *Ramayana* to the god Ganesh. He is, however, mistaken; it was in fact Vyasa who is said to have dictated *The Mahabharata* to Ganesh at the beginning of that other Sanskrit epic (see Narayan).

Macedonio Fernández has written a novel, *The Museum of Eterna's Novel (The First Good Novel)* (1967), half of which is composed of more than fifty prologues. Italo Calvino expresses a fascination with narrative beginning in *If on a winter's night a traveler* (1979), a book largely composed of the first chapters of several different novels. The narrator states: "The romantic fascination produced in the pure state by the first sentences of the first chapter of many novels is soon lost in the continuation of the story: it is the promise of a time of reading that extends before us and can comprise all possible developments. I would like to write a book that is only an *incipit,* that maintains for its whole duration the potentiality of the beginning, the expectation still not focused on an object" (177). Although there is a rather traditional frame story woven around the volume's many opening chapters, the sense of the power and possibilities of beginnings is never lost in the novel.

Beginnings have always been part of critical discourse, though often in a way that has belied the complexities and ramifications of this deceptive, rich, and elusive topic. In antiquity, two statements stand out. The first is Aristotle's observation that "a beginning is that which itself does not of necessity follow something else, but after which there naturally is, or comes into being, something else" (94, §7.3), a claim that is much more problematic than Aristotle imagined. The other famous ancient dictum is Horace's injunction to begin the telling in the middle of the story, in medias res, rather than from the strict beginning; Homer, he notes approvingly, begins the *Iliad* with the wrath of Achilles near the end of the Trojan War, not with Leda's egg (ab ovo), from which Helen emerged. With this, the opposition between the beginning of the story (fabula) and the beginning of its telling (syuzhet) first emerges in literary criticism.

Other classical critical traditions offer additional insights. In the *Natyashastra*, Sanskrit dramatic theorist Bharata devotes several lines to the proper arrangement of the preliminary stage matter and to prologues of classical Indian dramas as found in plays like Kalidasa's *Shakuntala* (2nd century CE). This type of recessed opening entered Western drama after being incorporated into the triple beginning (dedication, prelude in the theater, and prologue in heaven) of Goethe's *Faust* (1808), as Ekbert Faas remarks (161–62). Concerning the events of the story, Bharata defines the beginning (*prarambha*) as the part of the play that creates a curiosity about the attainment of the major objective (379), in which the seed of the plot (*bija*) is created and "scattered in small measure" (381); the *prarambha* produces the opening (*mukha*) and provides the source of the play's many objects, events, and sentiments (384).

Modern theorists of beginnings have generally gravitated toward one of three positions: (1) the attempt, like Aristotle's, to establish a fixed point where the sequence of events commences; (2) the identification of two paradoxically opposed trajectories which writers must navigate between; and (3) the hypothesis that all beginnings are somehow arbitrary, fabricated, or illusory. I will discuss each of these types in the following three sections.

Fixed Beginnings

Vladimir Propp imagined folktales as discrete entities with unambiguous starting points ("The king sends Ivan after the princess"). The subsequent structuralist tradition would continue to articulate story beginnings in a similar fashion. Todorov would formalize Propp's analysis into the general claim that an initial state of equilibrium is disturbed by the introduction of a serious disequilibrium; the narrative then attempts to reestablish a new equilibrium that is similar but not identical to the original state (50–52). Other structuralists would employ comparable formulations (Bremond; Prince *Grammar*), as would Peter Brooks in his study of plot (38). This general stance would also inform cognitive approaches as well as work in the social sciences, for example, the positions of J. M. Mandler and Nancy Stein, both of whom stress the establishment of the setting and the initiating event (see Stein and Policastro [113–27] for an overview of these and related positions). Meir Sternberg, in his seminal account of narrative exposition, gives signal importance to the first scene represented in a narrative: this act establishes the work's "fictive present," and all temporally prior material belongs to the exposition, regardless of where it appears in the text. "The exposition always constitutes the beginning of the fabula, the first part of the chronologically ordered sequence of motifs as reconstructed by the reader; but it is not necessarily located at the beginning of the sujet" (*Expositional* 13–14). Using the example of Henry James's *The Ambassadors*, Sternberg states that "the beginning of the fabula is the earliest event in Strether's history that we learn about in the course of the novel (namely, his marriage); while the beginning of the sujet coincides, of course, with the beginning of the first chapter" (9–10). I also situate James Phelan's concepts of "launch" and "initiation" here, with the important caveat that Phelan's rhetorical conception of narrative insists on dialectical interactions among beginnings, middles, and endings ("Beginning").[1]

Paradoxes of Beginnings

Edward Said analyzes a number of paradoxes and oppositions inherent in the concept of beginnings. Beginnings seem always predetermined, yet they also appear to mark a distinct break from that which precedes them. He approvingly quotes Valéry's pointed remark: "We say that an author is *original* when we cannot trace the hidden transformations that others underwent in his mind" (15). Though the notion of genuine originality is fallacious, the artist may produce an intentional beginning act that "authorizes" the work. He goes on to identify two types of works that center on beginnings, one whose starting point is "hysterically deliberate" (e. g., *Tristram Shandy*), in which "the beginning is postponed, with a kind of encyclopedic, meaningful playfulness" (44). The other category includes *Paradise Lost* and *The Prelude*; in both of these instances, "what was initially intended to be the beginning became the work itself" (44).[2] Stephen Kellman, in his study of opening lines of a work, has posited a different opposition, noting that opening lines generally do one of two things: either "[to] thrust us immediately into the text or to retard our

---

1. For Phelan, *launch* refers to the introduction of a work's global instabilities or tensions; *initiation* specifies the initial narratorial dynamics, including the narrator's original relation to the text and the implied reader (see Herman, et al., *Narrative* 57–62).

2. Said also differentiates the human, secular, consciously intentional, and ceaselessly reexamined concept of *beginnings* from the idea of *origins*, which are instead theological, mythical, and privileged. Thus, "an origin *centrally* dominates what derives from it" (373), while the beginning encourages nonlinear development, relations of adjacency, and a movement toward dispersion.

encounter until we are prepared for it" (146). A. D. Nuttall outlines a comparable though rather more cosmic dichotomy, the artificial versus the "natural" beginning, and focuses on "the various tensions which exist between the formal freedom to begin a work where one likes and an opposite sense that all good openings are somehow naturally rooted, are echoes, more or less remote, of an original creative act: *in medias res,* as against 'In the beginning'" (vii–viii). By the end of his analysis he finds both terms of this dichotomy to be problematic. Niels Buch Leander's study, *The Sense of a Beginning: Theory of the Literary Opening,* identifies and examines several oppositions, including origins and beginnings, "natural" and artificial beginnings, and abrupt and extended openings. The studies identified here, it should be noted, are primarily concerned with the rhetoric and effects of opening passages of works of fiction.

Beginning as Fabrication

J. Hillis Miller suggests that "the paradox of beginnings is that one must have something solidly present and pre-existent, some generative source or authority, on which the development of a new story may be based. That antecedent foundation needs in its turn some prior foundation, in an infinite regress" (57). Melba Cuddy-Keane, looking at modernist narratives (especially those by Woolf), likewise takes up the question of the foundations or grounding that beginnings seem to imply; her essay draws important attention to beginning's "ragged edge," starting points that always turn out to be provisional or arbitrary and point back to still earlier (though no more definitive) beginnings, suggesting the possibility of what might be called an endless "writing before the beginning." My own approach continues in this direction and emphasizes unresolvable problems in the establishment of definitive beginnings in a work's story (fabula), discourse (syuzhet), and preliminary epitext.

Multifaceted Theories of Beginnings

The most comprehensive works that delineate a number of distinct starting points are those of Andrea Del Lungo, James Phelan, and Catherine Romagnolo. Del Lungo offers four points of approach: "commencer le texte (fonction codifiante); intéresser le lecture (fonction séductive); mettre en scène la fiction (fonction informative); metre en marche l'histoire (fonction dramatique)" (138); that is, beginning the text, interesting the reader, setting the scene, and starting the story. Phelan similarly outlines four different starting points in narrative which, with the partial exception of the final one, match up with Del Lungo's, though Phelan's development of these categories is rather different: (1) the exposition or setting; (2) the launch, or opening instability that sets the plot in motion; (3) the initiation, or commencement of engagement between author or narrator and audience; and (4) the entrance, which initiates the reader's entry into the narrative proper. Romagnolo offers an equally thorough modeling of the various types of beginning, which designate a work's discourse (primary and secondary), story (chronological), and plot (causal) (xix–xxvii). Significantly, she also includes another category, "conceptual," for thematic beginnings, since works that foreground formal beginning strategies regularly interweave thematic discussions of origins into their texts. This daring move helps push narrative theory toward a constructivist perspective that refuses to separate strategies of narrative composition from the larger conceptual issues that inspire those techniques.

A Theory of Narrative Beginnings

To determine the beginning of a narrative, I suggest we identify three distinct kinds of beginning: one in the narrative *text* (syuzhet), one in the *story* as reconstructed from the text (fabula), and one in the prefatory and framing material provided by the author that circumscribes the narrative proper (*authorial antetext*). There is also what may be called an *institutional antetext* that frames (or attempts to frame) the book before it is read. My concept of the beginning of the story or fabula corresponds more or less to Del Lungo's starting of the story (*histoire*), Phelan's launch, and Romagnolo's beginning of the story (chronological); my idea of the beginning of text or syuzhet corresponds to Del Lungo's starting of the text, Phelan's entrance, and Romagnolo's primary discursive beginning.

The Beginning of the Syuzhet

In nearly all cases (except those that are touched by a Shandean playfulness), there is no ambiguity concerning the beginning of the syuzhet: in written narratives, it is the first page of the narrative proper.[3] It is perhaps the very fix-

---

3. For a discussion of beginnings in oral narratives and the ritual formulas that explicitly mark the beginning of the story, see Jean-Louis Morhange, pp. 389–93.

ity of the syuzhet that is the ground for play with beginnings in the other two areas. Several postmodern narratives have appeared that dislodge this stability; there is the "novel in the box" by Marc Saporta (*Composition No. 1*, 1962), a series of unnumbered autonomous pages which the reader is invited to shuffle before reading as one would a deck of cards. Ana Castillo's epistolary novel *The Mixquiahuala Letters* (1986) extends the compositional technique of Julio Cortázar's *Rayuela* [*Hopscotch*, 1963]) and offers different points of entry for different readers: cynics are advised to begin with the second letter, while the quixotic are told to begin with letter number three. Many hypertext novels have several possible points of entry, as Jessica Laccetti explores. At the end of the section called "Begin" in Michael Joyce's *afternoon: a story*, the text asks, "Do you want to hear about it?" and offers two different narrative paths, depending on whether the reader clicks on "yes" or "no."

The Beginning of the Fabula

The important question of exactly where the story or fabula begins is, by contrast, a difficult one to determine with precision. Is it the chronologically first dramatized scene, narrated incident, mentioned act, or inferable event? Each possible answer is problematic. Sternberg, as I have just noted, states that the beginning of the fabula of *The Ambassadors* is the first narrated event in the history of Lambert Strether. But Sternberg does not indicate the criterion he uses for this determination, nor does he consider other possibilities of establishing the origin of the fabula, such as the earliest recounted or summarized event in the history of Strether's life; or the story of his family; or the stories of related figures, such as the account of the fortune assembled by Chad Newsom's grandfather, money which helps enable Chad to live in Paris and thus bring Strether deep into the novel's plot. Neither does Sternberg mention the difficulties that would be posed by more ambiguous, recessive, or irretrievable beginnings of the fabula in more elusive texts. And there are texts in which the first dramatized scene is not part of the story proper, as in Joseph Conrad's depiction of the misadventure of the legendary gringos on Azuera at the beginning of *Nostromo* (1904).

Even a seemingly straightforward example can reveal how hard it is to come up with a definitive beginning that does not require several interpretive decisions that are unlikely to be agreed upon by many readers. We will start with a text that contains several references to the past, James Joyce's "The Dead" (1914), and ask where its story begins. If our definition is that of dramatized scenes, then it begins as the guests are arriving at the party at the

Morkans': with one partial exception at the beginning of the text, there are no analepses; the entire narrative is told in a completely linear manner, as any reference to the past comes from memory or a conversation in the "narrative present tense." But this response is clearly inadequate, since the point of the story is the revelation of a significant past event, the death of Michael Furey, and its powerful transformation of the protagonist, Gabriel Conroy. This centerpiece of the story, narrated by Gretta, would have to be part of the fabula, I believe. Otherwise, to take another example, all the past events of Oedipus's life would not be part of the fabula of Sophocles's *Oedipus Rex* (429 BCE); this is clearly an unsatisfactory conclusion, since the story has to stretch at least as far back as the prophecy that stated that Oedipus would kill his father and marry his mother. Mieke Bal is one of the few theorists to discuss this possibility; she calls it an "embedded fabula that explains and determines the primary fabula" (144). However, this ingenious delineation will seem inadequate to most theorists, I suspect: to refer to the cause of the central story as an embedded fabula would seem to imply it may not be the same story, simply because it is disclosed by a character's speech rather than through stage enactment or authorial narration.[4]

But if we allow narrated events into the fabula, and it seems we must, where do we stop? Should we not consider any other anterior events that are discussed or alluded to by the characters equally part of the story proper? Through conversations and free indirect discourse in "The Dead," we learn of Lily's leaving school; last year's party; Freddy Malin's penchant for borrowing; Gabriel's attending the university with Molly Ivors; his deceased mother's disapproval of Gretta when they married; virtues of long-deceased tenors; and, in what may be the oldest recalled event, the story of Gabriel's grandfather's horse (an episode, it might be noted, that is unconnected to the main story line but that acts as a mise en abyme of Gabriel's situation). Is this the beginning of the fabula? There are of course many other earlier events implicitly alluded to as well: the statue of Daniel O'Connell, the Wellington monument, and even the picture of the two princes murdered in the Tower of London all attest to distant historical events. For that matter, the references to Christmas

---

4. We can get a clear sense of what is at stake in these different positions by probing deeper into the example of *Oedipus Rex*, which Sternberg refers to as a "plot-type sujet" due to its chronologically "deformed causal disposition of motifs" (*Expositional* 12). The story of Oedipus's birth and abandonment is, of course, not dramatized; it is only deducible from the various (and contradictory) oral accounts given by the various personages during the unfolding of the drama. As Sandor Goodhart has shown, it may well be that the backstory that everyone ends up believing has some interesting discrepancies and may not, in fact, be entirely true. This should warn us against uncritically including uncorroborated episodes derived from characters' narratives as part of the fabula. Sometimes they are, and sometimes they aren't.

presume the birth of Jesus, while the allusions to ancient Greek divinities and an enemy hero (Paris) take us further back to the time of the Trojan War—we have now arrived at the literal *ovo* that Horace had admonished us about.

This line of argumentation can be pushed even further. The opening sentence of Beckett's *Murphy* (1938), "The sun shone, having no alternative, on the nothing new" (1), both invokes the statement from Ecclesiastes and may imply an earlier time before the sun could be said to shine. Amos Oz, in his book on narrative beginnings, takes this position even further, and asks: "Isn't there always, without exception, a latent beginning-before-the-beginning? A foreword to the introduction to the prologue?" (8–9). He goes on to suggest that any story, "if it is to live up to its ideal duty, must go back at least all the way to the Big Bang, that cosmic orgasm with which, presumably, all the smaller bangs began" (10). Not only is there a definite logic in Oz' playful statement, but the fact of the matter is that such an infinite regress of antecedents not only can be but actually has been put in practice. It is not unusual for Native American autobiographers to begin with the story of their ancestors or their nation, or to go even further back: Geronimo's story of his life starts with the words "In the beginning the world was covered with darkness. There was no sun, no day" (59); only after several creation stories and a brief account of the various Apache groups does he arrive at the moment when he is born (69).

In the realm of popular fiction, one may similarly point to the epic sagas of James A. Michener, which often begin with the geological origins of the setting of the work, followed by accounts of the earliest human habitation, and then stories of wave after wave of immigration over the centuries. *Hawaii*, for example, starts with the words "Millions upon millions of years ago, when the continents were already formed" (1) and goes on to narrate the emergence of the Hawaiian Islands from the seafloor. We might also note that at the beginning of the Spike Jonze/Charlie Kaufman film, "Adaptation" (2004), the question "How did I get here?" is answered by a very rapid presentation of the history of the world beginning with the cooling of the earth 4.4 billion years ago and concluding with the protagonist's birth.

So where, then, does the story really begin? I don't think there is an easy solution to this dilemma. One other obvious possibility is to take the first incident that is causally connected to those that follow; such a choice would correspond well to a number of different accounts, including Aristotle's definition of "that which itself does not of necessity follow something else, but after which there naturally is, or comes into being, something else" (94, §7.3), as well as the statement in Gerald Prince's *Dictionary of Narratology*: "the incident initiating the process of change in a plot or action. This incident does not necessarily follow but is necessarily followed by other incidents" (10). Also consonant with this approach are Peter Brooks's identification of the beginning as the initiation of narrative desire, Phelan's notion of "launch," and the theoreticians who, drawing on story grammars, identify the beginning as the first item in the sequence of connected significant events (Tomashevsky's bound motifs, Barthes's cardinal functions [*Image* 93–97], and Chatman's kernels [*Story* 53–56]).

But if the idea of the first event referred to by the text is far too inclusive, the idea of the first function is much too restrictive. Most of the events narrated in the early portions of "The Dead" (and many of the subsequent ones until Gabriel's encounter with Molly Ivors) are not directly connected to the events that follow; they are, rather, what Tomashevsky would call "free motifs," Barthes "indices," and Chatman "satellites." The main drama at the beginning of "The Dead" is the fear that Freddy Malins will, once again, drink too much and spoil the party. It never happens; Freddy turns out to be just fine. This non-event is instead an example of what one might designate, adapting Phelan's term, a "false launch."[5] Our perception of the beginning of the story or fabula can be complicated by the proliferation of minor anterior events or digressions that are not necessary to the unfolding of the plot. They are red herrings that promise to produce conflicts that do not in fact appear and that, to vary the metaphor, constitute a series of visible pistols that, despite Chekhov's dictum, are never fired.

In many seemingly "plotless" modernist works, many events are included for their thematic, symbolic, or analogical relation to the main events of the text, not because they partake in an unbroken chain of causally connected events such as that found in a novel by Jane Austen. The sequence of the bound motifs must thus be reduced to a subset of the story, and determining the first instance of the former will not help us establish the beginning of the latter. Bound motifs, those "which may not be omitted without disturbing the coherence of the narrative" (Tomashevsky 166), are useful concepts for the analysis of many tightly plotted works, and we may understand why many theorists like Propp, Brooks, Phelan (launch), and Romagnolo (causal beginnings) wish to employ this as a central category of analysis, even as some (like Romagnolo xxvii) note how difficult it can be to find the precise origin of this elusive thread. In between the bound motifs and the free motifs there often exists a hazy realm of ambiguous motifs that are neither entirely bound nor exactly free. Thus, Gabriel's brief encounter with Lily near the beginning of the text almost certainly has no consequences for the chain of events that later unfolds; it anticipates rather than precipitates them. The

---

5. On this subject, see Werner Wolf's essay, "Defamiliarized Initial Framings in Fiction."

same can be said of his later encounter with Molly Ivors. One could imagine a more deterministic reading that affirms that this later encounter makes him more uneasy about his status, actions, and relations with women and thereby aggravates his final unfortunate scene with his wife. However, even in this case, the earlier episodes could be removed without significantly impacting the central drama in the last third of the text.

I conclude from this investigation that if we are to determine the actual beginning of a story, which seems a basic narratological objective, we need to critically sift through the various possibilities—whether dramatized, narrated by a character, or otherwise alluded to—until we arrive at the first substantial event of the story or, stated more precisely, *the earliest event that significantly impacts later events in the story.* Our definition will thus be a somewhat fluid one, and one that thereby points to the elusive and often arbitrary nature of beginnings. The consequence for our reading of "The Dead" is thus a paradoxical one: a strict reading will establish the beginning with Michael Furey's infatuation with Gretta, or even Gabriel's unnarrated childhood, which, one may postulate, forms his insecure personality. On the other hand, building on recent postcolonial criticism of the text, it could also be argued that the first essential event of the story is an unnarrated one that colors all the subsequent material, informs every major scene, is implicit in Gabriel's three encounters with women who symbolize Ireland, and is embodied by the stunning presence of the dead Michael Furey that is the culmination of the novella's plot, that is, the English occupation of Ireland.[6] This occupation, it might be added, is one that itself lacks a fixed beginning but can be fairly accurately said to have taken place in stages over the course of several centuries.

Finally, we may identify an impossible kind of beginning found in the type of text that circles back to its starting point, like *Finnegans Wake,* Nabokov's "The Circle," and Beckett's "Play," where the last sentence is also the first sentence. Such works are literally endless, their fabulas infinite. Such fabulas have no fixed beginnings; they are everywhere.

The Beginning of the Authorial Antetext

What I call the *authorial antetext* is the totality of authorial material that precedes the first words of the narrative. In most cases, this material includes the

---

6. It is the insistent causal web stretching from the occupation to the events of "The Dead" that suggests we consider this the beginning of the story rather than mere backdrop. See Cheng, pp. 128–47, for a reading that emphasizes the text's colonial and nationalist figures and discourse.

title, dedication, epigram, table of contents, author's note or preface, and other related material. Though independent of the story proper, these elements are often integral components of the work. To take the standard example articulated by Genette, imagine how differently we would read Joyce's novel if it were not titled *Ulysses*. Likewise, the familiar list of "other works by the same author" helps identify the work and direct its appropriate reception, including times when the author is using a nom de plume and is not revealing all the other books actually written by them. Caroline Heilbrun addresses this issue by listing "Other Books by Amanda Cross" inside the cover of the pseudonymous mysteries she has penned. Naturally, this practice can be parodied; the Loki Principle suggests it must be. The prefatory material to Nabokov's *Look at the Harlequins!* includes a list of "Books by the Narrator," a collection of titles that parodies the one usually found at the beginning of the author's own books. Thus, Nabokov's *King, Queen, Knave* becomes the narrator's *Pawn Takes Queen*; *Ada, or Ardor* becomes *Ardis*; *The Real Life of Sebastian Knight* is turned into *See Under Real*; and Nabokov's *Laughter in the Dark* becomes the narrator's *Slaughter in the Light*. Even the copyright notice can disclose an interesting story, as in the case of suppressed works like D. H. Lawrence's *Lady Chatterley's Lover*, as John Sutherland has explained in his discussion of beginnings (*How* 65–71). Especially important is the antetextual designation of a work as fiction or nonfiction; its significance is obvious when it is absent or incorrect, as happened when James Weldon Johnson's *Autobiography of an Ex-Colored Man* was published without the name of the author or the information that the book was a work of fiction. Readers naturally assumed that the book was an autobiography and that the fictional narrator was actually the book's author (see Rohy 80–87).

We may start by differentiating two types of authorial antetext, one discrete, the other fluid. In the first, each element is clearly separated from what follows it. Thus, in the case of *Nostromo* in the Doubleday collected edition of Conrad's works, we are first presented with the title but not the subtitle. On the next page we get the list of other volumes in the set, and then the full title page appears with both the main and the subtitle, *Nostromo: A Tale of the Seaboard*, and the name of the author. On the same page there is an epigraph from Shakespeare: "So foul a sky clears not without a storm" that both identifies it as a serious work enmeshed in the richest vein of literary history and also promises riveting events in the plot. This is, in turn, followed first by the copyright page (listing only the date of the collected edition). Then, on the opposite page, there is a dedication to John Galsworthy, a personal gesture that may also help situate the reception of this work, since Galsworthy was a highly regarded novelist of the period. After this comes an "Author's

Note," which was written for the collected edition, published seventeen years after the novel was first issued, and which retrospectively discusses the book and its origins. This prefatory note points to a curious feature of the authorial paratext that reveals that new beginnings can be added indefinitely; their proliferation can be stopped only by death—or by the fear of unprofitability: as long as the author is alive to reintroduce the material and a publisher can be induced to reprint the work, yet another introduction can always be added. Conrad's text then presents a table of contents that materially divides the book into a tripartite form, a culturally rooted division that spans the most austere (Dante's *Commedia*) and most popular ("The Three Little Pigs") forms, and then we finally get to the words "Chapter One" and the opening, the temporally sweeping first sentence of the syuzhet, "In the time of the Spanish rule, and for many years afterward, the town of Sulaco . . . ."

In other types of text, the various prefatory materials can bleed into each other. Vishakadhatta's Sanskrit drama *Rakshasa's Ring* begins with an actor declaiming a benediction. This is followed by an enacted prologue in the theater as another actor portraying the director enters and, referring to the benediction, shouts, "Enough! Enough!" Next he begins his introduction to the play that is about to be performed. He goes on to recite a verse stating that the moon, or "Chandra," was about to be eclipsed, or "overthrown." At this point a voice offstage protests vigorously. It turns out to be a character in the play who has metaleptically overheard (and misunderstood) the framing dialogue and vows to defend his emperor, Chandragupta Maurya, against any who would presume to overthrow him. With this, the play proper begins. For a more familiar example of this kind of permeable framing, we need only think of the title and opening credits of a film shown on a white background to jaunty music that, once the paratextual matter ceases, is revealed to be the white wall of a room inhabited by the protagonist, who then turns off the radio that we discover has been emitting the music we were hearing as the film commenced. That is, the nonnarrative paratext briefly shares the same narrative space as the story it precedes.

Each type of beginning contains the seeds of its own violation; these too must be reckoned with and included in a comprehensive theoretical account. We have already seen how the beginning of the syuzhet can be subverted by the texts that refuse to present themselves in any fixed order, and this includes the more playful kinds of hypertext fiction. The narration of the first event of the syuzhet may also be deferred as descriptions, or other expository material may be set forth, occasionally at unusual length. For example, the first chapter of Hardy's *The Return of the Native* does not contain any represented events but is composed entirely of a description of Egdon Heath; many *nouveaux romans* also start with a seemingly unnatural amount of nonnarrative description.

The Loki Principle insists that the conventions of the antetext will be violated, and we find two common ways. The first is to include all the appropriate introductory units but to situate them in all the wrong places, a familiar practice since Sterne's *Tristram Shandy*, where the preface is placed in the middle of the third book and a dedication does not appear until the fifth volume. Similarly, the first pages of Ishmael Reed's *Mumbo Jumbo* present the novel's first chapter; after it comes the conventional prefatory material such as title page, list of other works by the author, copyright information, epigraphs, and dedication. Only then does the second chapter appear; this arrangement defamiliarizes the conventional order and draws immediate attention to the first words of the story.

The other common method of dislodging convention is to introduce fictional elements into the conventionally nonfictional apparatus such as the author's preface. Hawthorne's "The Custom House" which precedes and introduces *The Scarlet Letter* is one such document; the fictional elements in it are subtly situated and gradually developed, and they are easily missed by casual readers (see Pearson). Near the middle of the Author's Note that prefaces *Nostromo* and explains its genesis, Conrad states: "My principal authority for the history of Costaguana is, of course, my venerated friend, the late Don José Avellanos," author of a volume of local history, unpublished ("the reader will discover why," Conrad adds slyly), titled *Fifty Years of Misrule* (x). This figure, we quickly discover, is a character in the novel; Conrad pretends to derive his story from a book he has invented. These two portions of the text, which in almost all cases also separate the nonfictional work of the author from the fictional words of the narrator, can be further collapsed (as in some of the more extreme texts of Nabokov) and thereby problematize the very boundary that separates fiction from nonfiction (see Richardson, "Nabokov"). We may also note the paradoxical case of Faulkner's *The Sound and the Fury*, for which Faulkner wrote an appendix seventeen years after the book was first published. The appendix contains statements that contradict some of the material in the text proper, which Faulkner refused to standardize. Furthermore, Faulkner insisted for many years that the appendix be placed at the beginning of the book; in this position, it radically changed the effect the volume's baffling opening section produces on readers, as some critics have noted, and seems to alter the characterizations and sense of inevitability of the original text, as Stacy Burton observes in her overview of these issues. This antetext is attempting to revise the original story, it seems.

The Institutional Antetext

We also need to include what may be called "the institutional antetext" (the subject of exhaustive analysis by Genette) which includes variable and nonauthorial framing elements. I believe that it is important to move beyond Genette's concept of the paratext and distinguish authorial from institutional antetexts because of their different authorities and, often, dissimilar purposes. In fact, the purposes of each may well be opposed.[7] The status of the authorial antetext is often fairly clear in most recent works, as we have just seen; it includes all the authorial material in the book that frames the narrative proper. We need to distinguish this authorized antetext from that provided by other sources (including the publisher), such as the cover design, frontispiece, lettering, illustrations, the collection of favorable critical notices the book has received, and even the book's binding. Insofar as these entities conform to the tenor of the text, they may be seen as extensions of the authorial antetext; insofar as they contradict or are irrelevant to the work, they may be dismissed as temporary devices to satisfy economic, ideological, or private demands.

There is obviously a considerable gray area between these two poles. The cover illustration, for example, may be created with the input from the author (the original edition of *Ulysses*), or it may be done by the author him- or herself (Alasdair Gray's *Lanark*). Vanessa Bell's many designs for the covers of books by her sister, Virginia Woolf, occupy a wide range of effectiveness, relevance, and suitability (see Lee 363–64). There have been many cases in which the author was confused, annoyed, or outraged by the cover design. Among the most unfortunate examples of the latter are the cheap 1950s pocketbook editions of various modernist classics that displayed dizzy-looking women whose ample breasts could not fit properly within their blouses, an advertising gimmick that might have sold a few more copies to lascivious males but otherwise contradicted the austere prose, experimental narration, and philosophical themes of the work. Likewise, titles may be imposed on the author (*Sartoris* for Faulkner's *Flags in the Dust*) or supplied by an editor to an ultimately grateful author (Maxwell Perkins for Thomas Wolfe). As these examples should reveal, the importance of the distinction between authorial and institutional antetexts is most clearly evident when the two are opposed or contradict one another.

---

7. Thus, Genette's concept of the peritext includes dedications, prefaces, titles, subtitles, introductions, and postscripts, regardless of their author; it seems to me very important to differentiate between the different authors and intended audiences of each. In general, I feel that Genette's massive study of the various kinds of paratext would be more useful if it focused on authorial insertions and additions.

In addition to many of the paratextual features already mentioned, John Frow includes the following framing devices: the publishing house; inclusion in a prestigious series; and editorial exegesis, such as "an introduction stressing the canonical status of the text" (334). I will add parenthetically that many of these conventions are transformed by postmodern authors, as we will see in chapter 6. In his discussion, Frow avers that the actual condition of the physical book affects its reading and that a book's reception can be altered by a sumptuous binding, a mass printing, or a tawdry cover. I have never, however, met a scholar who claimed that his or her interpretation of a book varied with its typeface or binding; no one would ever assert "I have a more conventional reading—but then I was using the deluxe edition. In it, the aristocrats really seem more genteel." These are, rather, reactions we suspect may be true of other, more credulous readers, but never ourselves. In Virginia Woolf's *Night and Day* (1920), there is a character who, presenting a valued book to a friend, exclaims: "'The Baskerville Congreve,' said Rodney, offering it to his guest. 'I couldn't read him in a cheap edition'" (73), but this exchange merely served to indicate Rodney's superficiality.[8]

In the rest of this chapter I will briefly examine the problematics of beginnings in the work of Samuel Beckett. The first sentences of most of Beckett's texts do not sound anything like typical opening lines; they tend to problematize rather than inaugurate the act of beginning: "Finished, it's finished, nearly finished, it must be nearly finished" (*Endgame*); "I shall soon be quite dead at last in spite of all" (*Malone Dies*); "I gave up before birth, it's not possible otherwise" (*Fizzle* 4); "For to end yet again" (*Fizzle* 8); "I don't know when I died" ("The Calmative"); "All that goes before forget" ("Enough"); and "Try again. Fail again. Better again. Or better worse" (*Worstward Ho*). These opening sentences repeatedly problematize the act of beginning, as textual openings often fail to begin properly or refuse to point to any plausible subject of narrative interest and instead announce conclusions or endings. As each text continues, however, the act of beginning irrupts into the text at repeated and unlikely moments. The beginning, it would seem, is arbitrary, inessential, or useless, yet it cannot be dismissed and keeps returning in the text: the first sentence of the eighth *Fizzle* just quoted, "For to end yet again," continues with the following words: "skull alone in a dark place pent bowed on a board to begin." Thus,

---

8. In this regard, we might also note, as Porter Abbott has pointed out to me, the different-colored binding of copies of Dorian Gray's favorite novel, with colors chosen to suit his different moods.

the ending announced at the outset immediately (and paradoxically) yields to an originary scene and a declaration of the intent to begin.

One of the more illustrative beginnings is that of *Molloy,* and examining it can help illuminate both the issues involved in the theory of narrative beginnings as well as the difference between modernist and postmodern kinds of opening. *Molloy* is composed of two ambiguously related narratives: a first-person account by a man who claims to be Molloy, and another account by Jacques Moran who describes his quest for a man who seems to be named Molloy. In Beckett's trilogy, this text is followed by *Malone Dies,* a novel that seems like another version of the first half of *Molloy* and is itself followed by *The Unnamable,* a narration about the impossibility of narration (*Three Novels*).

The first words of the syuzhet of *Molloy* and the trilogy are: "I am in my mother's room. It's I who live there now. I don't know how I got there" (7). This is a typical Beckettian beginning that defies the basic rules of the narratable and does not lead to any narrative tension or insufficiency. It precedes, appropriately, the retrospectively narrated story of a failed quest, of a wayward journey with a most dubious goal. Unlike a modernist text, where the narrative tension might center on Molloy's discovering how he came to be where he is, just as Proust's novel ultimately reveals how Marcel became a writer, Molloy will never learn how he got to his mother's room, and he doesn't especially care to find out. After additional discussion of the setting of the writing, the narrator gives a confused account of two figures he seems to have observed walking toward each other, unless he is mistaken, which he admits could easily be the case. After several pages of rumination on the possible encounter of this pair, he decides to go to visit his mother. He relates his erratic and largely futile journey, during which he forgets the reasons that impelled him toward her. In the end of his narrative, he collapses in a forest after hearing a voice call to him. Causal progression is minimal and dubious, and every form of teleology is vain; the beginnings of the action of the novel, like all the other actions, seem to lead nowhere.

The discourse about beginnings by the narrator and the status of the various texts within the work are equally inconclusive. On the second page of the text we are given a confusing statement about beginnings. We are told that a man comes every Sunday to take away the papers that Molloy writes. The narrator continues: "It was he told me I'd begun all wrong, that I should have begun all differently. He might be right. I began at the beginning, like an old ballocks, can you imagine that? Here's my beginning. Because they're keeping it apparently. I took a lot of trouble with it. Here it is. It gave me a lot of trouble. It was the beginning; do you understand? Whereas now it's nearly the end. . . . Here's my beginning. It must mean something or they wouldn't keep it. Here it is" (8). A possible gloss on these ambiguous words might give us the following: "In an earlier draft, I had told my story chronologically, beginning with the first event. But they [*pace* Horace] rejected that method. Now I begin my text retrospectively, describing the scene of writing after all the events have taken place. This other method seems to be the one they want, since they seem to be retaining this version." (It should be noted that, in typical Beckettian paradox, Molloy cannot know that the pages he is currently writing are the ones that will be retained by "them.") Since the Moran section of *Molloy* does more or less start at the beginning, there is a fair chance that it may be the earlier draft that is referred to here.

The prefatory account is rapidly followed in the English translation by the promise of still more beginnings: "This time, then once more I think, then perhaps a last time, then I think it'll be over, with that world too" (8). It is not clear whether the same story will be begun again and again, or whether new stories will be produced (or retrieved), and it is precisely this question of narrative identity that in numerous forms suffuses the ensuing texts. The overarching sense is that beginnings constitute nothing new, and that endings likewise resolve nothing. Or in the words of Malone, "I knew that all was about to end, or to begin again, it little mattered which, and it little mattered how" (161). The basic frames of beginning and ending are eviscerated, just as the notion of any teleological progression is exploded. Beckett will only give us one damned thing after another, with an arbitrary beginning and an inconclusive ending. In doing so, he resists (or parodies) the entire logic of plot in traditional narrative. He does not even allow one to posit that the same events are beginning again, since he so problematizes the concept of identity. There is only the repetition of the ineffectual act of starting yet again.

The theoretical categories outlined above are likewise tampered with by this author. The beginning of the syuzhet, normally the first page of the narrative proper, threatens to become unfixed by the fact of the book's two disjointed parts and the suggestion that the version that is placed second, Moran's narrative, might just be the prior one and that the reader could therefore begin equally well with it. More recent authors intensify this conundrum by constructing books with inverted type that can be started from either cover, such as Carol Shield's *Happenstance* and Mark Z. Danielewski's *Only Revolutions*, which I discuss in chapter 7. The Molloy narrative likewise reprises key episodes of Homer's *Odyssey*, although in an oblique and intermittent fashion (and through the mediation of yet another text, Joyce's *Ulysses*), thus inviting us to see Odysseus's desire to return home near the beginning of Homer's narrative as an originary source and Beckett's as a second or repeated beginning (see Michael Robinson 157–58). Finally, we may ask which text should be considered the primary one. The original French version differs from the English translation at points; most significantly for our purposes the early line "This time, then once more I think, then perhaps a last time, then I think it'll be over, with that world too" (8) expands significantly on the French edition by adding one more time: "Cette fois-ci, puis encore une je pense, puis c'en sera fini je pense, de ce monde-là aussi" (9). *L'innommable* does not seem to have been imagined as part of the original sequence.

The status of the beginning of the fabula of *Molloy* is still more elusive. Playing with the trope of birth as beginning, the narrator claims to remember his entry into the world. But since he "remembers" emerging from his mother's rectum rather than her womb ("first taste of the shit"), we may safely conclude that this origin is literally false, however resonant it may be as metaphor or metafiction (excretion is regularly equated with writing in Beckett). In fact, every recollected past event is qualified, doubted, or denied ("I say that now, but after all what do I know now about then" [31]). Or major narrated events are subsequently "denarrated" ("I went back into the house and wrote, It is midnight. The rain is beating on the windows. It was not midnight. It was not raining" [176]). There is no solid set of facts we might assemble together into a fabula; we are left with only the ambiguous discourse of the text. The beginning of the fabula is thus negated.[9]

Even the work's antetext is somewhat unclear. When John Calder was preparing to publish the three novels together, he asked Beckett whether he could call them a trilogy. Beckett refused, and later refused the word *trinity*. After another request for *trilogy* from his American publisher, Barney Rosset of Grove Press, Beckett responded, "Delighted you are doing the 3 in 1 soon. Simply can't think, as I told Calder, of a general title and can't bear the thought of [the] word trilogy appearing anywhere. . . . If it's possible to present the thing without either I'd be grateful" (cited in Gontarski xii). Though he promised to "cudgel his fused" synapses to come up with a word or two to describe the relation of the three texts, no such word ever emerged. The three books remain in a partially indeterminate relation to each other, unexplained by any antetextual indicator.

For Beckett, every beginning is false—a clumsy artifice or a deliberate lie. The unbroken plenum of his characters' experience does not allow for the crisp, distinct segregation of events into a framework that permits beginnings or endings to arise. Most modern authors and theorists might well agree that a fluid representation of human experience is more accurate than those who,

---

9. I discuss *denarration* at more length in chapter 7 and in *Unnatural Voices* (87–94).

following Aristotle, would bracket off one segment as that "which itself does not of necessity follow something else" (94). Beckett's works are much more effectively modeled by Henry James's opposite affirmation that "really, universally, relations stop nowhere" (171–72).

Beckett affirms the continuity of relations but refuses to provide the illusion of a "natural" starting or stopping point. This perception is widely shared by modern and contemporary authors. One of André Gide's central characters observes: "I consider that life never presents us with anything which may not be looked upon as a fresh starting point, no less than as a termination. 'Might be continued'—these are the words with which I should like to finish my *Counterfeiters*" (335). In *If on a winter's night a traveler* Calvino's narrator similarly wonders "how to establish the exact moment when a story begins? Everything has already begun before, the first line of the first page of every novel refers to something that has already happened outside the book." He goes on to reflect that "the lives of individuals of the human race form a constant plot, in which every attempt to isolate one piece of living that has a meaning separate from the rest—for example, the meeting of two people, which will become decisive for both—must bear in mind that each of the two brings with himself a texture of events, environments, and from that meeting, in turn, other stories will be derived which will break off from their common story" (153). Insofar as a work is mimetic and has a significant scope—that is, insofar as it describes a social world—every beginning will be provisional or arbitrary, just as Patrick Colm Hogan ("Stories") and Philippe Carrard ("September 1939") have suggested that almost all beginnings of historical narratives commence with an ultimately fabricated (and invariably debatable) starting point.

Discussing Aristotle's definition of ending and his exemplary text, *Oedipus Rex*, J. Hillis Miller argues: "It is not really the end. It cannot be said that nothing follows causally from it. . . . As the audience well knows, the events of the day are only an episode in a story that leads to Oedipus' own death and transfiguration" (11). It can be similarly affirmed that the play's beginning is equally woven into earlier events. We may easily go further into the past of the myth and recover more-distant beginnings: Laius, while being given shelter by the king of Pelops, abducted and raped the king's son and carried him off to Thebes. As a result of this crime, Hera sent the Sphinx to ravage the Thebans, and Laius was warned never to procreate. Though he married Jocasta, he followed this injunction until one night when he became intoxicated. From this act, Oedipus was conceived. One might easily write a play about these events and push the beginning back still further, and it seems that Euripides did, although it is no longer extant. And of course we may go still further back to the anterior story of his ill-fated great-grandfather, Cadmus, whose killing of the sacred dragon set in motion a series of misfortunes for himself and his descendants.

As we may infer from the examples of the ancient cycle of Trojan epics (of which only Homer's are extant), the fictional worlds of Balzac or Faulkner, or the latest additions to the "Star Wars" set of films, there is always the possibility of a prequel to explain how events had arrived at the beginning point of the chronologically later narrative. As Porter Abbott has observed, the prequel indicates that "beginnings are not sacred, but can be pushed back endlessly into the past" (*Cambridge* 57). Jeremy Hawthorn similarly notes that in Conrad's "Malay trilogy"—*Almayer's Folly* (1895), *An Outcast of the Islands* (1896), and *The Rescue* (1919–20)—each successive narrative moves deeper into the past, as the chronology of the narrated events is the reverse of the chronology of publication. He concludes: "If the deferral of closure is, by common consent, a standard element of modernist fiction, right from the start of his writing career Conrad seems intent on establishing that all openings, all beginnings, are provisional" (85). These sentiments tend to confirm the statement of Sartre's Roquentin: "Les décors changent, les gens entrent et sortent, violà tout. Il n'y a jamais de commencements" (60) [The scenery changes, people go in and come out. That's all. There are no beginnings (39)]. This is also true of non- or antimimetic fiction, in which an author may always create an anterior beginning to any such narrative, as Beckett so insistently demonstrates. Even an origin myth can be reframed by an earlier origin tale from before the beginning. At every level, then, beginnings are provisional concepts, inherently unstable, typically elusive, and always capable of being revised or retold. Every beginning is always already in medias res.

CHAPTER 3

Narrative Middles I

Plot, Probability, and Tellability

PLOT IS probably the most widely discussed aspect of narrative in the history of narrative theory; in fact, it was being discussed even before there was a known account of narrative. Decades before Aristotle began teaching, Euripides, in his play *Orestes,* critiqued numerous improbabilities of the recognition scene in Aeschylus's *Libation Bearers.* Aristophanes would go on to satirize several of Euripides' own unlikely rescue scenes in his *Thesmophoriazusae.* Later, as we know, Aristotle would conceptualize plot more generally in terms that continue to resonate in narrative theory. He gave plot (*mythos*) pride of place in his model, considering it to be the most important aspect of a tragedy, more so than character, language, or spectacle. For him, a plot needed to be complete and of a certain magnitude, and its beginning and end must not be arbitrary. It should have an organic unity and be free from irrelevant incidents; the events that compose it should be conjoined in a probable or necessary connection. Bharata, the theorist of ancient Sanskrit drama whose *Natyashastra* is in many ways analogous to Aristotle's *Poetics,* referred to plot as the *body* of drama and differentiated between the principal and subsidiary story lines. He identified five means of developing the plot: the seed (*bija*) of the story will scatter and grow; the vital drops (*bindu*) will restore continuity after narrative interruptions; the episode (*pataka*), though not centered on the hero, does aid him in achieving his goal; the more oblique incident (*prakari*) may contribute to the central action but is not itself continued; and the goal (*karya*) describes the efforts made by the characters to achieve their ends. As R. L. Singal observes, the unity of action emphasized by Aristotle is equally present in the *Natyashastra*: its "division of the plot into five stages was itself designed to ensure unity of action" (119; see also 120–23). In my discussion below, we will find that many of these concepts continue to resonate.

While a detailed examination of discussions of plot in the twentieth century would reveal some significant disagreement (e.g., the structuralist emphasis on a grammar-like order of events versus the neo-Aristotelian stress on the affective consequences of a trajectory of action), stepping back from specific divergences reveals substantial areas of general agreement, even among theorists who otherwise have little in common.[1] Paul Ricoeur, writing from the perspective of hermeneutics, asserts that plot is "the intelligible whole that governs a succession of events in a story. . . . A story is made out of events to the extent that plot *makes* events *into* a story" ("Narrative" 167). Not only is this stance congruent with Peter Brooks's psychoanalytic approach; it is actually cited by him in support of his own position (13–17). Brooks uses *plot* as a term to embrace "the organizing line and intention of narrative" (37) and "the design and intention of narrative, a structure for those meanings that develop through succession and time" (12). This view, in turn, is consonant with the other major strand of theorizing plot: the emphasis on unity, design, completion, and effect produced by neo-Aristotelian or rhetorical narrative theorists associated with the University of Chicago, beginning with R. S. Crane.

Also noteworthy is the structuralist notion of the most general parameters of story: a basic pattern of a state of harmony, a disruption of that harmony, and an attempt to restore the original harmony. D. A. Miller has developed and refined this position; for him, the narratable emanates from what he calls a condition of "disequilibrium, suspense, and general insufficiency from which a given narrative appears to rise" (ix) More simply, a problem appears at the beginning of the story: Odysseus wants to return to his home, a plague is ravaging Thebes, a ghost tells Hamlet to avenge his father's murder. The initial disequilibrium leads to a desire to rectify the situation; for most of the narrative the protagonist seeks to alter the problematic situation; the end is signaled when the problem is resolved (or, in some cases, shown to be unresolvable).

In what follows, I will examine the varieties of ways in which plots are constructed, noting the goals and functions of each, without privileging any particular type. There is, as noted above, considerable agreement on the basic task of plot: to tie the collection of events together into a seemingly organic

---

1. Even Hilary Dannenberg, who at the beginning of her entry warns that "plot is one of the most elusive terms in narrative theory," goes on to note the convergence of meaning in the usage of many theorists ("Plot" 435).

whole or, in the words of Brooks, "the dynamic shaping force of the narrative discourse" (13). We will explore the ways in which authors follow, alter, or reject this stricture. In the next chapter, I will continue this account by identifying ways of ordering events that are independent of plot-based concerns. In my discussion, I will suggest that authors regularly pit plot against its opposite, the lack of any governing order, to enhance the ultimate effect of the thread of connection. There is often a keen tension between a seemingly wayward or random accumulation of events and the moment at which these events are brought together into an overarching trajectory. But this dialectic of dispersal and merging applies only to those writers who accept the framework of the plot, and, as we will see, many do not.

Parameters of Plot

It is generally agreed that events in a narrative may be either episodically conjoined or be more tightly woven together in a more or less continuous causal chain. There is considerable agreement on the relative value of each (which I will try to jostle somewhat in my remarks below), but less agreement on their general relation to each other. Aristotle strongly favored a plot that consists of a single action and denigrated episodic kinds of construction, noting that those who believed they have a unified subject by dramatizing the life of an individual were mistaken, since the incidents of a person's life are many and wayward. Meir Sternberg takes this idea further, writing that "a narrative must necessarily have a story as its compositional backbone; but it can do without a plot or make do with scattered causal elements (as in most picaresque novels)" (*Expositional* 11). Peter Brooks, by contrast, argues that "a narrative without at least a minimal plot would be incomprehensible. Plot is the principle of interconnectedness and intention which we cannot do without in moving through the discrete elements—incidents, episodes, actions—of a narrative" (5). He concludes that "even such loosely articulated forms as the picaresque novel display devices of interconnectedness, structural repetitions that allow us to construct a whole" (5).

In part, this dispute reenacts an earlier debate; E. M. Forster famously differentiated merely episodic narratives from plots proper due to the causal connection binding the scenes together in a plot (93–94). Seymour Chatman, however, has persuasively argued that, unless otherwise instructed, readers will assume a connection between successive events involving the same characters such that, to take Forster's example, "the king's death has something to do with the queen's"; thus, "'The king died and then the queen died' and 'The king died and then the queen died of grief' differ narratively only in degrees of explicitness at the surface level; at the deeper structural level the causal element is present in both" (*Story* 46). I agree with Brooks and Chatman here concerning mimetic narratives: there is almost always some connection, however minor, among many of the episodes in a picaresque tale, while there is almost always something extraneous in a tightly plotted work. For example, a ballroom scene need not be so elaborately depicted, a minor character could be excised, and subplots could be curtailed. Even in the *Odyssey*, we could easily question the necessity of including many of the events that occur during Odysseus's journey home, as well the need for him to relate so many of his substantially episodic adventures to the Phaeacians. Aristotle recognized this, and even as he praised Homer for not narrating the entire account of Odysseus's adventures in Troy (95), he admitted that many of the adventures recounted in the *nostos* are mere episodes (103). Consequently, it seems much more cogent to view the two as opposite poles of the same spectrum. By contrast, the real distinction that needs to be articulated is, on the one hand, between essentially mimetic plots and, on the other, unnatural plots that are based on parodies or rejections of probability in their stories.

Episodic Plots

Plots can be more or less episodic, but it is very rare for there to be no connection among the events. As Robert Fiore observes about the sixteenth-century novella *Lazarillo de Tormes*, the protagonist "is modified and molded" by his experience; he changes from the innocent at the outset of the work to a more cunning and retributive figure after he is struck over the head by his master (84). Furthermore, different genres have different requirements; surely there is nothing terribly wrong with a picaresque novel being picaresque. Many kinds of comedy require only a string of humorous incidents that may end fairly arbitrarily rather than forming a unified totality that culminates in a decisive resolution; Ejner Jensen argues that such works do not rely on fixed or conclusive endings to tie the scenes together (21). It is useful to refer to Roy Jay Nelson's metaphor here: an episodic structure "provides a unifying central track, along which a number of side tracks branch off. . . . The branches are not causally connected to one another, except insofar as each has some causal bond to the main line" (105). Many postmodern works test or refuse the idea of a unified plot and therefore need to be judged by different criteria. Rachel Cusk pushes the episodic form to new extremes in her novels *Outline* (2014) and *Transit* (2017), both of which assemble a minimally connected series of events that happen to the narrator, even though the narrator is barely characterized, generally passive, and little affected by the events. Jennifer Egan's *A Visit from the Goon Squad* (2011) invites us to speculate on exactly how different individuals and groups can in fact become conjoined as they age, move, and shift from state A to B, to employ one of the images of transformation she employs in the book.

The "Classic" Plot

On the opposite end of the spectrum from the episodic plot is what we may term the *classic* plot: the kind that theorists from Aristotle to Dryden to Brooks have considered to be normative. A classic plot comprises a causally entailing series of events, none of which is extraneous or adventitious, that progress to heightened drama that is resolved in its ending. Especially compelling examples of these kinds of plots are present in most of the novels of Jane Austen and the tragedies of Racine. By contrast, ties between events are less rigorous in multigenerational novels like Joseph Roth's *Radetzkymarsch* (1932)—in fact, generational disintegration is one of this novel's central themes.

It is not easy to match the genre requirements of a work with the demands of verisimilitude, so, understandably, the aesthetics of a well-crafted classic plot is widely appreciated. One may argue with Coleridge's opinion that Ben Jonson's *The Alchemist*, along with *Oedipus Rex* and *Tom Jones*, deserves to be judged one of the three "most perfect plots ever planned" (I prefer *Emma*'s plot myself); no one, I suspect, will suggest that *Don Quixote* should be among them, despite its numerous other virtues.

Subvarieties of the classic plot include **formulaic plots,** which can be driven by a simple sequence: the hero strives to prevent the disaster; the secret agent seeks to defeat the enemy; the thieves want to get the jewels; the detective needs to catch the killer; and the young man desires to get the young woman (it is rare that this happens the other way around, though Shakespeare does it in *Much Ado about Nothing,* and we now have numerous novels in which the woman tries to get the woman). Many genres are partially defined by the strictness of their plot patterns, including mysteries and thrillers—the ultimate plot-based narratives as testified to by the rigorous guidelines publishers often provide to their aspiring authors.

An interesting modern variation of the classic plot is what I will call the **obscured plot.** A number of works, especially shorter ones, present a series of events that are brought together and united into a whole by a final climactic scene, often with an ironic twist, that produces a crucial illumination in the central characters' minds as they perceive the overarching, final connection. In Katherine Mansfield's "Bliss," for example, the central consciousness, Bertha Young, experiences extreme bliss, feels fascination for her new female friend, and develops her first real sensual desire for her husband. At the end of the story, she discovers that her friend and her husband are having a torrid affair; from this time forward, her life will be radically changed. Discussing this story and others like it (including Wharton's "Roman Fever" and Kleist's "The Marquise of O"), Armine Kotin Mortimer calls the hidden material the "second story" and observes that "it is the function of the first story to create before the eyes of the reader the entire second story, insinuated into the devious structures of the first, and bring it forth full blown in a final blaze of glory" ("Romantic" 191).[2] One may quibble with the terms invoked. For example, is it the second story or the completion of the first? For whom is it the second story—not the adulterers—or the re-reader? But it is easy to recognize that Mortimer has effectively isolated and described an important and indeed favorite plot pattern in modern fiction. In particular, the "recognition" effect at the end of these works is especially powerful because the reader usually learns of it at the same time the character does. Novels that effectively employ this kind of delayed and often private *anagnoresis* include Shirley Hazzard's *The Transit of Venus* (1980) and Lauren Groff's *Fates and Furies* (2015).

Fragmentary Plots

More extreme are fragmentary works that require the reader to assemble them, to make the sequences into a genuine plot in a more conscious and concentrated manner than we are normally accustomed to do with more straightforward works. For the most part, the paradigm for this kind of plot is an extension of typical modernist practice; the gaps one is required to fill are simply larger, more frequent, and more prominent. Ted Gioia has recently commented on the proliferation of fragmentary narratives and their frequently paradoxical status; he observes that "the new fragmented novel is holistic and coalescent. It resists disunity, even as it appears to embody it" ("Rise" 4). Works presented as fragments, like many of Beckett's, invariably invite the reader to connect the pieces in some way. We see this dynamic in *How It Is* (1961), a work that foregrounds and thematizes its own fragmentariness ("my life in bits and scraps" [20]) even as it repeatedly invokes—and mocks—

---

2. See also Dan Shen's comparable work on Mansfield's shorter texts and James Phelan's analysis of "Roman Fever" in *Experiencing Fiction* (95–108).

a larger governing trajectory: "how it was I quote before Pim with Pim after Pim how it is three parts" (7); the narrator even insists "we follow I quote the natural order more or less" (7). Intriguingly, a fragmentary plot often functions largely in the same ways as more standard or classic plots do, although its scope is typically more constrained.

Double and Multiple Plots

Many narratives have more than one story line. Some of these are deftly woven together; others can be quite independent, as in Middleton and Rowley's *The Changeling* (1622). Many Restoration comedies have two parallel plot lines, one involving a rather flirtatious couple and the other a pair of more sentimental lovers; the success of one pair often depends on the success of the other. Such an arrangement has several potential virtues and possibilities. Having two different individuals or couples in roughly the same situation allows for more nuanced characterizations, as the reasoning, decisions, and results of one party will be quickly contrasted with those of the other. The relative value of different approaches to the same problem is often part of the work's larger thesis, as in Terence's *Adelphi* (*The Brothers* 160 BCE; see Levin 226–32). Authors may also employ a multiplot structure to provide a larger social canvas, to disclose the web of connection between distant events, to provide architectural and thematic parallels, and, as we will see, to provoke readers' perceptions of relevance and unity as they process seemingly unrelated scenes.

John Dryden cited Ben Jonson on the virtues of the "underplot" and observed: "'Tis evident that the more the persons are, the greater will be the variety of the plot. If then the parts are managed so regularly, that the beauty of the whole be kept entire, and that variety become not a perplexed and confusing mass of accidents, you will find it infinitely pleasing to be led in a labyrinth of design, where you see some of your way before you, yet discern not the end till you arrive at it" (245). One of the narrative challenges of the double- or multiplot work is how far apart the separate story strands are allowed to diverge and, once separated, how they can be effectively brought together as part of the same plot. This compositional drama can be thematized in the narrative itself, as when, at the beginning of its sixteenth chapter, the narrator of Dickens's *Bleak House* rhetorically asks: "What connexion can there be, between the place in Lincolnshire, the house in town, the Mercury in powder, and the whereabouts of Jo the outlaw?" and goes on to ruminate: "What connexion can there have been between many people in the innumerable histories of this world, who, from the opposite side of great gulfs, have, nevertheless, been very curiously brought together!" (186). Peter Garrett does a fine job of explaining how George Eliot dialectically manages her many plots in *Middlemarch*, noting that "the narrator's alternation between individual and general is . . . not an effortless tracing of connections, not the natural pulsation of an organic rhythm, but a series of small collisions and reversals, a perpetual process of 'checking' one perspective against another" (139; see 135–79).[3]

As noted in the first chapter, Shakespeare keeps his co-plots far apart in *King Lear* for most of the play before bringing them into intimate and mortal conjunction by the end. In *Henry IV, Part 1*, the king's court, the rebels' camp, and the rogues' tavern are deftly interwoven; the physical placement of the characters onstage also points to insidious similarities between the rebels and the royals. George Eliot keeps the main plots far apart in much of *Daniel Deronda*, while Virginia Woolf's *Mrs. Dalloway* sets out a number of different consciousnesses and gradually connects them all to the main plotline, delaying the connection with Septimus Smith until the final pages of the text. In *How to Be Both*, Ali Smith, as we have remarked, pushes the separation of two plots still further; in many ways they mirror each other's concerns, though they remain too distant for a single narrative.

Corinne Bancroft has recently employed the concept of the "braided narrative" to discuss the practice of novelists like Nicole Krause, who in *The History of Love* (2005) "plait[s] together different narrative threads, distinct in terms of both narrator and story" (Bancroft 262). Though the juxtaposed narrative segments often seem more divergent than those in a familiar multiplot novel, the distinct segments do ultimately come together into a single narrative in almost all the examples Bancroft adduces. She has identified an interesting new subtype of narrative, though I feel that it can largely be analyzed with the same tools we employ for interpreting narratives with multiple plots.

Pseudoplots

Authors like James Joyce both invoke and reject the principle of plot—a not uncommon stance among the modernists. James Phelan's account of narrative progression (*Reading* 15–20) can help clarify the dynamics at work in "The Dead," a piece that ingeniously plays with the idea of plot. Phelan differentiates "between two main kinds of instabilities: the first are those occurring within

---

3. See also Richard Levin on the practice and limits of multiplotted works in English Renaissance drama.

the story, instabilities between characters, created by situations, and complicated and resolved through actions" (15). The second kind are those created by the discourse, and include dissonances "between authors and/or narrators, on the one hand, and between readers, on the other" (15). He calls these *tensions* and identifies them as instabilities of value, belief, opinion, knowledge, and expectation. If two characters desire the same object, we have an instability; if the narrative takes a very strange turn, we have a tension.

As we observed in the previous chapter, as the text of "The Dead" begins to unfold, the reader is quickly presented with an instability: his aunts' annual party is well underway, but Gabriel has not yet arrived. His presence is especially important for the supervision of another guest, Freddy Malins, who is notorious for turning up drunk. Gabriel quickly appears, however, and the aunts are relieved. Malins appears in passable shape, is handed a glass of lemonade, and behaves himself the rest of the evening. The anticipated instability proves to be a nonissue. Gabriel has a failed conversation with Lily, the caretaker's daughter, who is helping out at the event. Another potential instability now emerges: Gabriel mentally goes over the speech he will give; he fears that he has chosen the wrong tone, that its allusions will backfire, and that the speech will be a failure. General conversation ensues in which further potential instabilities are adumbrated (the pope's recent banishment of women from church choirs; Mr. Browne's Protestant questioning of Catholic practices), but these too produce no significant incident. A piece is performed on the piano, the guests participate in a formal dance, and Julia Morkan sings a song.

During the dance, Molly Ivors accuses Gabriel of turning his back on Ireland and writing reviews for a conservative paper that opposes Irish home rule: "'I'm ashamed of you,' said Miss Ivors frankly. 'To say you'd write for a rag like that'" (188). Finally, we have the first genuine instability in the story. Gabriel is annoyed and flustered and does not offer a satisfactory response to her accusations. A major political argument, like the one early in *Portrait of the Artist as a Young Man*, appears imminent. Miss Ivors then takes Gabriel's hand and says "in a soft, friendly tone" that she was only joking (188); shortly thereafter, she departs. Gabriel gives his speech and it is a success. The party continues and then the guests start to leave. The text is now two-thirds complete; up to this point, we have had no significant instability, with the sole exception of Gabriel's private resentment of Miss Ivors's words. This fact, in turn, provokes the work's most important tension (one that has been present for sometime): why are we being given such a detailed account of an inconsequential chronicle of minor events? All the carefully prepared disruptions—Freddy showing up drunk; an animated argument between Gabriel and Miss Ivors; other potential religious or artistic controversies; the failure of Gabriel's speech—have all been deflated. The text's instabilities have evaporated; nothing significant has occurred. Many first-time readers legitimately wonder: where is the plot?

Gabriel then sees his wife listening to another song. She is quite moved by it, though Gabriel mistakenly thinks she is becoming sexually aroused. The final pages dramatize a series of misunderstandings and suspicions in the mind of Gabriel as his wife unfolds the story of her affection for a young man, Michael Furey, many years before in Galway. Though very ill, Furey sang the same song to her in a cold rain as she was about to leave for Dublin; he died a few days later. Gabriel is miserable; he feels his own affection is pathetic compared to a love that is happy to risk death. He questions the basis of his marriage, the extent of Gretta's and his love for one other, the general pattern of his life, and his own sense of self.

Even more interesting, current Joyce scholarship tends to doubt the depth and consequences of Gabriel's apparent "epiphany."[4] It is not a pivotal moment that finally allows him to accurately see and judge his life and perhaps change it for the better. It is not, that is, a moment that brings the evening's events together in a single plot. Instead, it is most likely a moment of romantic self-pity on Gabriel's part; he will probably not change his behavior, learn anything from it, or even remember the events of the night for very long. It is, in fact, only a "pseudo-epiphany"; in "The Dead," Joyce does not so much provide a plot as the illusion of one.

Plotlessness

Contra Coleridge, T. S. Eliot praised Ben Jonson not for his skill in plotting but for his skill in doing without a plot (75). In the twentieth century, we have seen plot atrophy much more than in any previous period. Brian McHale has used the term *weak narrativity* to depict a spectrum of modern and postmodern ways of "telling stories 'poorly,' distractedly, with much irrelevance and indeterminacy, in such a way as to invoke narrative coherence while at the same time withholding commitment to it and undermining confidence in it" ("Weak" 165). My sense is that we will do best to imagine weak narrativity in two forms: one which is uninterested in traditional, especially Victorian, devices for generating narrative interest; and another which mocks the narrative interest it proposes to generate—in short, a modernist and a postmodern kind of plotlessness, respectively. The first type is explored by Bo Pettersson,

---

4. See Bowen.

in his article "What Happens When Nothing Happens: Interpreting Narrative Technique in the Plotless Novels of Nicholson Baker." This article analyzes some of Baker's novels, including *The Mezzanine* (1988), whose "plot" consists of the narrator's ten-second ride up the escalator after his lunch. The obvious question that is raised by such works is: how are such novels readable, let alone worthwhile? Pettersson explains that Baker's miniaturist fiction is so enjoyable "because description, narrative, and argument go seamlessly together by presenting the digressive logic of [its] diffident and learned narrators. What Baker achieves, then, by slowing down the action and all but obliterating the plot is a kind of defamiliarization" (53). To some extent, he makes seemingly trivial events interesting and surrounds this minimal story line with other engaging narrative components, including plenty of backstory. In fact, an examination of the novel reveals that most of the text is narrative, though most of it is analeptic: flashbacks that stretch back to the immediate, middle, and distant past of the protagonist. In this case, I would suggest that we see the basic challenge of the modernist plot at work: the author selects the most unpromising set of (non)events and accepts the challenge of creating something readable, ultimately even compelling, out of it. Postmodern plotlessness by contrast is more radical, more satirical, and at times more plotless. An example frequently brought up in this context is Beckett's "Ping"; we have seen that it is not only virtually plotless but almost devoid of any action. Nevertheless, reading it can be as compelling as it is challenging. Taken together, these issues foreground some of the questions surrounding the concept of tellability, which will be discussed at the end of this chapter.

Unnatural Orders

Standard mimetic plots have been explored and analyzed quite thoroughly and effectively; in addition to the work of Brooks, Phelan, Sternberg, and Ryan, we may point to Benjamin Harshav (Hrushovski), Raphael Baroni, and Roland Barthes's account of the proairetic code in *S/Z*. Taken together, these accounts offer differing though overlapping theories of the ways in which a mimetic plot, employing probability and developing readerly interest, binds events together into a unitary structure. But there are other forms of organization, some of which have hardly been examined. The Loki Principle insists that every literary law will produce its own violation, and this is certainly true of the standards of conventional plot construction. Many authors have joined together a preposterous sequence of events that elude or parody standard plots as they defy the laws of probability and move quickly into the realm of the impossible. The following sections will examine three such violations of mimetic emplotment: oneiric, carnivalesque, and contradictory.

Oneiric Plots

Many oneiric narratives refuse to employ a probabilistic progression; their events unfold in an unpredictable, haphazard manner. We see this in the more extreme works of Kafka like "Ein Landartz" ("A Country Doctor" 1919) as well as in many recent fictional texts by Can Xue, such as "The Lure of the Sea" (*Blue* pp. 56–90). In Kafka's story, the patient's wound is first imperceptible, then large and filled with worms; it is then described as a birth defect, a flower, and a couple of glancing blows from an axe. These sequences fascinate us in large part because of their utter rejection of the probable; at the same time, they reproduce the familiar associations of dream logic. I would also suggest that that some of the uncanny power of texts like *Der Process* (*The Trial* 1925) and *Das Schloss* (*The Castle* 1926) comes from the ways in which a naturalistic canon of probability is alternately followed and eluded throughout each work.

Carnivalesque Plots

In Aristophanes' *Thesmophoriazusae*, the character Euripides learns that the women of Athens are angry about his depictions of them onstage and are meeting to avenge themselves. He goes to great (and outrageous) lengths to have the all-female assembly infiltrated by a man who will defend him, and he starts by asking the effeminate playwright Agathon to go. Later, Euripides will persuade his servant, Mnesilochus, to infiltrate; he is then depilated onstage the better to pass as a woman. Once there, he is quickly exposed and restrained. As often happens in Aristophanic comedy, the preposterous plots instigated by the characters fail utterly. Mnesilochus then tries to get himself rescued by imitating the rescue scenes of several of Euripides' plays. None of these attempts work. Euripides does arrive, and, after promising to stop slandering the women, the two are allowed to depart in peace—thus easily voiding the "problem" that motivated the plot in the first place.[5] The events and their motivations are largely incommensurate in most carnivalesque plots. The trigger of these acts is almost a parody of teleology; the events are bound together not so much with a chain as with a breath.

---

5. See Richardson, *Unnatural Narrative*, pp. 95–96, for additional analysis of this work. There is nothing probable in any scene of the play.

We find this kind of narrative assemblage throughout the history of literature and in both high and popular narrative forms in works by Lucian, Rabelais, Ludwig Tieck's *Die verkehrte Welt* [*The Upside Down World*], Lewis Carroll's Alice books, Edward Lear's nonsense poems, Gilbert and Sullivan operas, Oscar Wilde's *The Importance of Being Earnest*, many absurdist dramas, Bob Hope–Bing Crosby *Road* movies, Looney Tunes cartoons, Monty Python movies, and several postmodern texts. What is common among such works is their flouting of probabilistic progressions and their replacement by seemingly gratuitous ones, although these often follow a broadly comic path based on exaggeration. In general, what would be a cheap plot trick in a mimetic narrative becomes an excellent gimmick in a carnivalesque plot: there can never be too many timely coincidences in a play like *The Importance of Being Earnest*. In Lucian's *A True Story*, the protagonists' ship encounters a storm so fierce that it blows them to the moon. Back on earth, they are swallowed up by a 150-mile-long whale; they live in its belly for twenty months before they move on to their next adventure. Nothing is too preposterous for this narrative, which mocks the exaggerations of those who, since Homer, have composed extravagant tales about amazing voyages.

Mikhail Bakhtin observes that in works with a Rabelaisian chronotope, we find "the destruction of all ordinary ties, and of all the *habitual matrices [sosedstva]* of things and ideas, and the creation of unexpected matrices, unexpected connections, including the most surprising logical links ('allogisms') and linguistic connections" (169). In carnivalesque plots, we encounter things like metaphors made literal, as when, in Aristophanes' *The Frogs*, a contest in which Hades attempts to determine whether Aeschylus or Euripides wrote the "weightier" lines. A large scale appears to have been brought onstage, and a line from each playwright is assessed. The words of Aeschylus denote larger, heavier objects than do those of Euripides, so Aeschylus is declared the victor.

There may be a kind of development in these works as we find a cluster of unlikely coincidences that bind a preposterous totality together. We often see increasingly extravagant and outrageous events building up as the narrative approaches its ending, and metafictional acts of frame breaking may appear toward the end. But this is not always the case. In many such plots, cumulative development is eschewed. Instead of a series of connected events that combine to produce a single, comprehensive effect, each event is intended to produce essentially the same comic response. The one rule that seems to govern such progressions is the simple one that each event needs to be amusing. Thus, one cannot repeat the same stunt too often. In Aristophanes' *The Frogs*, when Dionysus, dressed like Hercules, enters Hades, he encounters Aeacus, who mistakes him for Hercules and threatens him with several monsters. Afraid, Dionysus then has his servant Xanthias exchange clothes with him. At this point an attractive woman appears who is delighted to see Hercules and invites him to a feast. Dionysus, who always likes a good party, then exchanges clothing again with the servant and prepares to enjoy himself. At this point, Aeacus returns, and one more exchange of clothes occurs. Three switches are the usual limit of this device; after that, something different must transpire.[6] And in this play, it does—Xanthias offers up Dionysus, disguised as a servant, to be tortured by Aeacus until he tells the truth. He is whipped and tries to explain that he is really a god.

In *Endgame* (1957), Samuel Beckett offers a dark version of the carnivalesque. In this work, there is no single, unified action, no dynamic chain of events, but merely a series of largely gratuitous doings. The play is an assault on the teleology implicit in much traditionally plotted drama. As one arbitrary or meaningless event follows another, the question is not how tightly they are all connected but whether there is any substantial connection there at all. To interpret this play, one does not follow the trajectory of its plot so much as attempt to determine whether it has any significant plot. Early on, Hamm asks Clov whether or not he has "had enough." Clov responds he has always had enough, to which Hamm responds, "Then there is no reason for it to change" (5). Here, Beckett seems to be challenging the basic premise of dramatic narrative—transformation—and instead constructs a static play, devoid of all that makes a story tellable. There is a disequilibrium, even a conflict: Clov's continued subservience to his blind, immobile master. But, as we quickly realize, this situation too will not change. When Hamm asks, "Why do you stay with me?" Clov replies, "There's nowhere else" (6). For characters and audience, this amounts not to a plot but to a refusal of plot. Despite repeated claims "We're getting on" (9) and "Something is taking its course" (32), there is no cohesive grouping of events, but rather an avowedly arbitrary conglomerate of random actions that lead nowhere. *Endgame* is thus a defiantly anti-Aristotelian drama. Manfred Pfister has referred to Beckett's tendency to reduce the story to a mere sequence of events. In *Waiting for Godot, Endgame,* or *Happy Days,* "the immutability of the situation in which the dramatic figures find themselves—something they accept as a foregone conclusion—and their constant verbal and mimetic activity are no longer designed to bring about a

---

6. Here, I am again alluding to the general Western preference for tripartite units, including compact narrative units. Myths, legends, tales, and jokes typically offer an event, a slightly varied repetition of the event, and a third, very different instance that transforms the situation. If you tell a joke that begins, "A minister, a priest, and a rabbi walk into a bar," you cannot either add or subtract an episode without disappointing your audience.

change in the situation through action but have decayed into a form of game that merely serves to pass the time" (201).

Contradictory Plots

A growing number of extended texts build numerous contradictions into their story lines. These include Robbe-Grillet's *La Jalousie* (1957), Anna Kavan's *Ice* (1962), Harold Pinter's *The Basement* (1967), Robert Pinget's *Passacaille* (1969), Robert Coover's "The Babysitter" (1969); and feminist authors Caryl Churchill's *Traps* (1977), Jenny Erpenbeck's *Aller Tage Abend* (2012), and Kate Atkinson's *Life after Life* (2013). Though one might think that a series of major contradictions in the story line would kill off narrative interest, it turns out that many of these works are compulsively readable despite the contradictions—including the multiple deaths of the protagonists. I will briefly look at Atkinson's novel to try to determine how this is achieved.

Atkinson's *Life after Life* (2013) offers several mutually inconsistent plotlines, most of them the forking-path type of progressions where first one and then the other mutually exclusive events transpire. Most of these involve the death of the protagonist, Ursula Todd. Thus, near the beginning of the narrative, a snowstorm is raging as Ursula's mother is about to give birth to her. The snow prevents the doctor from arriving in time, and the baby girl dies as she is being born, choking on her umbilical cord (4). In the next chapter, the scene is replayed, but the roads are open, the doctor arrives, he snips the cord, and Ursula lives. She goes on to die several times in the book in a variety of ways. As a small girl, she drowns at the seaside (28); later, she falls to her death from a slippery roof (59); during the 1918 epidemic, she dies of influenza (84); she is killed by a gas leak (84); she is murdered by her husband (241); and so forth. After each death, the narrative returns to an earlier moment, a different path is taken, and the death is erased or denarrated.

In her review of the book, Francine Prose describes her experience of encountering these contradictory events: "The first few reverses are startling, but after a while it begins to seem quite normal (if still pleasantly jolting) when a character who, we think, has left the narrative forever reappears in another guise or is seen from a new perspective." Curiously, Prose deploys the language of modernism to describe these effects, although it is not the same scene viewed from a different perspective but a total transformation of the event itself that is occurring. Prose further notes that "the surprise of what happens is less intense than the unexpectedness of what doesn't happen:

what seemingly irreversible damage exists is repaired with the 'delete' key." She explains that "it's interesting to note how quickly Atkinson's new rules replace the old ones, how assuredly she rewrites the contract: we will stay tuned as long as she keeps us interested and curious about what all this is adding up to." Thus, "each tragedy continues to surprise and disturb us, even as we learn to expect that the victim will be all right in the morning" ("Review").

James Phelan's conception of narrative dynamics can again help us understand how the effects noted by Prose are attained. They also show how we are regularly entangled in an interconnected web of both instabilities and tensions, local and global. The book's first chapter, dated November 1930, depicts someone who we will later learn is Ursula as she attempts to assassinate Hitler. She gets a shot off just as Hitler's attendants fire their guns at her. Darkness then is said to fall and the chapter ends. At this point, there is a major instability as we wonder about the fate of the shooter and her target. There is also a significant tension, for we are curious about the genre of the book: perhaps a kind of alternative history that assumes that Hitler had been assassinated in 1930. Both of these leads prove to be empty. We soon learn that "darkness falls" is an indication that the focalizing figure is dying. Likewise, no alternative history will emerge; Hitler lives on and World War II will take place.

We will, however, be invited to speculate on more-general questions concerning the many directions a life can take. The narrative continues by moving into the past: February 11, 1910. This segment is the one in which the baby is born and dies, followed by the one in which she is saved. The same instability, that is, is resolved in an opposite manner, thereby producing a vast tension concerning what kind of book this really is. A global pattern soon develops in which a death occurs every few chapters; then the path is usually retraced, and a different, viable fork is provided instead. The narrative's main tension is largely resolved as we get a feeling for the way in which this extraordinary sequence tends to unfold; at the same time, our interest in its instabilities is restored as we want to discover what will happen next.

The danger with such a narrative technique is that death, since it has no irreversible consequences, can become trivial and thus lose its tellability. This is essentially what happens during the disappointing war in heaven among the immortal angels in *Paradise Lost*. At one point Ursula observes, "'What a world of difference there was between dying and nearly dying. One's whole life, in fact'" (200). But, of course, this isn't true for this novel. Marie-Laure Ryan has stated that "the intensity of suspense is inversely proportional to the range of possibilities"; thus, at the beginning of a story, anything can happen, "and the forking paths into the future are too numerous to contemplate. The future begins to take shape when a problem arises and confronts the hero with a limited number of possible lines of action. When a line is chosen, the spectrum of possible developments is reduced to the dichotomy of one branch leading to success and another ending in failure" (*Virtual* 142). What happens in *Life after Life* and other contradictory texts is exactly the opposite of what Ryan accurately posits for mimetic narratives. We are right to wonder how such an author can possibly maintain both suspense and tellability in her narrative.

Atkinson negotiates this hurdle in a couple of ways. Some of the deaths are rather sudden and thus take the reader by surprise. They vary in their causes and the agency of the relevant individuals: some are caused by neglect, some by bad luck, and others by a catastrophic consequence of ordinary children's behavior. Ursula's death at the hands of her husband is especially unjust and horrific, and it raises the violence level quite a bit. Once World War II begins, however, a different pattern emerges. In a bombing raid during the Blitz in November 1940, Ursula is killed while taking shelter (289). When the scene recurs in slightly different circumstances, the German bomb explodes again, and again Ursula dies (314). The reader may feel surprised or even shocked at this violation of the rule of reversible death that has been in place so far in the book. A few pages later, the scene is replayed, and Ursula, instead of going into the shelter where the bomb will strike, tries to rescue a terrified dog. She is away from the scene when the bomb detonates, and she survives, standing beside a large brick wall. The reader is assuaged; the protagonist will live.

But then the wall abruptly collapses on her and she dies again (321); a major tension returns, intensified. The rules have all been changed; we have to wonder whether this death is the "real" one that will not be undone even though its precise form may vary. Early in the book, Ursula's mother "wondered when death would seek its revenge" (31); perhaps this is it. The next chapter takes us back to 1926; the one following to 1933; and the next to August 1939. The hopeful reader appears to be rewarded in the chapter that follows, dated April 1945 and centered on Ursula. Unfortunately, this is the wrong story line. In this thread, Ursula has married a German before the war and was stuck in Germany for its duration. Now her husband is dead, she is hungry, exhausted, desperate. Her child is gravely ill and she has no money. There is gunfire around her, and British bombs are falling close by. She places a poison capsule in her daughter's mouth and both drift off into death. Something has changed radically: "She had never chosen death over life before and as she was leaving she knew something had cracked and broken and the order of things had changed. Then the dark obliterated all thoughts" (379). Having followed Ursula through so many deaths, we feel for her in part as we might for a mimetic character who has had until now survived many near-death scrapes.

The following chapter returns to September 1940, and the reader may well feel divided anticipation. There are well over one hundred pages remaining in the book; surely Ursula will come back to life for good? Then again, she may just die again and again during the war, quickly and slowly, killed alternately by German and British bombs, done in by others and by her own hand. Finally, we return to November 1940. The bombing starts again. One hundred pages after its last incarnation, the scene in the shelter is replayed once more, but this time she is finally able to elude her demise (430–32). A more linear narrative returns; later, we even get a glimpse of 1967 when she is enjoying her retirement party.

In this narrative, Atkinson uses three ways of sequencing the events: the primary one is that of false turns in the story line that are promptly corrected as the story moves on along its "normal" expected trajectory. There are also "dead ends": story lines that appear and then are abandoned after one or two iterations, like the book's first scene where Ursula shoots Hitler—it seems that only the fates of fictional characters, not historical ones, can be rewritten.[7] There are also serial repetitions; for example, the events of the day of Ursula's birth, February 11, 1910, are narrated twelve times throughout the course of the work. Many of these versions extend the narrative or present it from another perspective; sometimes the story is negated or altered, as when the cat smothers the baby but she is revived by her mother (132). In the first narration of the time the baby is saved, her mother makes a mental note "to buy just such a pair of scissors" in case of an admittedly unlikely emergency (11). In the penultimate iteration of the scene near the end of the novel, the doctor is again absent, and after giving birth to the blue-faced baby, her mother heaves herself up, opens a drawer, pulls out a pair of surgical scissors, and cuts the umbilical cord. "One must be prepared," she mutters (320), as little Ursula begins to breathe.

I suspect that our response to these extraordinary events is somewhat similar to our response to comparable events we might find in an ordinary mimetic narrative. We can imagine the author writing the book such that the protagonist keeps barely avoiding death rather than dying and being returned to life.[8] I am not here attempting to naturalize the exquisite contradictions that Atkinson builds into her narrative but rather merely suggesting the presence of

---

7. This scene is also repeated near the end of the book, but it has no discernible consequences for the story.

8. Marina Lambrou, in her article on the disnarrated events in the film, *La La Land*, draws on the work of social psychologists Roese and Olsen, who point out that "recent research has focused on the beneficial effect of generating such counterfactuals, in that they may often elucidate plans of behavior that lead to future betterment" (forthcoming).

somewhat comparable situations in our lives. It is obvious that many thematic elements are also implicated in this kind of emplotment. Precisely because the basic characters of the individuals are largely the same whatever their circumstances, we see the enormous power of chance events or bad decisions, the plasticity of destiny, and the precariousness of human life. Jenny Erpenbeck's narrator reflects on these mortal contingencies in terms that apply equally well to the events in *Life after Life*: "There was an entire world of reasons why her life had now reached its end, just as there was an entire world of reasons why she could and should remain alive" (114). There are numerous metafictional implications as well, such as the relative (but nevertheless self-limited) flexibility of the author's control over the construction of events and the general play with our ordinary expectations of how narratives progress. Authors normally do not kill off their central protagonist shortly after the narrative has begun. Atkinson makes us wonder how many more times Ursula will die, what kinds of death with they be, how frequently they will occur, and, especially, whether one of them will be definitive. Ursula may have nine (or twenty-nine) lives, but at some point she may not be revived. We also wonder who else will get to live again and, above all, how such a narrative will finally end. These questions form the book's "unnatural plot," and most readers, like Prose, seem to find the answers largely satisfactory. The local instabilities of the characters' lives are juxtaposed with these global tensions throughout the novel.

Concerning the reception of the work's construction, I suggest that with a contradictory narrative, many of us move from confusion, to wonder, to curiosity, to pattern recognition, and to the appreciation of repetitions and variations as we mark the first presentation of new events and the rewriting of earlier ones. Our immersion is interrupted, dissolved, and largely restored, though in a diminished form; our focus shifts between the characters' perspective and that of the author as the drama of the story alternates with the story of its telling. Not all contradictory plots are as successful in producing such engagement; one finds considerably more immersive possibilities in Kavan, Pinter, and Coover than in Robbe-Grillet, Pinget, or Churchill, many of whose readers never get beyond the wonder, or, in some cases, the confusion.

Narrative Dynamics

While some narratives are, in fact, little more than the sum of their episodes, other types, most notably those utilizing a classic kind of plot, often create or at least strive for cumulative effects, as the events gain in cohesion and intensity and come to a climax. This plot can be especially strongly felt since, as Phelan and Rabinowitz observe, "The logic of the text's movement encompasses not only the interconnections among events but also the interaction of those story-level dynamics with the discourse-level dynamics arising from the interrelations of implied author, narrator, and audience" (Herman, et al., *Narrative* 58). When done well (usually, this means without violating too egregiously our sense of probability), such effects are powerful and enjoyable and largely explain the fascination with this kind of emplotment throughout the history of literary criticism. Antiprobabilistic narratives work somewhat differently; they can move vigorously toward a silly goal in a parody of the classic plot, and contradictory narratives can generate their own curious momentum as normal causal progressions are abandoned or rearranged. For these effects, we may extend Marie-Laure Ryan's concept of "metasuspense" (*Narrative as Virtual Reality* 145) to include our curiosity over what an unpredictable author will do next.

Numerous terms have been used to describe the general trajectory of typical plots; the best-known include Brooks's *arousal, climax,* and *detumescence*; and Gustav Freytag's pyramidal form to graph a narrative's exposition, *rising action, climax, falling action,* and *denouement*. As we will see, Brooks's model has been decisively critiqued by Susan Winnett, who has shown that neither all plots nor all sexuality can be encompassed by his nineteenth-century, androcentric model. Freytag's figure draws important attention to a general trajectory we find in many plots, but the pyramidal shape distorts the actual effects experienced by audiences.[9] In the case of many of Shakespeare's mature works, further refinements are necessary: there is often a miniature climax near the end of the third act that anticipates and prefigures the larger climax at the end of the play.

Tellability

We may now move on to the related question of "tellability," or what makes a narrative worth hearing and telling. As Wolf Schmid states, tellability "designates something that is *worth* telling, the *noteworthiness* of a story" (13). Raphael Baroni goes on to further clarify that tellability is dependent on the nature of specific incidents judged by storytellers to be significant or surprising and worthy of being reported in specific contexts, thus conferring a "point" to the story ("Tellability" 1). Generally, theorists of tellability always note the

---

9. If one insists on geometrical shapes, a more accurate one would have a long isosceles triangle resting on its side; the thick end would represent the resolution.

contextual nature of the tellable, pointing out that last week's news is not as tellable as today's and that a bad storyteller can ruin the tellability of otherwise interesting material. Nevertheless, in practice the concept is often treated as a constant, as if we all more or less agree on what is and is not tellable.

The history of the British novel, however, suggests that the case may be quite different; successive periods may even be analyzed in terms of the kind of tellability they promote or contest. The concept is strongly connected to the arrangement of the plot proper and is frequently felt to be part of it, such as in Samuel Johnson's famous complaint, "Why, Sir, if you were to read [Samuel] Richardson for the story, your impatience would be so much fretted that you would hang yourself" (Boswell 353). Romantic authors typically opted for a high degree of eventfulness, narrating unusual adventures in exotic locales or intense inner dramas of emotional turmoil. In the Victorian period this approach was transmuted into two basic forms. First, the realist novel typically revolved around issues important to most people's lives, like love, marriage, professional success and failure, death, and inheritance. The second form is the melodramatic narrative, packed with mortal dangers and death-defying escapes from imminent destruction.

Marie-Laure Ryan does point out the role of genre in such cases, stating that "whereas popular literature invests heavily in the tellability of plots, high literature often prefers to make art out of the not-tellable" ("Tellability" 590). In the case of modernism, the situation is much more extreme. The title of Chekhov's "A Boring Story" (1889) typifies the new direction away from traditional adventures and incontrovertibly major events that modernist narrative would take. When one of Joseph Conrad's early works was criticized for having an insufficient amount of compelling incidents, Conrad wrote to a friend, admitting that the work in question did lack incident, but countered, "It's life. The incomplete joy, the incomplete sorrow, the incomplete rascality or heroism—the incomplete suffering. Events crowd and push and nothing happens. . . . The opportunities do not last long enough. Except in a boy's book of adventures" (*Collected Letters* 1:321). He would go to further limit his incidents' tellability and mock the kind of book that possesses it. In *Lord Jim*, we learn of the hair-raising events of the near-sinking of the *Patna* and the fates of all aboard in summary form, after they have occurred, as Conrad foregoes narrating an amazing adventure of the kind that fills Jim's mind: "the sea-life of light literature. He saw himself saving people from sinking ships, cutting away masts in a hurricane, swimming through a surf with a line" (6). Naturally, he always imagined himself as "an example of devotion to duty, and as unflinching as a hero in a book" (6); Conrad soon reveals that such books are false and their effects pernicious (see Wegner).

Other modernists came down still harder on tellability. Dorothy Richardson stated that "plot nowadays, save the cosmic plot, is inexcusable. Lollipops for children" (139). E. M. Forster famously excoriated those who demanded tellable incidents: for him, "Curiosity is one of the lowest of the human faculties"; a simple sequence of compelling events is suitable to recount to "a gaping audience of cavemen or to a tyrannical sultan or to their modern descendants, the movie public. They can only be kept awake by 'and then—and then—'" (*Aspects* 71). Woolf praised Chekhov for his narration of ostensibly minor events with minimal apparent connection, noting that "we have to read a great many stories before we feel, and the feeling is essential to our satisfaction, that we hold the part together, and that Chekhov is not merely rambling disconnectedly, but struck now this note, now that with intention, in order to complete his meaning" (*Common* 176). Elizabeth Abel observes that "Virginia Woolf disliked the fixity of plot: 'This appalling narrative business of the realist,' as she called it" (93). Woolf's opposition to traditional plotting is also more philosophical—she felt that, whether in a fictional or a nonfictional form like the biography, traditional plots betray rather than reveal lived experience. She is also eager to move beyond the conventions of Victorian plotting and create something very different. In her essay "Modern Fiction," she complains that almost every writer seems "constrained, not by his own free will but by some powerful and unscrupulous tyrant who has him in thrall, to provide a plot, to provide comedy, tragedy, love interest, and an air of probability embalming the whole" (*Common* 150). These are the snares that she would try to elude in a series of works, beginning with *Jacob's Room*, that reconfigure the relations among events, progression, response, and real and assumed significance as she refashions the very concept of tellability, finding importance in a dinner party, a brushstroke, and a wave as she demythologizes war, political power, hierarchy, and the postulated great deeds of great men.

Contradictory narratives pose a particular challenge to ideas of tellability based on mimetic and other conventional narratives. Marie-Laure Ryan has observed that "some events make better stories than others because they project a wider variety of [possible] forking paths on the narrative map. Even though the story can only follow one path, the understanding of these events involves a consideration of the 'virtual narratives' of the unrealized sequences that branch out of the event" ("Tellability" 590). As we have seen, incompatible narrative paths *can* be followed and can generate substantial narrative interest.

Brian McHale, discussing narrative poetry in words that are equally applicable to prose fiction, observes that "with postmodernism, narrativity returns, but with a difference," as postmodernists "recoil from the modernist recoil" from conventional narrative ("Weak" 162). The most conspicuous such strategies are parody and pastiche; authors are thus able to deploy narrative momentum without having to pretend to believe in it. Tellability has returned, but in a form that mocks itself. We see this opposition forcefully in the tabloid headlines cited in postmodern works like Don DeLillo's *White Noise* (1985), a work that thematizes plotting ("Wonder drugs mass-produced onboard UFO . . . will lead to cures for anxiety, obesity" [146]), as well as in Jay McInerney's *Bright Lights, Big City* (1984): "COMA BABY SIS PLEADS: SAVE MY LITTLE BROTHER" (11). It is, after all, in the tabloids that we get the most compulsive kind of tellability, and this suggests that both the modernist aversion and postmodern parody have something significant to inform us about the nature of tellability.

Peter Brooks suggests that plot is an arousal of desire whose climax is delayed until the narrative's end (111). He goes on to expand his notion of desire to include many nonsexual desires and needs, all of which can be thwarted. Expanding this concept still further, we can find a comparable set of oppositions in almost every plot. Looking back over this variety of techniques of emplotment, we may observe that plot is a continuous movement against its own negation. Such movement can happen in a number of different ways; for example, a sequence of events may fail to come together in a plot, or a pair of story lines may fail to properly merge. In an ordinary story, a protagonist must overcome a series of obstacles or a series of opponents who seek to prevent the objective from being reached and, thereby, the story being concluded: if Odysseus dies or gives up early in his attempt to return home, there is no more story.

Beyond the primary plot and its storyworld there are also a number of antagonistic devices that threaten the satisfactory completion of a story. These threats to the narrative's integrity include the seemingly trivial events that can potentially reduce a work's tellability, descriptions that go on too long, separate narrative strands that threaten to fail to merge, and gaps that keep fragmenting the text, as ever smaller, more dispersed, more unconnected scraps accumulate that may not be able to be made to cohere. Among postmodern and antimimetic plots, we see nonprobabilistic plots that are produced by a parody of plot itself or, more radically, the plot threatened by contradictory versions of the same events, as authors seek original ways to form a plot out of the material that would seem to threaten its very possibility, or the metaleptic intrusion of one storyworld into an ontologically distinct one.[10]

---

10. Dannenberg states that sophisticated narratives "use the temporal orchestration of multiple possible worlds to frustrate" the desire for a "causal-linear sequence of events through linear time" (45); this is another way that the movement of the plot can be challenged or retarded.

It has long been understood that there is a dual movement in emplotment: plots work toward their own solution and seem to defer or prevent that resolution. What is interesting to observe is that this dynamic can also appear in the discourse. It is in this sense that Sterne's *Tristram Shandy* is the most typical novel in literary history, as Shklovsky provocatively asserted; the book simply exaggerates the delaying and dispersing movements common to all narratives. J. Hillis Miller, referring to the novel's plot, even remarks that "the interest of a narrative lies in its digressions, in episodes that might be diagrammed in loops, knots, interruptions, or detours making a visible figure" (68). Similarly, some late modern, postmodern, and antimimetic narratives disclose the unnatural aspects potentially present in all narratives.

We see the extensiveness of modernism's rejection of the rule of a conventionally compelling plot and observe that this is almost certainly the first time in the history of literature that an engaging plot has been overthrown as the driving force of narrative. This practice is still inadequately recognized. Porter Abbott writes: "All successful narratives of any length are chains of suspense and surprise that keep us in a state of impatience, wonderment, and partial gratification" (*Cambridge* 57). This claim ignores the modernists' and many postmodernists' successful attempts to elude or transcend these chains. It is thus important that we devote more attention to the other traditions of emplotment, analyzing the progression of seemingly plotless narratives, episodic works, and works that employ an antiprobabilistic progression of events.

CHAPTER 4

Narrative Middles II

Non-Plot-Based Narrative Progressions

THERE ARE many ways other than that of standard forms of plotting to arrange the sequence of events in a narrative. Some are independent of principles of classic emplotment, while others are opposed to and work against it. In this chapter, I will identify the most salient varieties of non-plot-based narrative orderings in recent fiction, point out relevant historical antecedents, and note how these strategies supplement or supersede more traditional modes of sequencing.[1] This inventory will have its own sequencing principle, moving from the most familiar to the most counterintuitive orderings, that is, from those that almost invisibly accompany the movement of story to those that threaten to overthrow it. Each instance, however, will fit within the causal definition of narrative I have argued for, although in some extreme cases the definition will be slightly modified. I will also look for the presence of each strategy in Joyce's *Ulysses*, a novel that employs a rather large number of ordering techniques other than those of traditional emplotment.

Ulysses is particularly interesting concerning the progressions of its events. On the one hand, the work seems to lack what might seem to be the minimal

---

1. I will note at the outset of this chapter that Ralph Rader presented an important early attempt to move beyond what he terms "the realism-plot-judgment" model of narrative he identified with the earlier Chicago School theorists; his account, while disclosing three very different forms a realistic narrative progression may take, nevertheless remains grounded in a mimetic framework and thus does not encompass antimimetic patterns.

necessary plot: event after event appears to occur largely adventitiously, even randomly, as stray thoughts and minimally motivated events are noted. Terence Killeen observes that nothing much happens in the "Lestrygonians" episode: "Bloom meanders along through Dublin's centre, has the odd encounter, reflects on this and that, has a bite of lunch, makes his way to the museum" (83). He goes on to add that "something *almost* happens; he nearly runs into Blazes Boylan, but this encounter, which would have been dramatic enough, does not occur" (83). The first linear sequence centers on Stephen Dedalus from 8:00 AM until 11:00 AM (chapters 1–3); this progression is interrupted, and the clock is reset to 8:00 as we meet Bloom in chapter 4. The two main story lines, centered on Stephen and on Bloom, often approach each other but never fully merge in any significant way until the end of the work; and the final chapters resist any mechanism that will tie the events together as the two men part ways like two ships passing in the night, as a common description of the book's inconclusive ending avers. There does not appear to be any resolution that binds the varied events together into a classic plot. Many shorter sequences seem adventitiously conjoined and are often unconnected by any large causal chain among events; "The Wandering Rocks" episode, which traces the essentially noninteractive movements of several spatially adjacent Dublin citizens, can even be seen as a kind of quintessence of the work's refusal of traditional plot. Timothy Martin observes that "many of the later episodes betray principles of wholeness independent of *Ulysses* as a whole" (208); the rest of his essay provides an impressive study of the connections and ruptures among the novel's events.

The book's frequent use of interior monologue and free indirect speech makes the sequencing of still shorter passages seem even more adventitious; to say that sentence B follows sentence A simply because that thought just popped into the character's mind is often not much of an explanation at all. Todorov goes so far as to state that "the most striking submission to the temporal order is *Ulysses*. The only, or at least the main, relation among the actions is their pure succession" (*Introduction* 42). Though Todorov significantly overstates the case, such a sentiment was common among the book's earlier readers.

Intertextual Ordering

One obvious method by which these ostensibly gratuitous events and episodes are patterned is by their reproduction of the order of an earlier text. The dual linear progressions noted above appear in *Ulysses* because the same sequence occurs in the *Odyssey*: Joyce puts Stephen's otherwise unmotivated and inconsequential encounter with the Protean ocean (chapter 3) after his meeting with the Nestor figure (chapter 2) because Homer's Telemachus speaks with Nestor (Book 3) before doing battle with Proteus (Book 4). Homer's largely causal sequence becomes the template for Joyce's otherwise seemingly random conjunctions. This ordering continues for much but not all of Joyce's text. His Lotus Eaters, Aeolus, Lestrygonians, Sirens, and Oxen of the Sun episodes follow the same order as that used by Homer; other episodes, however (Hades, Cyclops, Circe), are rearranged to suit different purposes. As Hugh Kenner explains, since "funerals are morning affairs in Catholic Dublin, 'Hades' comes before 'Circe'" (26), as the episode is reordered to conform to the book's fidelity to realism.

Rhetorical Ordering

Sheldon Sacks has provided another useful way in which we may think about narratives that are organized in a manner largely independent of the customary qualities of plot. Discussing the genre of the apologue, or the fictional exemplification of a thesis or worldview, such as *Candide* or *Rasselas,* he points out that the episodes are "related to each other in a rhetorical order" rather than a probabilistic one. "There is no fictional 'probability' that Rasselas, after he leaves the haunts of gay young men, will meet a sage committed to controlling the passions" (56); such a sequence, however, does appropriately follow from the demands of the novella's argument. This kind of rhetorical sequencing is found in the more ideologically charged turns of many novels. Joyce often uses rhetorical progressions in this way, though in a more subtle manner. Thus, Deasey asks Stephen why Ireland was the only nation that never persecuted the Jews. Answering his own question, he says, "Because she never let them in" (30). Two chapters later, we are introduced to Leopold Bloom, one of about 5,000 Jews living in Ireland at the time of the book's setting. We can see numerous miniature and oblique rhetorical sequences in the dialectical progression of the events in "Scylla and Charybdis," in which the many idealistic theses propounded by the figures in the library are followed by the crassly materialistic positions of Buck Mulligan, whose entry into the room is synchronized with the model of thesis/antithesis. In a related manner, the catechistic structure of "Ithaca" is minimally narrative and is sequenced instead by the linked series of questions and answers; as C. H. Peake observes, this "is not naturally a narrative method; it implies a static situation which is being examined and analyzed rather than the unrolling of a concatenated series of events" (283; see also Fludernik, "Ithaca"). Aspects of the progressions common to apologues also appear in the numerous rhetorical trajectories present in the "Aeolus" chapter which is set in a newsroom and thematizes the art of rhetoric.

Aesthetic Ordering

It is easy to move from a sequence of events that exemplifies an argument to a more general, motif-based alternation or progression. But while these modes of composition are similar, their motives may be opposed. Rhetorical sequencing is an intentional arrangement set forth as advantageously as possible to produce a particular effect: generally, to bring the mind of the reader into closer conformity with the beliefs of the author. In this sense, it is every bit as functional as traditional emplotment, whose purpose is to impel readers from chapter to chapter by having them observe how sympathetic protagonists attempt to overcome adversity and attain their desires. Motif-based, architectonic, numerological, or geometrical kinds of sequencing are primarily formal designs that may have little function other than that of satisfying a desire for symmetry. I will refer to these forms as *aesthetic* orderings. It often happens that after a certain point, the motif does not merely accompany the narrative; instead, the narrative events are produced to accommodate the development of the motif.

Numerous other such aesthetic progressions may be enumerated, including the familiar circle pattern that returns important aspects of the narrative to their starting points; another is that which E. M. Forster described as the hourglass shape of Henry James's *The Ambassadors* (*Aspects* 153–62), as Chad Newsome and Lambert Strether exchange roles for a while at the end of the work. A more straightforward, antimimetic example of such an exchange of roles and personal ties occurs in Pinter's *The Basement*; the primary function of this reversal is arguably to produce the unrealistic inverted symmetry. We may also point to Tolstoy's insistent alternation of light and dark scenes throughout *Anna Karenina*. In "The Dead," as noted in the previous chapter, we do not really find much of a sustained plot; instead, however, we do find other forms of progression, including the parallelism of the positioning of the three scenes that depict Gabriel's unsuccessful encounters with women associated with the West of Ireland, the area least affected by English conquest and that thus represents Ireland herself. Though minimally connected by the succession of events, they form a structural design that helps explain the totality of the work and its movement toward ever more powerful and personal expressions of repressed Irish culture and history (see Cheng 134–47).

When examining any of the many scenes in *Ulysses* that do not obviously impel the plot forward, one may often explain a scene's placement in terms of its motif function rather than as part of any causal chain of events. Joyce is quite adept at these kinds of progressions: each of the final fifteen chapters of *Ulysses* thematizes a different organ of the human body, and, similarly, a different art or science is foregrounded in each. The specifically generative functions of these themes occur more at the level of individual events than at the chapter level, as Joyce dramatizes a specific organ (lungs) and discipline (rhetoric) in the Aeolus episode, although several smaller events (including mental events) may take place primarily for the purpose of illustrating the themes of breathing and of rhetorical symmetry, including metabole: "The door of Ruttledge's office whispered: ee: cree. They always build one door opposite another for the wind to. Way in. Way out" (97).

Still other kinds of symmetrical arrangements of chapters and events can be identified; these do not merely provide a structure for an otherwise unorganized conglomeration of events but at times go on to actually *produce* some of those events. Viktor Shklovsky identified a number of formal arrangements of narrative materials, including repetition, parallelism, antithesis, and triadic patterns, and pointed out that much of the *Chanson de Roland* is composed around dual and triple repetitions of the same set of scenes and events ("Novel" 15–51). In fact, many of these actions are present *only* because they complete the formal pattern that animates the rest of the text, in contravention of other compositional principles like causal connection, verisimilitude, or rhetorical efficacy. William W. Ryding carries this kind of analysis much further, describing how a number of medieval narratives eschew narrative unity in favor of "artistic duality, trinity, or some other form of multiplicity" (116), including the multiplication of parallel or antithetical story lines exclusively for this effect. Thus, the second part of *Beowulf*, which takes place fifty years after his victory over Grendel and the hag, is an entirely new (though fully symmetrical) story of the aged Beowulf's battle with the dragon. This work, like the *Chanson de Roland*, "has in fact two beginnings, two middles, and two ends. The central discontinuity that seems so clumsy to us appears to have served the medieval writer as a means to a particular esthetic end—it was, we may suppose, a special grace in story-telling" (43). Ring structures form patterns that are arranged in symmetrical and inverted orders, such as A, B, C, D, E, D', C', B', A'. Mary Douglas has analyzed these patterns across several cultures; Tom Stoppard's *Artist Descending a Staircase* (1972), which I will discuss in chapter 6, provides a recent, vivid example of this kind of arrangement. Other comparable methods of production and ordering of narrative segments are common in numerous periods of literary history.[2] These various architectonic progressions are no doubt understudied because in many cases they may seem to be less important than or a mere appendage to the unfolding of the progression of the story's main events; so powerful is the pull of the plot in the perception of narrative that it may need to be abandoned or suppressed for alternative ordering systems to become visible. Nevertheless, these methods of sequencing do help explain why a given narrative has the events and arrangement it does. Even if Dante's story were largely completed halfway through the *Paradiso*, he would have had to stretch his material out until he had reached the structurally requisite thirty-three cantos to maintain the symmetry of the work's three parts.

The arrangement of a cluster of literary motifs may be modeled on or borrowed from standard musical patterns. Many authors have utilized the general structure of the sonata (Strindberg's *Ghost Sonata*) or the symphony (Gide's *La Symphonie pastoral*); the framework of jazz (Toni Morrison's *Jazz*); and the prescriptions of the classical Indian musical form, the *raga* (Amit Chaudhuri's *Afternoon Raag*). A trajectory provided by the fugue has at times proven irresistible, as evidenced by Thomas Mann's *Der Tod in Venedig*; there is also the *Fuga per Canonem* that orders the "Sirens" episode of *Ulysses*.[3] These last two examples point to an important distinction in non-plot-based ordering devices: often these are unobtrusive, working in tandem with more conventional modes of story sequencing, producing a trajectory of otherwise largely unmotivated sequences or (as in the case of Mann) an overdetermined narrative progression. That is, Aschenbach dies in Venice *both* because he has chosen to stay in the city as cholera spreads *and* because it is the final expression of the bass theme—death—as it merges with its contrapuntal theme of sexual desire. Many of the sequences in Joyce's "Sirens," however, make little or no sense if approached from the traditional perspectives of story or plot; indeed, the episode's first set of words make no virtually sense from most any conventional framework: "Bronze by gold heard the hoofirons, steelyringing. / Imperthnthn thnthnthn. / Chips, picking chips off rocky thumbnail, chips. / Horrid! And gold flushed more. / A husky fifenote blew. / Blew. Blue

---

2. For a comprehensive overview of symmetrical and numerological progressions in narrative literature, see R. G. Peterson. For a study of symmetries in chapter sequencing in the traditional novel, see Marshall Brown.

3. There is still some disagreement on just how closely this episode approximates a musical composition. For a compelling recent approach, see Susan Sutliff Brown.

bloom is on the. / Goldpinnacled hair. A jumping rose on satiny breast of satin, rose of Castile. / Trilling, trilling: Idolores. / Peep! Who's in the. . . . peepofgold?" (210, Joyce's ellipsis). As an overture that previews the primary versions of the major themes and motifs to follow (and roughly approximates the order of their appearance), it is an accurate and useful compendium that performs the same function as a musical overture—that is, a very daring one that offers such disparate motifs that we are unsure whether they can in fact come together in the development of the text that follows.

Visual Event Generators

One might designate the presentation of the opening phrases of "Sirens" as foreshadowing or announcing the material to follow, but one may equally effectively view them as generating the rest of the chapter. This type of oscillating perspective is frequently relevant to narratives that are or seem to be generated by (fictional) pictures within the text. Longus's second-century novella, *Daphnis and Chloe,* begins with the partial description of a narrative painting, which the narrator finds so wonderful that he decides to narrate in prose the story it depicts. In Goethe's *Novelle,* we are presented with drawings of an abandoned castle, the story of a fire in a marketplace, and the picture of a tiger leaping on a person. As the tale unfolds, the protagonist visits the castle; observes a fire break out in the marketplace; and witnesses a real tiger, having escaped from its enclosure, leaping on a person. Such unlikely repetitions may be properly viewed as uncanny coincidences or an overactive display of irony; one might also more effectively read them as a cunning, proto-Borgesian play with narrative sequencing in which simulacra come to engender the objects and events that they had represented.

For a Joycean example we may turn to the phantasmagoric "Circe" chapter, in which images Bloom has seen earlier in the day now come alive, such as the Greek nymph in the painting in his bedroom (444–51). This kind of "pictorial genesis" is also found in many *nouveaux romans,* perhaps most memorably in Robbe-Grillet's *In the Labyrinth* in which a number of shapes described at the beginning of the book go on to generate objects having a similar shape which then become foci of unfolding narratives (*Two Novels*). Thus, the layer of dust in the room engenders the snow that appears in the story that grows from it; the image of the cross-shaped object on the desk is transformed into the bayonet of the soldier in the inner story; the rectangular shape produces the box he is carrying; and the painting, *The Defeat at Reichenfels,* after being described in impossible detail, comes alive and turns into a narrative, as a description becomes, through metalepsis, a sequence of events, and the opposition between temporal and spatial art forms dissolves.[4]

Verbal Event Generators

Other forms of event generation are common in the *nouveau roman* and its various antecedents; a particularly seminal type is the way in which a few select words go on to generate the object or actions they depict. Jean Ricardou has called it a *structural metaphor* and describes it as a trope that is made literal and takes on life in the text (*Problèmes* 135–41). I will refer to it as a *verbal generator* and use it to refer to a practice that names an object or event which then appears or occurs in the narrative. In a traditional work, there may well be an ironic verbal foreshadowing of an event before it occurs; in the *nouveau roman*, this becomes an alternative principle of narrative progression as individual words or images produce the events of the text (see Sherzer 13–36; Hayman 104–46).

Thus, in Robbe-Grillet's *Project for a Revolution in New York*, the concept "red" in all its permutations generates many of the events (including murder and arson); still more primary is the juxtaposition of contraries, as Thomas D. O'Donnell has explained. Noting further narrative proliferation, O'Donnell traces the avatars that produce the rat in the book. "Very early in the novel, the narrator informs us that Ben Said is wearing black gloves; when writing in his notebook, Ben Said tucks the gloves under his armpit. Another glove appears on the cover of Laura's detective story"; this in turn suggests that "Ben Said may be responsible for the fate of the girl on the story's torn cover. Upon closer examination, it is noted that the "glove" is in reality an enormous furry spider. Laura found the book on top of the bookcase while trying to escape from a giant spider or a *rat*; henceforth, spider and rat form an elementary combination that may not be dissociated" (O'Donnell 192). These examples, O'Donnell points out, "illustrate Robbe-Grillet's thematic generative technique to provide a long range 'plot' for his novel" (192).

---

4. For an example of this kind of text generation, see Claude Simon's *Triptych* (1973). For the opposite movement, in which a narrative progresses only to end up as a painting, see Alejo Carpentier's El siglo de las luces (*Explosion in a Cathedral* 1962); the metaphor of spatial form becomes literalized, as it were, in this text. Emma Kafalenos has compellingly discussed images that generate or otherwise alter stories (*Narrative* 179–96).

In Joyce's "Circe," we find a clear example of a verbal generator producing a substantial stretch of text. As Bloom denigrates the use of tobacco, Zoe retorts: "Go on. Make a stump speech of it." What immediately follows in the narrative is the figure of Bloom in workingman's overalls, giving an oration on the evils of tobacco before an adoring populace (390–93), as the phrase "make a stump speech" announces the event it produces.

In many of the compositions of Jean Ricardou, on the other hand, individual French words produce slight lexical variants which go on to generate the newly named objects or relations in the text as it unfolds. Even the name of the press that appears on the title page (*"Les Éditions de minuit"*) can serve as a textual generator: thus, in *La Prise de Constantinople*, the word *Éditions* engenders the characters Ed and Edith, as well as the idea of the hill of Sion, while *Minuit* determines that the book will open late at night (384). Though common in avant-garde texts, such verbal generators can actually be traced back as far as the thirtieth canto of Dante's *Purgatorio*, where the elders call out, *"Manibus, oh, date lilia plenis"* [With full hands, give me lilies]. At this moment literal flowers fall out of a cloud.

Verbal generators are present in Sterne's *Tristram Shandy*. Tristram's father, Walter Shandy, actually writes a book that attempts to prove that the name one is born with strongly influences one's fortunes in life; or, in his words, "that magic bias which good or bad names irresistibly impress upon our characters and conducts" (Book 4, chapter 8). This is certainly true for Tristram's sad destiny as well as that of others in the narrative: Dr. Slop makes his entry covered in mud after having just fallen off his horse. Walter Shandy wants to give his son a great name that will ensure a superior life and tells his servant Susannah to have him christened Trismegistus (Book 4, chapter 14). He then calls her a leaky vessel and says he doubts that she will remember the name. What is spoken comes to pass: Susannah partially forgets the name and the child is mistakenly christened as Tristram.

An interesting variant of the verbal text generator is that of the metaphor made literal. In Ben Jonson's *Volpone, or The Fox* (1607), the insistent animal names and imagery seem to produce the otherwise odd scene in which Sir Politic Would-Be climbs into a giant tortoise shell onstage (see Richardson, "Words"). Nabokov has identified a similar set of generators at work in Gogol's *Dead Souls* (1842), as metaphors and similes generate objects and personages (*Nikolai* 77–84). Stanley Corngold has further argued that clichés and dead metaphors have "the uncanny power to come to life when taken literally" (225); they can help explain many of the transformations in Kafka's work. Rushdie's work frequently employs such figures, as in the Sunderbans episode in *Midnight's Children*, where the moral darkness that consumes the narrator produces a single night that lasts 635 days. Borges has written a story about the verbal generation of physical entities in a fictional world that then crosses over into the narrator's world in "Tlön, Uqbar, Orbis Tertius" (1940).

Alphabetical Orderings

Alphabetical patterns can also serve as a means of ordering events. Such a progression, as Roland Barthes once remarked at the beginning of one of his own such compositions, has all the order and arbitrariness of the alphabet itself. This kind of movement, which will be further explored in chapter 6, may trace its descent from Raymond Roussel. It is not inherently a fictive one and can be readily found in nonfiction and nonnarrative forms (e.g., Barthes's *A Lover's Discourse*) as well as in works that straddle the line between narrative and nonnarrative, such as Michel Butor's *Mobile*, which Dina Sherzer describes as "semiotic catalogue" (46). In some works, like Walter Abish's *Alphabetical Africa*, the ordering principle is partially generating what is depicted in the novel. Its first chapter, titled "A," only uses words beginning with the letter *A*. The second chapter ("B") only allows words beginning with either *A* or *B*, and so on. Thus, in the first chapter we have unusual sentences like "As alien airforce attacks Angola, Albert asks, are anthills anywhere about, agreeing as Alex asserts, all Angolans are assholes" (2). Roy Sommer observes that "the first chapter begins with a puzzle: how is Antibes, the French city, linked to Africa? Why is the assembly of an African army described not as an event in the fictional world but as the outcome of an argument, and in which part of the African continent can antelopes and alligators coexist? Alligators don't normally live in Africa, and yet they are mentioned, like the argument, because the word begins with the letter a" ("(Un)Natural Response"; see also Orr 113–16). In many cases, however, alphabetical arrangements do not stray too far from the standard progression of emplotment, as we will shortly see. Though Joyce delights in the play of individual letters and is intrigued by the alphabet (Ahbeesee defeegee kelomen opeeque rustyouvee" [48]), I don't find any strictly alphabetical orderings in *Ulysses* of any scale (although the letters of the last word of the book, *yes*, are contained, in reverse order, in its first word, S*tately*).[5]

---

5. There is, however, plenty of alphabetical play in "Ithaca" (anagrams, acrostics, etc.).

Serial Ordering

Another generating mechanism used by many postmodern authors and a few filmmakers is based on repetition of events rather than on a progression from one event to another. Anna Kavan has used the metaphor of the recurring dream to describe the obsessively repeated and internally contradictory quest of the protagonist to find and rescue the victimized heroine in her novel *Ice* (1967). Caryl Churchill constructs "Heart's Desire" as a series of repetitions and variations of an opening scene; while the performance progresses, certain plotlines are developed, some of which move far from the first scene and others of which appear once or twice and then are abandoned—something we saw in play in Atkinson's *Life after Life*. A classic instance of this practice is probably Robbe-Grillet's *Jealousy*, in which a number of the same set of events are presented nine consecutive times, with each version containing significant variations. As Robbe-Grillet has explained, in a traditional narrative, "what follows phenomenon A is a phenomenon B, the consequence of the first," while in a *nouveau roman* like *Jealousy*, "what happens is entirely different. Instead of having to deal with a series of scenes which are connected by causal links, one has the impression that the same scene is constantly repeating itself, but with variations; that is, scene A is not followed by scene B but by scene A', a possible variation of scene A" ("Order" 5). This technique is variously designated by its theorists; the most useful term is probably that employed by Dina Sherzer, who calls this kind of progression "serial constructs" (13–36).[6] Serial constructs may be further sequenced according to other patterns of progression; for example, the depictions in *Jealousy* move toward greater intensity and violence before the last segment provides a final, sedate set of events.

Stephen Dixon's *Phone Rings* (2005) is especially interesting in developing the possibilities of beginning, repetition, contradiction, and progression. The novel begins with several brief, self-negating accounts of a very disturbing phone call:

Phone rings. "It's for you," his wife says. "Manny. He doesn't sound—"
 The phone rings. "Should I get it," his wife says, "or do you want to?"
 "I'll get it," he says, and picks up the receiver and says hello. "Uncle Stu," his nephew says, "It's about Dad. . . ."

---

 6. This term is intended to loosely suggest but not insist too systematically on the kind of serial form used to structure and generate modern twelve-tone music. It is merely an analogue of the musical practice.

Phone rings. He's lying on his bed reading and thinks "Why didn't I shut the ringer off?" and yells out, "Anyone going to get it?" More rings. Nobody answers him. (11)

Another, different version follows; we quickly learn that the call reports the sudden death of the protagonist's, Stu's, beloved brother, Dan. The text then moves back in time to several earlier encounters with Dan, all begun by or involving a phone call. Once again the phone rings, and we are given yet another variation on the scene: "Manny says he has very bad news, the worst imaginable. 'I'm sorry, I don't know how to say this'" (22). Chapter 2 begins with the phone ringing and Stu thinking how much he would like to talk to his brother; over the course of several pages, no one appears to answer it. Then Stu picks it up on the fifth or sixth ring and learns in different words that something terrible has happened to his brother (31). Stu then dials the phone and calls Dan. Dan answers, and Stu asks whether it's true that he just died. Dan responds, "It isn't. You hear me; my voice? I'm alive as you are" (31). At the end of the chapter, news of his death is again delivered by the telephone. As the book progresses, other ominous phone calls are recounted, usually at the beginning of a chapter: the death of their father and the impending death of their mother. The reader begins to dread any new mention of ringing. The rest of the novel consists of flashbacks of the brothers' shared experiences and accounts of Stu's attempts to move, gradually and with difficulty, beyond his grief. The phone calls diminish, until the last chapter returns us once more to the primal scene of the dreadful message; this time, it may be the "definitive" account that hitherto had been partially repressed—or it may be just one more possible version.

We also note that in each episode of *Ulysses*, Joyce includes echoes of other episodes, some of which can feel quite out of place and seemingly present only for their echoic function, but, other than this, cannot be said to generate the text. Miniature reproductions of the string of events of the entire book (that is, mises en abyme) are also present at several points in Joyce's text (543, 552).

Collage Composition

A related technique is "collage" composition: a collage in which several key elements are recombined in a number of different arrangements and contexts, and which constitutes the nexus that connects the different units (see Sherzer 37–76). This order may be present (and is no doubt less jarring) in nonnarrative texts; it is also more of a principle of coherence rather than progression per se, since after a certain amplitude is reached, there is no inherent reason for the text to continue. Nevertheless, to answer the question "How are the third or fourth sections related to the opening units?" a plausible response is that they are recombinations, analogues, or variations of some of the elements present in the earlier segments; the collage technique, that is, necessitates such a progression. As Dina Sherzer remarks, such texts "are open in that no one referential or morphological element brings about the sense of an ending or a feeling of completion; other variations and repetitions could be added to the existing ones, lengthening the text but not changing it otherwise" (14). This observation is a fairly good depiction of Lyn Hejinian's text *My Life,* a partially autobiographical collage that was originally published in 1978, when the author was thirty-seven. At this time, the work consisted of thirty-seven sections, each with thirty-seven sentences. The second edition, published eight years later, had eight new sections of forty-five sentences, and eight new sentences had been added to all of the previously published sections. Hejinian has expressed her fascination with texts that can include "analogues and coincidences, resemblances and differences, the simultaneous existence of variations, contradictions, and the apparently random" (*Language* 117).[7] *Ulysses* can function as a model for such practices, as its central figures, motifs, tropes, and elements are recombined in successive chapters, sometimes in ways that violate the book's mimetic stance, as Hazard Adams has pointed out in his study of these deviously "wandering rocks" ("Critical"). They can be thought of as the revenge of the text against the demands of the plot.

Random Ordering

We arrive now at our final strategy, or rather antistrategy, of narrative progression: the aleatory. Popularized by Dadaists who would select phrases that had been cut out of newspapers and thrown into a hat, a number of authors and composers, including William Burroughs and Karlheinz Stockhausen, have utilized this technique. Beckett's "Lessness" is a short text randomly assembled: Beckett ordered 120 sentences by drawing numbers out of a container; he then did it again so that the text contained two sequences of the same sentences, each in a different random order. Interestingly, the numerous interconnections among its elements tended to make any order in which they appeared seem purposive. There are no aleatory elements in *Ulysses*—Joyce once won-

---

7. Oneiric ordering, which mimics the associative conjunctions of dream sequences, can be situated with collage composition.

dered whether it wasn't too meticulously structured—and it may be that there is only a single aleatory phrase in all of Joyce's works. As Richard Ellmann recounts, Joyce was dictating part of *Finnegans Wake* to Samuel Beckett. "In the middle of one such session there was a knock at the door which Beckett didn't hear. Joyce said 'Come in.' and Beckett wrote it down. Afterwards he read back what he had written and Joyce said, 'What's that "Come in"?' 'Yes, you said that,' said Beckett. Joyce thought for a moment and then said, 'Let it stand.' He was quite willing to accept coincidence as his collaborator" (649).

Conclusion

It is clear that this overview of non-plot-based forms of narrative progression suggests how prevalent these forms are and how significant they can be. Some of these, like rhetorical or aesthetic ordering, can be seamlessly complementary to more usual kinds of emplotment; they add an additional motivation for the precise narrative trajectory that emerges. Traditional emplotment often or even typically works in a kind of unacknowledged counterpoint with other methods of progression. At times these diverge or come into collision, a situation most evident when ideological trajectories displace probability in a realist work, like the ending of D. H. Lawrence's "The Fox," which I will discuss in chapter 7. By contrast, radical aesthetic ordering techniques, such as verbal event generators, are quite disruptive in a different, more obviously deliberate, manner and regularly defy conventions of mimesis and supplant plot altogether. Though dispensing with the ordering principles of plot, these works remain narratives. There is still a causal connection, although a tenuous or unusual one, between successive events in these works. The connections may be slight, as in collage compositions, or unexpected, as in some geometrical patternings. At times they may seem to move beyond the principles of plot and probability in order to create instead an aesthetic order. Serial constructs and verbal and visual generators produce a chain of linked events, even though they are not linked through the agency of actors or events. Instead, it is the generator that is the cause of the events, and the characters experience those effects.

It may be that many of the more vigorous non- or antiplot mechanisms of narrative sequencing presume the awareness of standard forms of emplotment, forms that these mechanisms work in a dialectal way to attenuate or negate. Thus, while the concept of plot alone cannot describe the various sequencing patterns present in many recent works of fiction, most of those patterns can be fully comprehended only in relation to plot. Even chance compositions are interesting not for any intrinsic reason but for the ways they appear to mimic or contravene the kind of order produced by emplotment. The symbiotic relation between plot and other antithetical orderings is especially pronounced in the arrangement of the chapters of Robbe-Grillet's *Jealousy*. The shifting intensity of these descriptions, as Jean Ricardou has pointed out, nevertheless traces the conventional structure of slowly rising and rapidly falling action typical of the traditional novel ("Naissance"). A more elaborate development of this pattern is found in the many deaths near the end of the multiple contradictory scenarios represented in Coover's "The Babysitter": the baby is both choked to death and drowned by the babysitter; the babysitter herself is drowned in the tub and then lies dead on a rug; the husband experiences several humiliating denouements; and his wife finally hears that her children are murdered, her husband is gone, and there is a corpse in her bathtub. We also note that the sequence of variants that compose the experimental film *Run, Lola, Run* follow the general pattern of comedy, with a successful conclusion of the elaborate efforts of the protagonists at the end of the final sequence. Traditional formulas of narrative progression are partially represented, the better to be parodied.

We may affirm that narrative progression is a protean, dynamic process, with multiple sources of narrative development operating at different points in the text, as *Ulysses* exemplifies so clearly. The concept of plot alone is not adequate to explain all the sequences even of many plot-driven compositions, let alone the more experimental event generators identified above. I prefer to think of plot as a component of narrative sequencing that is independent of and working in varying degrees of complementarity with or opposition to other kinds of progression, especially rhetorical, generic, and aesthetic orderings, some of which will be discussed more fully in chapter 7. Looked at from the vantage point of literary value, it may well be that some of the most compelling narrative sequences are those that seamlessly interweave two or more strategies of progression, making the independent orderings seem to be coextensive and unobtrusive.

CHAPTER 5

The Varieties of Narrative Time

TEMPORAL EXTENSION is one of the most basic aspects of narrative. Narratives unfold in time, typically relate events from multiple periods, and are composed in time. Time has rightly been singled out by theorists of narrative for intensive analysis; Paul Ricoeur even claims that "I take temporality to be that structure of existence that reaches language in narrativity and narrativity to be the language structure that has temporality as its ultimate referent" ("Narrative" 165). Temporality has routinely been a subject of exploration (and critical evaluation) in the history of criticism, from the neoclassical critics' fascination with the relation between a play's represented story time and the time of its presentation to formalist explorations of modernist temporal constructions. Many creative authors have recently fabricated ever more fascinating temporal arrangements. As Elizabeth Deeds Ermarth has stated, "While all narrative is temporal by definition because its medium is temporal, postmodern sequences make accessible new temporal capacities that subvert the privilege of historical time and bind temporality in language" (11). In this chapter, I will attempt to modify and extend the concepts of time set forth by Genette just as Genette modified and extended the ideas of the Russian formalists, especially Viktor Shklovsky.[1]

---

1. Genette, of course, is aware of many texts that elude his narratological system. He admits that there are some narratives that will not allow a consistent story and its attendant temporality to be inferred: "Obviously, this reconstitution is not always possible, and it becomes

For a comprehensive account of narrative temporality, several basic concepts are required. First we need the complementary ideas (as will be discussed in at greater length in chapter 6) of the **(1A)** story or **fabula** (Genette's *histoire*) and **(1B)** text or **syuzhet** (Genette's *récit*)—which are, respectively, the chronological sequence of events that can be derived from the text, and the sequence in which they are actually presented to the audience. Take a simple sequence like: (a) John died today. (b) He fell sick a year ago. (c) In his youth, he seemed to have much promise. (d) He was often sick as a child. (e) He was born in 1961. The syuzhet presents the events in a reverse chronological order; we rearrange them to get the sequence of the story, that is, (e), (d), (c), (b), (a). This distinction is essential for narrative analysis.

In fictions set in a recognizable historical period, we will also want to observe whether the events are congruent or incongruent with historical accounts, or what Dorrit Cohn refers to as the "referential level" (112), which we will call **historical time** and designate by **(1C)**.[2] Often, the more realistic a narrative attempts to be, the greater is the attempt to conform to, or at least to not contradict, the facts of history; this is especially true of historical fiction. *War and Peace* (1869) for the most part hews rigorously to the timeline of the Napoleonic campaigns; the anxious reader, worried about the fate of the Russian Army in late 1805 as depicted in Book III, need not skip ahead to later chapters of the novel but can instead look up the Battle of Austerlitz in a volume of European history. James Joyce is likewise meticulous in weaving the actual events of June 16, 1904, into the novel he set on that day. The musings, historical and other, that comprise Virginia Woolf's "The Mark on the Wall" (1917) are set in a vague, early twentieth-century time period until the work's final sentence which abruptly situates it in the middle of World War I. More recently, Jean-Paul Dubois's novel *Vie Française* (2004) frames the narration of the events of the protagonist within the history of the French Republic; the chapters are titled by the name and date of the prime minister at the time. Sometimes, the pairings don't match up especially well as the historical chronicle seems unrelated to the pattern of the life of the protagonist, and this disjunction is incorporated into the narrative. In the chapter titled "Georges Pompidou (June 20, 1969–April 2, 1974)," the narrator asks: "In those

---

useless for certain extreme cases like the novels of Robbe-Grillet, where temporal reference is deliberately sabotaged" (*Narrative Discourse* 35).

2. Cohn limits this level to nonfictional narratives; we may observe the "distinction of fiction" she affirms, even as we extend her ideas and utilize the concept for fictional narratives that refer to historical events. As she herself notes, "When we speak of the nonreferentiality of fiction, we do not mean that it cannot refer to the real world outside of the text, only that it *must* not" (15). Observing these correspondences can be important—even essential. At the same time, the *ontological* status of each realm still remains distinct. On this subject, see Richardson, *Unnatural Narrative*, pp. 67–88, especially pp. 83–88.

years, what could possibly have connected the France of a Georges Pompidou [...] to the slapdash universe of [the character] Mathias, a champion of invective, the 'Little Red Book,' and kung fu? For that matter, what could connect most of us to that president straight out of the Rothschild Bank [...]? Absurdity, perhaps, and ridicule" (67–68).

Jesmyn Ward's *Salvage the Bones* (2011) is set in coastal Mississippi at the end of August, 2005. To fully comprehend the story and experience its intensity it is necessary to know that the historical Hurricane Katrina is about to strike the community there with a force that none of the characters can imagine. It is necessary to perceive the narrator's mistakes about historical events in order to appreciate, for example, the full effect of Anthony Burgess's *Earthly Powers* (1980). Salman Rushdie offers a considerably more radical confrontation with the historical record in *Midnight's Children*, where Shandean narrative arabesques are fused with the history of modern India and Pakistan. The narrator, Saleem Sinai, observes: "Rereading my work, I have discovered an error in chronology. The assassination of Mahatma Gandhi occurs, in these pages, on the wrong date. But I cannot say, now, what the actual sequence of events might have been; in my India, Gandhi will continue to die at the wrong time" (189–90). This work's fabula distorts the historical timetable that otherwise structures much of the novel and thus opposes verifiable history to the fictionalized history in the text. This strategy is a typically postmodern reconstitution of history; at the same time, it also underwrites a distinct postcolonial political allegory—Gandhi's death will always be untimely for those on the subcontinent, as recent events there continue to demonstrate.

Many nineteenth-century novels have a setting that is deliberately vague in key specifics so as not to contradict real-world events; thus Hardy begins *The Mayor of Casterbridge* (1886) with the words, "One evening of late summer, before the nineteenth century had reached one third of its span, a man and a woman, the latter carrying a child, were approaching the large village of Weydon-Priors." We also find counterfactual histories, which presuppose that known historical accounts are correct except for some crucial alteration; in Philip K. Dick's *The Man in the High Castle* (1962), the alternate history postulates that the Axis powers won World War II and the United States was occupied by the Imperial Japanese armed forces. Finally, we may point to Guy Davenport's story "The Haile Selassie Funeral Train" (1979). In this unnatural text, Apollinaire and James Joyce are described as being on the funeral train. This, of course, is historically impossible, since Apollinaire died in 1918 and Joyce died in 1941, which makes them unable to be on the train of the dead emperor, who was alive until 1975. Knowledge of the way it contravenes the historical record is essential to appreciating its temporal reconfigurations.

We may add to these an additional category that is optional for authors: **(1D) the time of writing** that the narrator indicates elapses during the course of the text. In most novels with heterodiegetic narrators, this temporality is unmarked; it is as if the narration is produced all at once or at an unknowable interval after the narrated events have transpired. This category, however, is very important for diary fiction or other works that feature the act of writing. It is particularly visible when it produces a humorous effect: Tristram Shandy famously laments that the more he writes, the more he falls behind; Rushdie's Saleem Sinai also shares this problem at the beginning of his story and is appropriately scolded by his narratee, Padma, who complains that at his current rate of narration, "you'll be two hundred years old before you manage to tell about your birth" (37).

Also essential is **(2A)**, Genette's concept of **duration**, or the time it takes to read (or otherwise experience) a text, itself a development of the idea of *Erzählzeit* as established in the German critical tradition by Günther Müller and others; I will discuss duration at greater length below.[3] To this, we will want to add **(2B)**, a necessarily fuzzy but significant concept: **time of reception.** Although unmarked in most narratives, it can produce conspicuous effects. Charles Dickens's "A Christmas Carol" was first published several days before Christmas (December 19) in 1843. Contemporary serials, such as soap operas, routinely set the month's story events within the time of their reception in North America: the Fourth of July, Thanksgiving, Christmas, and New Year are experienced by characters and audiences at the same time each year. And as Tom Keymer explains, many eighteenth- and nineteenth-century novelists often referred to the time that elapsed between the publication of different volumes of the work. In 1765, the seventh and eighth volumes of *Tristram Shandy* were published, four years after the preceding volume had appeared. In the first chapter, the narrator apologizes for this gap and blames it on his ill-health (and Laurence Sterne, the author, was himself unable to write while he was ill during this period). Periodical publication also allows the author, whether during the nineteenth century or online in serial web narratives, to adapt the narrative to address emerging audience desires and contemporary events. Such interaction affected Eugène Sue while creating the ninety installments of *Les Mystères de Paris* (1842–43). As Peter Brooks notes in his foreword to the Penguin translation, socialist reformers offered Sue ideas and tracts; he responded to them in his novel by introducing various reformist schemes. By the time the novel was reaching its end, he was ready to

---

3. For an account of the subtle differences between Günther Müller's and Genette's conceptions, see Ricoeur, *Time and Narrative*, Vol. 2, pp. 77–88 and 178–82.

proclaim himself a socialist. Later, he would be elected to the National Assembly as a socialist delegate.

We may complete our survey of the most widely used concepts of narrative temporality by adducing Genette's notion of **frequency, (3A),** which details how many times events in the fabula are narrated in the syuzhet. Thus, a single event may be narrated several times, while several events may be narrated once ("every Friday that summer they went to the beach"). To this, we will want to add the idea of **pseudofrequency, (3B),** or the near-repetition of events with only a slight variation, a favorite technique of authors like Gertrude Stein and the *nouveaux romanciers*. The different versions of the same events in *Rashomon* are not the same thing as the partial repetition of altered events in Coover and others. For this reason, Genette's example of recurring events in the work of Robbe-Grillet is not accurate, since many of those descriptions are not "stylistic variations" of the same events but are in fact recountings of similar but different ones (*Narrative Discourse* 115).

Antimimetic Forms of Time in the Fabula

Most general accounts of narrative temporality still share the same general mimetic assumptions. In many cases, this is all that is required. Genette's widely used account of order, duration, and frequency is generally adequate to describe three aspects of the temporality of most nonfictional narratives and of the great majority of works of mimetic fiction that models itself on nonfictional modes (though it does not attempt to engage with historical time). Genette's model is also adequate for much modernist fiction; in fact, it was quite possibly the strikingly antilinear yet naturalistically recoverable texts of the modernists that inspired these investigations in the first place. However, these categories do not work if applied to many late modernist and postmodern texts, since they are predicated on distinctions that writers who are more experimental are determined to preclude, deny, or confound—and this is also true of some postmodern forays into nonfictional genres.[4] As Diane Elam suggests, "Postmodernism is the recognition of the specifically *temporal* irony within narrative" (217). Surveying the considerable body of avant-garde and postmodern narratives, we can, following out the logic of the Loki Principle,

---

4. See, for example, Christian Moraru's insightful analysis of the temporal curiosities of Nabokov's autobiography, *Speak, Memory* (40–54).

identify several significant varieties of temporal construction that exceed the mimetic framework.[5]

Among the numerous violations of realistic temporality present in recent texts, there are six kinds of temporal reconstruction that stand out as sufficiently distinctive to warrant particular notice. Many of these strategies, as we will see, are present in earlier narratives as well; furthermore, insofar as they engage in logical contradictions, they are usually only possible in works of fiction.

1. Circular

In "The Garden of Forking Paths" (1941), one of Borges's characters speculates on how a book can be infinite. He muses, "The only way I could surmise was that it be a cyclical, or circular, volume, a volume whose last page would be identical to its first, so that one might go on indefinitely" (*Collected* 125). As Borges was imagining such seemingly impossible works, they had just begun to appear, as I have noted in chapter 2. The locus classicus of this type is *Finnegans Wake* (1939); other earlier examples include Queneau's *Le Chiendent* (1933) and the fourth chapter of Nabokov's *The Gift* (1937–38).[6] Nabokov describes his short story "The Circle" (1936) as "a small satellite that separated itself from the main body of the novel and started to revolve around it" (*Stories* 653), and which also has a serpent-biting-its-tail structure. The story begins with the phrase, "In the second place" (375), a sentence that logically follows the story's final sentence, which begins, "In the first place" (384). The end of Beckett's drama "Play" (1963) consists of the direction, "Repeat play" (*Collected* 157); the work is then enacted again. Even as the performance ceases, the audience has a clear sense that the fabula is repeated infinitely. Brian McHale further points out that "other variants on the ouroboros-structure include Julio Cortázar's *Hopscotch* (1963/7), Gabriel Josipovici's 'Mobius the Stripper' (1974), and John Barth's minimalist Mobius-strip narrative, 'Frame-Tale' (from *Lost in the Funhouse*)" (*Postmodernist* 111). Perhaps the best-known type of impossible temporality, this kind of fiction, instead of ending, returns to its own beginning, and thus continues infinitely. Its circular chronology partially

---

5. My objections apply equally to accounts of narrative temporality deriving from philosophical hermeneutics. Ricoeur, for example, postulates a reciprocal relationship between narrativity and the structure of existence ("Narrative" 165). The narrative patterns I am about to discuss have never existed except on a printed page.

6. Leona Toker prefers to designate Nabokov's temporal structure as an infinite spiral; see her discussion of this point (*Nabokov* 158–63).

mimes but ultimately transforms the linear chronology of everyday existence; it always returns to and departs from its point of origin—which is also its conclusion. Shorter, miniature narrative loops can also appear in fiction, as can be found in Rushdie's *Two Years, Eight Months, and Twenty-Eight Nights* (2015). They may be also perceived by some characters. In Phillip K. Dick's "A Little Something for Us Tempunauts" (1974), one of the tempunauts is conscious that he is re-experiencing the accident that kills them: "We're in a closed time loop, he thought, we keep going through this again and again, trying to solve the reentry problem, each time imagining it's the first time, the only time . . . and never succeeding. Which attempt is this? Maybe the millionth" (260). In Harold Ramis's film *Groundhog Day* (1993), the variations made by Bill Murray's character on his previous actions are different events, though many of those of the characters around him are not (see Hermann).

2. Antinomic

As we will discuss more fully in the following chapter, there are several narratives that move backward in time, such as Elizabeth Howard's *The Long View* (1956) and Harold Pinter's *Betrayal* (1978). Most narratives can be easily situated within the standard temporal concepts that inform almost all contemporary narrative theory—that is, each segment is ordered chronologically, but the sequences themselves are ordered antichronologically; at this level, the order of the syuzhet is simply the opposite of the order of the fabula.

Other, more complexly retroverted narratives, however, present conundrums that are more recalcitrant; these include texts like Alejo Carpentier's "Viaje a la semilla" ["Journey Back to the Source," 1944], Ilse Aichinger's "Spiegelgeschichte" ["Mirror Story," 1952], and the final section of Angela Carter's *The Passion of New Eve* (1977). In these works, the narrative moves forward into the characters' past.[7] These temporal inversions are not confined to the syuzhet, but form the fabric of the fabula.

Ilse Aichinger's protagonist in "Spiegelgeschichte" (1952) goes from her burial forward in time to her birth, looking ahead to that which has already occurred, as it were. Thus, we get statements like: "Drei Tage später wagt er nicht mehr, den Arm um deine Schultern zu legen. Wieder drei Tage später fragt er dich, wie du heisst, und du fragst ihn. Nun wisst ihr voneinander nicht

---

7. Brian McHale identifies other examples of "reversal of process" in Pynchon's *Gravity's Rainbow*, such as rocket production ("faired skin back to sheet steel back to pigs to white incandescence to ore, to Earth" (*Gravity's* 139), which, he adds, "seems to presuppose the extension to reality itself of film's capacity to be run backwards" (*Constructing* 110).

einmal mehr die Namen [. . . .] Ein Tag wird kommen, da siehst du ihn zum erstenmal. Und er sieht dich. Zum erstenmal, das heisst: Nie wieder" (71). [Three days later he no longer dares to put his arm round your shoulder. And three days after that he asks you what your name is, and you ask him his. And now neither of you knows the other's name [. . . .] A day will come when you will see him for the first time. And he you. For the first time means: never again (74–75)]. The first meeting, from a mimetic perspective, is also the last one from the characters' perspective.

In a mimetic text, the narrator tells the story retrospectively (i.e., in the past tense), as the audience's reception of the story is prospective; the interested reader wants to learn what has already happened and moves ever closer to the time of the narrating. In antinomic narration, the narrator moves ever further away from the time of the narrating, and the reader is still moving prospectively, though time's arrow is reversed. This also means that causality is inverted, as what we think of as effects are presented as having caused their causes, as when the abortionist is made quite sober by drinking gin (71). Discussing the way one processes such antinomic texts, Porter Abbott writes: "Notice how in reading, your mind automatically sorts out the forward motion of the story. In fact, much of the curious appeal of this writing depends on this automatic reconstruction. And this reconstruction is required, too, for the overall effect of this novel" (*Cambridge* 17). Aichinger's story also includes jocular, tongue-in-cheek comments about this unusual temporal situation that mirrors its opposed chronological trajectories: "Vom Hafen heulen die Schiffe. Zur Abfahrt oder zur Ankunft? Wer soll das wissen?" (66) [Over in the harbour the ships are hooting. Does it mean arrival or departure? Who can know that (68–69)]. This kind of joke works only with an antinomic temporal construction.

Martin Amis's novel, *Time's Arrow* (1991) intensifies this effect by reversing chronology at a more minute level. Genette has written that "one can run a film backwards, image by image, but one cannot read a text backward, letter by letter, or even word by word, or even sentence by sentence, without its ceasing to be a text" (*Narrative Discourse* 34). *Time's Arrow* almost seems to have been written to refute these statements, as "Good" and "How're you" are rendered "Dug" and "Ooh Yirrah" (7). As Seymour Chatman remarks, "This is the vocal counterpart of characters walking backwards or [decapitated] heads returning to their bodies" ("Backwards" 36). He points out that the verbal reversals in *Time's Arrow* go to the phonemic level only twice. More typical is the reversal of sequence and trajectory of daily events. Thus, eating a meal is described in the following terms:

You select a soiled dish, collect some scraps from the garbage, and settle down for a short while. Various items get gulped up into my mouth, and after skillful massage with my tongue and teeth I transfer them to the plate for additional sculpture with knife and fork and spoon.... Next you face the laborious business of cooling, of reassembly, of storage, before the return of these foodstuffs to the Superette, where, admittedly, I am promptly and generously reimbursed for my pains. Then you tool down the aisles, with trolley or basket, returning each can and packet to its rightful place. (11)

Additional examples of this practice continue to appear, as Chatman documents in his article on the subject, "Backwards." Tamar Yacobi has similarly analyzed the work of Israeli poet Dan Pagis, one of whose poems employs antinomic temporality to "undo" the Shoah:

The scream goes back into the throat.

The gold teeth to the jaw.

The fear.

The smoke to the tin chimneys and further inside

Back to the hollow of bones.

And already you will be covered with skin and sinews and you will live,

You will still be living,

Sitting in the living room, reading the evening paper.

Here you are! All in time. (Cited in Yacobi 112)

Jonathan Safran Foer's 2005 novel, *Extremely Loud and Incredibly Close*, is a narrative about a boy's search for his father, who is believed to have been killed in the attack on 9/11. The narrator states that he took photos of a man falling from the top of one of the Twin Towers to his death below. The sequence of the photos is inverted: "I reversed the order, so the last one was first, and the first was last. When I flipped through them, it looked like the man was floating up through the sky" (325). The narrator goes on to speculate that had time been reversed; the figure in the picture, who might have been his father, "would have left his messages backward, and the plane would have flown backward away from him, all the way to Boston" (325). Then, "Dad would have gone backward through the turnstile, then swiped his Metrocard backward, then walked home backward as he read the *New York Times* from right to left" (326). The book ends with the photos in antichronological order, which the reader can physically flip to make the falling man seem to return to the top of the building, as the effects of time and death are movingly, if momentarily, vanquished. It is revealing to observe that this antimimetic form is often used to depict extreme, traumatic events: death from an illegal abortion, a postapocalyptic flight, the 9/11 attack, the Holocaust. Jim Crace offers a possible explanation for this preference following his own use of antichronological narration in his novel *Being Dead*, a temporally innovative work about a husband and wife who are brutally murdered: "To start their journey as they disembark, but then to take them back where they have travelled from, is to produce a version of eternity," Crace writes. "First light, at last, for Joseph and Celice. A dawning death. And all their lives ahead of them" (7). Fiction is able to briefly reverse the ravages of time and death, if only in a novel.

3. Hypothetical

This form originates with a new kind of narration, the hypothetical mode of second narrative composed in a recipe-like form. There is no fixed temporality, but a typical progression is indicated, as the following example from Lorrie Moore's "How" indicates: "Begin by meeting him in a class, a bar, at a rummage sale. Maybe he teaches sixth grade. Manages a hardware store. Foreman at a carton factory. He will be a good dancer . . . A week, a month, a year. Feel discovered, comforted, needed, loved, and start sometimes, somehow, to feel bored" (55). Matt DelConte has suggested that texts like this "do not have a story in the traditional sense: the entire action consists of discourse because the prescribed events are hypothetical/conditional; nothing has actually happened" (214). He concludes that "we experience time differently in these types of narrative, for without an actual story there exists no real storytime" (214). Nevertheless, there are variable indications of how much time elapses: "a week, a month, a year," not "after ten seconds" or "after twenty years." Radically different temporal parameters would produce a very different narrative. It is also the case that the story proceeds as if the originally hypothetical events had in fact taken place, in a form that had earlier been articulated as a possible one, as hypothetical future events become transformed into an incontrovertible past.

4. Contradictory

As we have noted, a prominent type of many of the more extreme postmodern narratives is the self-contradictory story, in which incompatible and irreconcilable versions of the events are set forth. In real life, such contradictions are not possible: a man may have died in 1956 or he may have died in 1967, but he cannot have died in 1956 *and* in 1967. But this law of noncontradiction does not have to be followed in antimimetic works of fiction. In Angela Carter's *Nights at the Circus* (1984), story time follows regressive paths, as when Big Ben strikes midnight three times in fairly rapid succession—there is no malfunction of the bells' mechanism; midnight arrives three different times that night. As we have noted earlier, there are many other works with contradictory story time, including J. B. Priestley's *Dangerous Corner* (1932), Coover's "The Babysitter" (1969), the mutually incompatible endings of John Fowles's *The French Lieutenant's Woman* (1969), and most famously (and egregiously) in Robbe-Grillet's later fiction.[8] Discussing *La Maison de rendez-vous* (1965), Ruth Ronen has observed that "fictional worlds can contain time paradoxes where time is presented as reversible or bilateral" (*Possible* 202).[9] In these texts, there is no single, unambiguous story to be extrapolated from the discourse; rather, there are two or more contradictory versions that seriously vitiate the very notion of fabula (*histoire*) insofar as it is conceived as a single, self-consistent series of events that can be inferred from the discourse. Genette's notion of frequency as well as his concept of story presupposes the existence of a fixed, retrievable, noncontradictory sequence of events, a sequence many postmodern writers refuse to provide. Ursula Heise, who deftly analyzes such contradictory temporalities in Pynchon and Robbe-Grillet (113–46, 179–219), explains this practice in these terms: "Postmodernist novels thereby project into the narrative present and past an experience of time which normally is only available for the future: time dividing and subdividing, bifurcating and branching off continuously into multiple possibilities and alternatives" (55).

Another version of this contradictory construction occurs when apparently different temporal zones fail to remain distinct, and slide or spill into one another. As the story segments merge, so do their respective temporalities. We find this in Pinget's *Passacaille* (1969) and in some of the later novels

---

8. Concerning the temporality of novels like *La Jalousie* or *La Maison de rendez-vous*, I must disagree with Ruth Ronen's claim that "chronology does not seem to condition narrative organization or to be relevant at all to the organization of the narrative world" (*Possible* 216). I suggest that it is more useful to affirm instead that the narrative world is ordered by (and indeed may be defined by) several independent, contradictory chronologies. Furthermore, its transgressive effects are dependent on the reader's perceiving and reflecting on the implications this chronology has on the fictional world.

9. See also Ursula Heise's theoretical analysis (113–46) of the contradictory temporality of Robbe-Grillet's *Topologie d'une cité fantôme* (*Topology of a Phantom City*, 1976),whose narrator "wanders down hallways and streets that always seem to give access to too many temporal dimensions, too many historical moments at the same time" (147).

of Claude Simon. Accounts of one set of events fold into a different set of events, presumably occurring at another time, without any framing device to clarify the relations between the disparate groups of events. In Simon's *Les Corps conducteurs* (1971), we find a retarded, minimal, and resolutely antiteleological temporality; the narrative moves from setting to setting, and invariably the "separate" times and spaces begin to bleed into each other, as the distinctions between each cluster of events collapse, and "now" and "then" no longer signify clearly disparate times.

There are also interesting variants of this practice, some of which rely on different historical times that are later merged together. We see this in the contamination of the basic eighteenth-century setting of Carpentier's *Concierto Barroco* (1974) by a brief and unexplained interlude in the twentieth century; in Ishmael Reed's superimposition of modern technology and consciousness onto a narrative otherwise set in the 1860s in *Flight to Canada* (1976); and in Milan Kundera's *Slowness* (1995), as the protagonist of the main, contemporary narrative is brought face-to-face with the hero of the eighteenth-century novel that has partially inspired the later fiction—and both characters are then encountered by the narrator/fabricator himself. An interesting recent example of this practice covering a briefer period of time appears in Peter LaSalle's story "Where We Last Saw Time" (2007), in which the character-narrator exists simultaneously in two time periods, two decades apart. He meets his girlfriend to try to dissuade her from a visit to Africa which his later self knows will prove fatal. This situation leads to a number of intriguing complications; as the narrator avers, "That made it trickier for me having to see her later, with my knowing what I did concerning what would happen to her there, and how poor Emily would, in fact, die in Cameroon a few years later. Maybe I could talk her out of going when we met at Hayes-Bickford later" (5). The play with verb tense here is illustrative of the text's paradoxical temporality.

5. Multiple

A curious temporality can be found in Woolf's *Orlando* (1928), in which the eponymous character ages at a different rate than the people who surround him (her), as one chronology is superimposed on another, larger one. Thus, twenty years pass for Orlando at the same time that three and a half centuries pass for those around her (him). This situation drives the narrator to some playful descriptions in which metaphorical statements about time take on a literal meaning when applied to *Orlando*, as the dual chronologies shrink and expand: "It would be no exaggeration to say that he would go out after breakfast a man of thirty and come home to dinner a man of fifty-five at least. Some weeks added a century to his age, others no more than three seconds at most" (99). This strategy is repeated (perhaps in homage to Woolf) by Caryl Churchill in her play *Cloud Nine*, which has the characters age twenty-five years as the society they inhabit gains a century. Borges' "The Secret Miracle" (1943) also employs a similar construction, as time slows down for a man awaiting execution so that he is able to finish composing a play even as the bullets from the firing squad move imperceptibly toward him; he experiences a year while his killers perceive an instant. An even more elaborate deployment of such disparate yet synchronized embedded chronologies can be found in Calderón's classic, *El gran teatro del mundo* [*The Great Theater of the World*, 1630], where both the history of creation and the time span of a human life are collapsed into the actual duration of the play's performance. It should be noted that Bakhtin's account of the chronotope of the medieval dream vision, which "synchronize[s] diachrony" to produce a time in which all events coalesce into "pure simultaneous existence" (157), is entirely consonant with the differential temporalities of Calderón and intriguingly anticipates some recent postmodern practices.[10]

In the works just discussed, different individuals in the same place experience time at different speeds; other narratives indicate that time elapses differently in separate locations. We may now move on to address a long-standing conundrum of Shakespearean criticism: the notorious "double time" of many of his mature plays, in which different plotlines, though beginning and ending at the same moment, nevertheless take different amounts of time to unfold. In *A Midsummer Night's Dream* (1595), a play replete with sly allusions to skewed chronology, four days and three nights pass for the duke and his entourage in the city while—at the same time—only two days and a single night pass for the lovers in the enchanted forest.[11] Spenser's *The Faerie Queen* (1590–96), as Rawdon Wilson has shown and J. K. Barret has more thoroughly discussed, also embodies similar temporal contradictions, as characters like Redcrosse both languish for a long time in captivity and are rescued swiftly from that brief captivity.

---

10. Another unexpected instance of this strategy can be found in Ben Jonson's masque, "A Vision of Delight," in which seasonal and diurnal temporalities are collapsed into the time of their enactment onstage. Though a notorious stickler for observing neoclassical temporal strictures in drama proper, Jonson utilized a very different poetics when constructing his masques.

11. For a discussion of the play's temporality from the perspective of narrative theory, see Richardson, "Time Is Out of Joint," pp. 302–4. This essay also analyzes the unusual temporalities of a number of other dramas, many of them mentioned in this essay, and discusses contradictions between the actual time of performance and the time said to elapse during that period.

Such a situation is present as well (and explicitly remarked on) in Byron's *Cain* (1821): after Lucifer returns Cain to Eden, Adah expresses her thanks that he has come back so soon, after only "two *long* hours" (III.i.54) according to the movement of the sun. Cain, understandably confused, responds:

And yet I have approached that sun, and seen
Worlds which he once shone on, and never more
Shall light; and worlds he never lit: methought years had
rolled o'er my absence. (*Poetical* III.i.56–59)

The temporally enchanted forests of Shakespeare and Spenser may have inspired "the time-shifting sorcery" of the jungle in the Sundarbans chapter of Rushdie's *Midnight's Children*. A creative variant of this strategy may be found in Ian McEwan's novel *The Child in Time* (1987), in which the protagonist observes as in a film his youthful parents discussing himself before he was born in two separate scenes that are repeated.

Interestingly, modern physics shows how, at least theoretically, two groups may realistically experience different chronologies—but only if one group is traveling at or near the speed of light. Peter Rabinowitz has also discussed some of the curious narrative aspects of time travel in which different "people experience events in different orders" ("'They'" 183); we see this when H. G. Wells's Time Traveler returns to his auditors' present and recounts what happened to him earlier in what for them is the distant future. Rabinowitz goes on to argue for the concept of "path" to identify this kind of chronological arrangement.[12]

6. Denarrated Temporality

Finally, there are also works like Beckett's *Molloy* (1951), which repeatedly negates the story it attempts to tell. Near the end of his narrative, Molloy wonders about an event he has just recounted: "Yes, it seems to me some such incident occurred about this time. . . . But perhaps I am merging two times in one, and two women" (75). Without a recoverable story, there can be no underlying chronological grid that is rearranged in the narrative discourse.

---

12. For additional accounts of skewed temporalities found in science fiction (especially works involving time travel), see Heinze; Ryan ("Temporal"); and Gallagher ("Undoing").

Duration

Genette's notion of duration—that is, the relation between the amount of time it takes for an event to occur and the time it takes for that event to be recounted—has not been developed as fully as it might be. Genette himself is a little apologetic about the necessary imprecision of its measurement (since reading speed varies greatly between individuals), and he resorts instead to the expedient of the number of pages devoted to an incident, although, of course, different editions vary considerably in the number of pages they allot the same text. Greater precision, however, may easily be obtained: a word count will be much more accurate for fiction, while the duration of the production of a play can be determined reasonably precisely, and the time of a film or video can be measured to the second. In the Fox television series *24*, the events of the story are for the most part sequenced to match as perfectly as possible the time of the show's reception, as the markers on the screen that indicate the time in the storyworld correspond exactly to the minutes of the actual time that is indicated on the cable box. There are also brief narrative gaps that match the interruptions of the show for commercial breaks, as economic concerns in the real world partially structure the presentation of the fictional story.

Genette outlined four different relations that can exist between the time of the story and the time of its presentation: (1) **pause,** where story time stops as discourse time continues; (2) **scene,** where there is a rough equivalence between the two, as in the narration of a dialogue; (3) **summary,** where the discourse time is much shorter than the story time; and (4) **ellipsis,** where discourse time skips to a later part of story time (*Narrative Discourse* 94–95). To this slightly asymmetrical group, Seymour Chatman has added the concept of **stretch** to designate events whose narration takes longer than the events themselves, as in a slow-motion movie sequence (*Story* 72–73). To these categories, we will add **contradictory** to designate cases where the story time and the discourse time cannot be made to agree.

The concept of duration is quite useful in describing certain postmodern practices, such as the equivalence Rushdie sets up between of an hour of the time represented and a second for its presentation, as he recreates the hours leading up to India's independence (and the birth of Saleem Sinai) in a manner generally associated with the launching of a rocket or the onset of New Year's Day: "But now the countdown will not be denied . . . eighteen hours; seventeen; sixteen . . . and already, at Dr. Narlikar's Nursing Home, it is possible to hear the shrieks of a woman in labour" (Rushdie's ellipses). After a vertiginous pause lasting a full paragraph, the countdown resumes ("fourteen hours to go, thirteen, twelve") before it's paused once more (124). Foregrounding duration in this manner points to the artificiality of the book's temporal construction even as it paradoxically enhances its dramatic effect.

Such extreme play with duration has some antecedents, including Heinrich Mann's "Drei-Minuten-Roman" ["Three Minute Novel," 1905] in which an entire life is recounted in some five hundred words, as well as in passages such as the following from Raymond Queneau's *Le Chiendent* [*The Bark Tree*, 1933], which shows the arbitrary nature of conventional novelistic observations once the time frame is expanded beyond its ordinary parameters: "At about 3 o'clock, the [figure in] silhouette blew its nose; at about 4, it spat; at about 5, it bowed; at about 5:50 it was already hearing the squeak of the little gate of its headless house. At 6, the other man was there, on the dot, at his cafe table" (10). Another playful example may be found in Virginia Woolf's *Orlando*: "It was now November. After November, comes December. Then January, February, March, and April. After April comes May. June, July, August follow. Next is September. Then October, and so, behold, we are back at November again, with a whole year accomplished" (266). The examples noted so far compress large swaths of time into brief periods of recounting; the opposite extreme also produces compelling effects. One of the most dramatic such instances appears in Ambrose Bierce's "An Occurrence at Owl Creek Bridge" (1894). A multipage depiction of a man's escape from hanging followed by his return to his home appears to take up almost a day of story time, but it is revealed in the end to be merely the few seconds between the beginning of the man's hanging and the moment he loses consciousness. Just as dying people are said to see their entire lives flash before their eyes, Bierce projects an imagined multihour future for the final moments of his protagonist. Tobias Wolff radically slows down the pace of narration as he elaborately depicts the movement of a bullet through the head of his protagonist in the last half of "Bullet in the Brain" (1995): as the narrator explains, once in the brain, "the bullet came under the mediation of brain time" (266; also see Phelan, "Privileged"). And some authors, as we will see, create works in which no story time elapses.

In drama, one may find many works in which the represented time of the story is contradicted by the time indicated in its presentation onstage. To take one of the best-known instances, Marlowe presents the final hour of Faustus's life onstage in a continuous soliloquy of fifty-eight lines, unpunctuated by any indication of temporal ellipsis, as the time of the story is radically shrunk. Shakespeare plays with this kind of construction as well, collapsing three hours of story time into a continuous twenty minutes of performance in the last scene of *A Midsummer Night's Dream* and compressing the unnatural night during which Duncan is slain in *Macbeth*.[13] Similarly, in *Hamlet*, the appearance of the ghost "that usurp'st this time of night" (1.1.46) twice impels the clock to hurtle from midnight to dawn in temporally uninterrupted periods lasting only a few minutes each (I.1; I.4–5). Hamlet is more prescient than he imagines when he complains: "The time is out of joint" (1.5.188).

Interestingly, Pierre Corneille reflected on this kind of temporal contraction. Breaking from appeals to verisimilitude that informed his positions in his essay on the unities, he states: "The fifth act, by special privilege, has the right to accelerate time so that the part of the action which it presents may use up more time than is necessary for performance" (296). The reason given for this rupture is the convenience of the audience, impatient to see the end of the play. Corneille explains he deliberately made use of this "privilege" at the admittedly overly compressed ending of *Le Cid* (1637); he also pointed to a classical precedent for this temporal telescoping in the final act of Terence's *Andria*.[14]

Comparable instances in fiction can also be found, such as the preternaturally fast death of Lolita's mother, who is killed by a car in the street while Humbert was talking to her in the next room of their house as he was mixing her a drink (98–99). As we have just seen in the previous chapter, the "Circe" episode of *Ulysses* abruptly collapses, expands, and distorts temporal duration, as eighteen pages of fantastic events occur in the pause between two sentences (390–407). An avowedly contradictory duration quite similar to that in *Doctor Faustus* appears in Paul Auster's *City of Glass* (1985), in which the delivery of an eight-page speech takes up an entire day—much to the surprise of the confused auditor of the monologue (*New York* 18–27). Still more radical violations can be found in stories by Calvino ("t zero," 1967) and David Foster Wallace ("Wiggle Room," 2009). Although Mieke Bal avers that "an event, no matter how insignificant, always takes up time" (7), in these works no time passes in the storyworld; there is only the duration of reading time, and the sustained temporal limbo in which the protagonists are playfully or painfully embedded. Together,

---

13. *Macbeth* is, in fact, still more temporally innovative. In the fabula, night stretches much longer than it should: "By th' clock 'tis day, / And yet dark night strangles the travelling lamp" (II.4.6–7). In the presentation of this scene, an equal and opposite chronological violation has transpired, as the duration of the entire night is radically compressed. For a full discussion of this play's temporality, see Richardson, *Unnatural Narrative*, pp. 104–10.

14. Through the device of the magic mirror in his *L'Illusion comique* (1636), he also devised an ingenious way to dramatize many years and still preserve the neoclassical "unity" of time.

these examples should demonstrate the usefulness of the concept of duration, as well as suggest that it can be measured more accurately, manipulated more playfully, and controverted more boldly than is generally recognized.

Length

The question of scale should also be broached. Aristotle warned against works that are either too enormous or too tiny to be properly perceived. Recently, this topic has provoked interest in narrative circles. Catherine Gallagher argues for an account of length that will include the reader's experience of narrative temporality. Lynette Felber has explored the *roman fleuve*, or, in her term, "novels without end"; Laurie Langbauer, Robyn Warhol (*Having* 71–119), and others have written compellingly of the narrative possibilities of extended serial fiction; many of these works were not intended to conclude. Since those studies were completed, much vaster works have started to appear, meganovels that dwarf *War and Peace*, *À la recherché du temps perdu*, and *Artamène ou le Grand Cyrus* (1649–54) by Madeleine de Scudéry. It has been announced that the world's longest work, Richard Grossman's *Breeze Avenue*, a five-thousand-volume, three-million-page "novel," is about to be installed as a reading room in Los Angeles; its precise contents, like Borges's "Book of Sand," will change regularly over time. Other meganovels include Mark Z. Danielewski's twenty-seven-volume novel-in-progress, *The Familiar*, and Mark Leach's open-sourced, seventeen-volume, ten-thousand-page work, *Marienbad My Love* (2008).

At the other end of the spectrum we find questions of shortness, some of which have accompanied the genre of the short story at least since Edgar Allen Poe argued that the optimal length was the amount that could be read at a single sitting. Recently, we have seen an increasing interest in short fiction, short-short fiction, and microfiction. The fountainhead of this movement is a six-word short story that is widely attributed to Hemingway: "For sale: Baby shoes. Never worn." It is pretty certain that Hemingway never wrote the text, but the genre proliferates through frequent contests in literary magazines. The length of a narrative certainly does affect its reception, though in highly variable ways that are difficult to accurately formulate. Clearly, economy and intensity are at a premium in a microstory—every word literally counts. A similar dynamic infuses very long works: the reader's attention must be maintained over very extensive stretches. David Letzler has recently pointed to the problems of attention, overload, and boredom in the meganovel, problems that seem to be inherent in the form (1–29). In general, it seems pointless to insist on a priori proscriptions; it is far superior to see whether the authors can achieve their goals. This happens in Proust and in the pseudo-Hemingway story; if Danielewski fails to create a successful meganovel, others may be able to produce one.

Tense

The vast majority of narratives are written in the past tense. Other possibilities also exist, as Genette has usefully noted. He identifies four types of time of narration: subsequent (the most common), simultaneous, prior, and interpolated (that is, discourse between the moments of narrated events, 217). Dorrit Cohn has more thoroughly analyzed first-person "simultaneous" or present-tense narration, in which events are narrated by the protagonist at the time they are occurring, thus producing impossible sentences such as "Face down. . . . I try to compose myself for a day of hiding. I doze and I wake, drifting from one formless dream to another," from J. M. Coetzee's *Waiting for the Barbarians* (1980, quoted in Cohn, *Distinction* 101). The events themselves may be reported in a simple chronological order, but they are completely "denaturalized," or removed from possible real-world, natural discourse, by being narrated in what Cohn has felicitously termed "the fictional present" (106); specifically, the narrator cannot be dozing when he writes the sentence stating that he is. As Cohn points out, this "form remains narratologically in limbo: neglected (if not denied) in theory, mis- or un- identified in practice, its anomaly falls between the cracks of established discursive norms" (101; see also Phelan, "Present"). Though Cohn's statement is largely true, we can still find some cases in which (roughly) simultaneous narration is not only possible but quite dramatic, as when Lord Byron is interrupted while writing a letter to a confidant about his latest attempted seduction ("billet") by the untimely entry of the husband of the woman in question: "My billet prospered, it did more, it even (I am at this moment interrupted by the *Marito*, and write this before him, he has brought me a political pamphlet in MS. to decypher [sic] and applaud, I shall content myself with the last; oh, he is gone again), my billet produced an *answer*, a very unequivocal one too" (*Selected* 143).

Future events can be presented in a few ways, most commonly through a prolepsis or "flash-forward" where an omniscient narrator indicates what will happen later on or a character narrator shifts from the narrative present to a future time. On rare occasions, narratives are written in the future tense, as happens in Christine Brooke-Rose's *Amalgamemnon* (1994): "He'll come back quick as a flash, would you separate fun from communication?

Well, because, well, no I wouldn't, and she'll laugh with him and cuddle up to him then add because there might be no ground to stand on if you didn't at all. And glancing up at his quizzical downward gaze she'll murmur, perhaps according to you there won't be? Because, he will announce slowly and softly, you will believe the absolute truth of your words and I shall forever be lost in the absolute relativity of mine" (33–34). In other situations, a character can see into the future, as happens in the case of prophecy, or when a character knows what will happen later in the narrative, as we have just seen in *Amalgamemnon*. In in D. M. Thomas's *The White Hotel* (1981), Lisa Erdman suffers from pains that will be inflicted in the future. As David Herman explains, this produces an inversion of cause and effect: the "pain is an effect of events that have not yet happened in the storyworld, a symptom that predates the condition it indexes"; her murder in 1941 "is, in fact, the cause of physical and mental problems that she began experiencing a quarter of a century earlier" (*Story* 252, 257; see also 251–61).

Recently, more authors have begun experimenting with the narration of future events. Don DeLillo's *Cosmopolis* (2003) contains three brief episodes in which the protagonist is able to perceive a few seconds into the narrative future: in his car, "Eric watched himself on the oval screen below the spycam, running his thumb along his chinline. The car stopped and moved and he realized queerly that he'd just placed his thumb on his chinline, a second or two after he'd seen it on-screen" (22). He later recoils after seeing a bomb blast outside, seconds before the bomb goes off (93–95) and finally previsions the image of his impending death (205–9), all without any supernatural intervention or science-fiction type of device. Eric can only speculate vainly, "Have all the worlds conflated, all possible states become present at once?" (205).[15]

Future-tense narration appears in every third section of Carlos Fuentes's *La Muerta de Artemio Cruz* (1962) and may also be present in Rick Moody's "The Grid" (*Ring* 29–38), which "begins in the present tense at a certain point in time, from which the narrative develops along a temporal line in the future tense" (Heinze 41); this situation produces sentences such as, "In the bar, in fact, she will be having her first kiss" (31).[16] In Ted Chiang's work of science fiction, "Story of Your Life" (*Stories*), one figure acquires a knowledge of future events that is comparable to her knowledge of her past; she is able to "remem-

---

15. Raphael Baroni likewise shows how, on a page of the graphic novel, *Watchmen*, Alan Moore and Dave Gibbons were able to illustrate the temporal experience of Dr. Manhattan, who gained, after an accident, the fabulous power of embracing the flow of time, past and future, all grasped in a single glance ("(Un)natural").

16. Second-person narratives of the hypothetical type generally use an imperative verb form that projects a set of events in the future: "Begin by meeting him in a class, in a bar, at a rummage sale" (Moore 55).

ber" events that have not yet occurred. Thus, it takes the reader some time to learn that a sentence that refers to the narrative present actually does so, and is not a flashback: "Right now your dad and I have been married for about two years, living on Ellis Avenue; when we move out you'll be too young to remember the house, but we'll show you pictures of it, tell you stories about it. I'd love to tell you the story of this evening, the night you're conceived, but the right time to do that would be when you're ready to have children of your own, and we'll never get that chance" (91). The narrator is speaking just before the time of her child's conception, even as she knows all the events in both their lives that will follow.[17] Future tense narration can take one of three forms, each grounded in a different ontological framework: the mimetic, which follows the probabilistic constraints of realism; the nonmimetic, in which a supernatural entity reveals future events; and the antimimetic or unnatural, which can only occur in fiction.

Other useful concepts for comprehending narrative temporality include what Genette calls "achronic" narratives, which designate works that contain numerous events that "we must ultimately take to be dateless and ageless" (*Narrative Discourse* 84); I will add, however, that this category should be greatly expanded and further delineated to include the various unknowable, self-negating, or inherently indeterminate story times present in numerous texts, such as Beckett's.[18] I also want to note David Herman's concept of polychrony, "a kind of narration that exploits indefiniteness to pluralize and delinearize itself" ("Limits" 75).[19]

---

17. In *Future Narratives*, Christoph Bode discusses a number of contradictory works like *La Jalousie* as future narratives. I feel this is mistaken, since such narratives, in the words of Ursula Heise, "project into the narrative present and past an experience of time which is normally only available for the future" (49).

18. As David Herman points out, "Temporal indefiniteness should not be conflated with timelessness or achrony: not knowing the exact temporal positions of several events occurring within a larger narrative sequence does not make those events achronic. Further, both the achronic and the temporally indefinite should be distinguished from the temporally multiple" ("Limits" 75). These are precisely the kinds of distinctions narrative theory now needs to be making.

19. Also worthy of note is Jesse Matz's concept of narrative "tenselessness" in Forster's *Maurice*, a novel that waited for the future for its completion, publication, and audience, but that also looks nostalgically to the past and employs various tactics of "detensing" (including iterative seriality) to achieve this effect.

Reading in Time

Reading is a temporal experience; we feel the effects of a narrative unfold over time. It is at least doubly temporal: Meir Sternberg points out that "narrative is composed of two sequences. There is the sequence of events in the world (the order of happening) and there is the sequence of events in the discourse about the world (the order of reading, or telling)" ("Reconceptualizing" 46). We may add that if the represented events are set in a historical period, there is also the relation (or nonrelation) between the time represented in the fiction and that of the actual historical events it invokes.

Several authors have foregrounded the incongruities between a symmetrical and a dynamic representation of events. Thus, Henry Fielding affirms, "When any extraordinary Scene presents itself (as we trust will often be the Case) we shall spare no Pains nor Paper to open it at large to our Reader; but if whole Years should pass without producing any thing worthy his Notice, we shall not be afraid of a Chasm in our History; but shall hasten on to Matters of Consequence, and leave such Periods of Time totally unobserved," since he does not feel that his narrative is "obliged to keep even pace with time, whose amanuensis he is, and, like his master, travels as slowly through centuries of monkish dulness, when the world seems to have been asleep, as through [a] bright and busy age" (*Tom Jones*, book 2, chapter 1, 52–53). Jane Austen refers to the projected time of future reading near the end of *Northanger Abbey* when she notes that her readers "will see in the tell-tale compression of the pages before them, that we are all hastening together to perfect felicity" (chapter 31, 540). It is precisely the flow of our processing of the narrative that Sterne (and others after him) so conspicuously interrupts.

Different works read much more quickly than others; an exciting thriller is rightly called a page-turner, while the pace of a novel by the later Henry James, who was accused of chewing more than he bit off, proceeds at a much slower rate. Modernists, eschewing Victorian notions of appropriate narrative pace, slowed down their narratives with poetic prose and philosophical speculations. At times, they paradoxically depicted the great velocities of modernity in prose that moves rather slowly, as Sam See discusses in "Fast Books Read Slow," an essay on depictions of speed in the contemporary world in works by Dos Passos and Hemingway. It is not clear how slowly a narrative can move and still remain readable; Dan Irving explores this limit in his essay "Eighteen Hours of Salmon: On the Narrativity of Slow TV," in which he analyzes the intense popularity of certain shows in which almost nothing happens for a very long time. Recently, Daniel Punday has brought a new relevance to the study of pace by looking at digital works and focusing on a user's interaction time. This temporality depends on, among other things, "an idleness that is quite different from our common ways of thinking about the temporality of reading" (202).

Sternberg's conceptual triad of suspense, curiosity, and surprise are also very helpful in analyzing the effects of key aspects of the reading process as they unfold over time. Marie-Laure Ryan further notes that "while spatial and spatio-temporal immersion invite us to slow down the pace of reading, and occasionally to reread a passage so we may linger on a particularly pleasurable scene, pure temporal immersion incites us to rush through the text toward the blissful state of retrospective omniscience" (*Narrative as Virtual Reality* 140). Immersion certainly enhances some aspects of the experience of the temporality of reading. It is also the case that, because these concepts are modeled for essentially mimetic narratives, they are imperfect guides for many antimimetic ones. Fortunately, Ryan has proposed the concept of "metasuspense" (145–48) that is more focused on the discourse because, in the words of Dannenberg, "it arouses the reader's curiosity about how the author will resolve the literary work's artistic design" (37). This experience is also at work when we encounter the kinds of unexpected types of duration I have noted above. In such cases, we have a critical, rather than immersive, experience of the multiple temporal flows as typical progressions and tempos are replaced by unusual or impossible ones.

The Temporality of *To the Lighthouse*

To help establish the utility of the theoretical model I have set forth, I will analyze the narrative temporality of a well-known work, Woolf's *To the Lighthouse*, to reveal just what this conception can produce in the way of critical analysis. The novel unfolds in three parts. The first depicts the Ramsay family's late afternoon and evening with friends at a summerhouse in the Hebrides; there, Lily Briscoe works on a painting, a couple gets engaged, a special dinner is served, and a trip to the lighthouse is planned. The second part briefly and highly selectively narrates the events of the ensuing ten years, including the deaths of Mrs. Ramsay and two of her children. The last section depicts the events of a morning and afternoon back on the island among the remaining members of the family and two returning guests; at the end, Mr. Ramsay and two of his children reach the lighthouse, and Lily finishes her painting.

Historical Time: In the first half of the novel, there are no specific historical markers. The work is set in a summer home on the Isle of Skye, and it could be taking place most any year from 1885 to 1913. Suddenly, in the second section of the work, we learn that the most brilliant of the Ramsays' children, Andrew, has died fighting in World War I: at once we are given a more precise time frame, 1915–17, for this event as history thrusts itself into the world of the novel. The relatively nebulous temporal setting has at once become more fixed; soon, the additional information that the family is returning to Skye after a ten-year absence shortly after the end of the war allows us to establish the historical period of the entire narrative with reasonable precision.

Order: For the most part, the narrative is largely linear.[20] This linearity, however, is an unusual kind insofar as it shifts rapidly from the thoughts of one consciousness to another, often with an overlapping set of perceptions from different vantage points, thus producing a powerful re-creation of simultaneity.

Frequency: The same event is occasionally narrated more than once, usually from the perspective of a different character; this happens most frequently in the first part of the novel. There is also an intriguing presentation of pseudofrequency, which I will discuss shortly.

Duration: One of the most powerful effects experienced by a first-time reader is the work's play with duration, that is, how many hours—or years—of story time are being represented per page of the text. In Part One, several hours of story time elapse over the course of 124 pages; in Part Two, this relation is reversed, as ten years are depicted in a mere nineteen pages. The original proportions are restored in the final section, as eighty-five pages are used to recount the events of several hours. The slow presentation of a few hours in over one hundred pages was extremely rare for its time (*Ulysses* had been published only five years before); the juxtaposition of exactly the opposite relation followed by a return to the original pace is unprecedented in the history of narrative. Almost equally striking are the brief summary statements of the deaths of Mrs. Ramsay and her two children, situated in between more leisurely depictions of the movement of breezes and the growth of plants in and around the house.

Unnatural Narration: Woolf's most radical play with temporality, however, has so far gone unnoticed; the perspective offered by unnatural narrative theory and analysis can allow us to retrieve it. The opening chapters of "The Window" section produce a very unusual sequence of events. In the third chapter, we learn that Mrs. Ramsay perceives "a loud cry, as of a sleep walker, half roused," declaiming lines from Tennyson's "The Charge of the Light Brigade": "*Stormed at with shot and shell*" (17, Woolf's italics). She turns

---

20. The main exceptions to linearity are the unmarked interpolation that depicts Mrs. Ramsay's visit to town with Charles Tansley some time earlier and the account of William Bankes's decision to join the family on the island.

apprehensively to see if anyone else had heard this embarrassing declamation and is relieved to observe that Lily Briscoe is the only one within earshot. The description of this scene continues seamlessly into the next chapter: "Indeed, he almost knocked her easel over, coming down upon her with his hands waving, shouting out, 'Boldly we rode and well,' but, mercifully, he turned sharp, and rode off, to die gloriously she supposed upon the heights of Balaclava" (17).

On the next page, William Bankes strolls over to Lily, and, after a pause, they begin a conversation. At this point we hear the lines declaimed, "*Someone had blundered*"; now "Mr. Ramsay glared at them [. . . .] Together they had seen a thing they had not been meant to see. They had encroached upon a privacy" (18). From the perspective of realism, one would conclude that Woolf has made a terrible error. The embarrassed Ramsay has again blundered into Lily; now she is with Bankes; some minutes have passed, but he is more shocked than the first time he did it. If this is a realistic representation of events, it seems that basic features of human psychology are being violated by an author routinely praised for her psychological insight. An approach alert to antimimetic techniques, however, suggests that Woolf is doing something much more daring: she is creating original representations that cannot be contained by the strictures of realism. Furthermore, Ramsay, who had earlier declaimed first the twenty-second and then the twenty-third line of the poem, is now shouting out the twelfth line. It thus appears that the same scene is not being repeatedly depicted, but rather it is being re-created.

In the next section, an even more egregious contradiction is depicted. Lily and Bankes walk off together; they have an extensive conversation (19). Jasper, the Ramsays' boy, walks past them carrying a gun. Lily and Bankes continue conversing. A shot is fired, a flock of starlings take flight, and the two of them "stepped through the gap in the high hedge straight into Mr. Ramsay, who boomed tragically at them, 'Some one had blundered!'" (25). This time, they are walking into Ramsay, not the other way around; for the third time, he is startled and embarrassed (he feels "an agony of peevish shame") at being seen in such a melodramatic act; once again (if that is the right phrase), he is booming out the twelfth line of the poem.

Contradictory Temporality: Woolf has just set forth a completely contradictory sequence of events that cannot exist in the real world and has subtly presented them as if they were merely different independent perspectives on the same fixed event. She has cunningly created a contradictory narrative temporality decades before Robbe-Grillet would do so. In addition, this looks forward to the more obviously impossible chronological progressions she would construct in her next novel, *Orlando*.

Reception and Time of Reading of Work: The time of the work's reception is relevant: published less than ten years after the devastation of the world war, the losses it abruptly depicts would resonate powerfully with its original audience in ways that most of us can now only guess at. Other families would have heard from neighbors or seen brief notices in newspapers naming people they had known; now without any advance warning they learn that their friends are dead. Thus, the time of reading of this narrative is also carefully crafted by Woolf. We are slightly disoriented by a beginning that plunges us deeper than usual into medias res, into what Melba Cuddy-Keane has called, "beginning's ragged edge." Our experience of the presentation of several perspectives is at first a little confusing for many, since it takes us so long to read about the events of an hour. Soon, however, we grow accustomed to the pace of the narration as we linger over the characters' thoughts and perceptions. The vast shifts in duration that occur in "Time Passes" are always felt as a massive change from the duration employed in the first part of the book—or of that used in almost any earlier novel. This no doubt invites us to share the shock of the sudden deaths of three of the characters and the shock of the Great War as well. Time is compressed as the war rages and the house decays. At the end of the narrative, Lily's completion of her painting occurs at the same time as the completion of the trip to the lighthouse, which takes place as Ramsay finishes reading his book, which creates the kind of merging of the reader with the author that Woolf advocated. As the children are depicted watching their father read, we see our own experience reflected at the same pace as it is described in the text: "Mr. Ramsay had almost done reading [. . . .] He was reading very quickly, as if he were eager to get to the end" (202–3). These descriptions may be equally applicable to our reading of *To the Lighthouse*; Woolf playfully enhances our merging with her text by producing in us the response it depicts, and it does so at the same speed that the characters experience it.

As we continue to explore contemporary temporal strategies, we would do well to recall Viktor Shklovsky assertion that "literary time" is a fabrication "whose laws do not coincide with the laws of ordinary time" (154); we also hark back to Bakhtin who, in his analyses of the chronotopes of the history of fiction, describes the Rabelaisian chronotope, the distinctive method of which consists "in the general destruction of all ordinary ties, of all the *habitual matrices* of things and ideas, and the creation of unexpected matrices, unexpected connections" (169), a practice that of course continues today in the more playfully disruptive and contradictory chronological formations typical of postmodernism. Since Bakhtin, important additional theoretical work on nonmimetic temporalities has been done, as we have seen, by Yacobi, Ronen, and Heise.[21] New work by Mark Currie, Jay Clayton, and Elana Gomel promise to expand our understanding of narrative temporality still further.

This chapter offers a more comprehensive model of narrative temporality that can do justice to antimimetic narrative practices. The history of fictional constructs of such temporalities stretches back almost to the beginnings of Western literature. In Aristophanes' *Peace*, Trygaeus's flight on a giant dung beetle to the halls of the gods is impossibly fast—so fast, in fact, that the protagonist metaleptically protests to the zealous prop man who is physically changing the scene. The concepts delineated in this chapter will help us describe more accurately and thoroughly the innovative use of narrative time in many works in the history of fiction and drama, and especially in modernist and postmodern texts.

---

21. Other useful earlier studies include A. A. Mendilow's suggestive account of *Orlando* (228–31) and David Leon Higdon's discussion of what he called "polytemporal time" in his book, *Time and English Fiction*, which does draw attention to the "destroying, ignoring or reconstituting clock time" (12) done by authors like Sterne, Lewis Carroll, and Beckett.

CHAPTER 6

Adventures of the Book

Fabricating Fabula and Syuzhet

ONE OF the most basic—in fact, foundational—concepts in narrative theory is the dyad of story and text, or fabula and syuzhet; that is, the distinction between (a) the story that we are able to infer from a text and reconstitute in its chronological sequence; and (b) the direct presentation of that text itself, word by word and page after page. Many kinds of works—folktales, myths, histories, traditional plays, bildungsromans, expressionist fiction, generational sagas, thrillers, and so forth—tend to be told in a largely linear fashion where story and text follow the same general trajectory. It is important to observe, however, that even in these cases there are always differences between the two due to the *duration* or pacing of the events in the text. Some are compressed, some stretched out, and some left largely untold; this is particularly noticeable in works that contain a large temporal ellipsis, such as Father Time's announcement "I slide / O'er sixteen years and leave the ground untried / Of that wide gap" at the beginning of the fourth act of *The Winter's Tale,* and the gap of several years that signals closure at the end of a novel like Flaubert's *L'Éducation sentimentale.*

Nonlinear works, in which the sequence of the story and the text don't match up, are common, from Homer's epics to daily accounts of athletic competitions in the sports section of the newspaper—the ending is usually presented first, especially if it is a dramatic one (see Carrard, "Telling"). *Tristram Shandy* inaugurates a tradition of narratives with extreme divergences between story and text sequences. These include Diderot's *Jacques le fatalist et son maitre*, Wordsworth's *The Prelude*, Lermontov's *A Hero of Our Time*, Heine's "Buch le Grand," Gerard de Nerval's "Sylvie," and Machado de Assis's *Dom Casmurro*. Modernist fiction and film have contributed still more divergent syuzhets, most notably in the work of Proust, Faulkner, and Kurosawa. This has led some (notably Genette) to postulate that nonchronological narratives are more advanced, but this thesis has not held up under scrutiny; Meir Sternberg has been particularly effective in presenting the case for linear narratives ("Telling").

In the 1960s and '70s, some narrative theorists assumed a primacy for the fabula as opposed to the syuzhet; Genette refers to the former as "the real order of events," the latter as "pseudo-temporal order of the narrative" ("Order" 25); Sternberg likewise writes that "the fabula involves what happens in the work (re-)arranged in the 'objective' order of occurrence" (*Expositional* 8). Such an affirmation discloses a pronounced mimetic bias: in nonfiction, there is an objective, preexisting order of events that can be either followed or inverted in its narration. As Monika Fludernik has stated, "Nonfictional narratives and remedializations clearly rely on a past story" ("Mediacy" 107–8). Similarly, mimetic fiction that models itself on nonfictional genres will utilize the pretense that the story exists independently of and prior to its narration.

Several narrative theorists subsequently argued for the opposite position. We are able to reconstruct the story only from the text in front of us. As Peter Brooks remarks, "The apparent priority of *fabula* to *sjužet* is in the nature of a mimetic illusion, in that the *fabula*—'what really happened'—is in fact a mental construction that the reader derives from the *sjužet*, which is all he ever directly knows" (13). Here, the stance is inverted and equally dubious: only in *fiction* is the discourse of the text our only source for the fabula (and realistic fiction that attempts to mimic nonfictional discourse will similarly attempt to provide the illusion of a fixed, preexisting fabula). The position articulated by Brooks has remained fairly common and may well be the dominant one today. Richard Walsh has recently claimed that "fabula is not so much an event chain underlying the sujet as it is a by-product of the interpretative process by which we throw into relief and assimilate the sujet's rhetorical control of narrative information" (67).[1] Nevertheless, the fact remains that the events of World War II occurred in a temporal progression before they were given narrative form, whether chronological or nonchronological. The Battle of Britain occurred before the Battle of the Bulge, no matter in which sequence this

---

1. Walsh's position refers to narrative in general but "especially to fiction" (67); I feel this partial qualification is inadequate to indicate the difference of fiction.

information is narrated, or indeed whether it is narrated at all. When Monika Fludernik states that "story [fabula] is always a construction and an idealized chronological outline" ("Mediacy" 107), she correctly limits this observation to fictional texts.²

A few other approaches have also appeared: Jonathan Culler made a case for fabula being in part a tropological construct that is retroactively created by the demands of the plot. Most theorists find this discussion ultimately misleading insofar as it conflates what happened with how we *learn* what happened; Fludernik has provided a sound critique (*Towards* 320–21). Other theorists who have recently contested the story/discourse distinction include Ruth Ronen, who uses the example of Robbe-Grillet's *La Maison de rendez-vous* "to demonstrate the impossibility of divorcing the order of events from modes of telling" (*Possible* 216); as we have seen, this distinction is often unable to be made usefully concerning the fiction of Beckett, Robbe-Grillet, and others. Patrick O'Neill has argued against the stability of this conceptual opposition itself and says that "perhaps the most striking thing of all with regard to the world of story, as far as narrative theory is concerned, is that ultimately we *cannot* ever 'say what really happened,' for that world, because of its status as a narrated world, finally both evades and exceeds description" (38). Nevertheless, meaningful aspects of the fabula can almost always be determined.

New Kinds of Fabula

Fludernik has also pointed out that "the story vs discourse opposition seems to repose on a realist understanding of narrative" (*Towards* 334).³ Moving beyond the mimetic perspective, we observe that perhaps the most important distinction has largely gone unremarked: the difference between texts with a single, retrievable fabula and those without one. Building on material presented earlier in this book, especially in the previous chapter, I will now identify some of these types. We may begin with the unknowable fabula, which can never be deduced from the text since it is too limited, vague, or unreliable. As Mieke Bal observes, "It is not always possible to reconstruct the chronological sequence. In many experimental modern novels, we find that these

---

2. Many of these and related issues are further clarified by Nelson Goodman's response to Barbara Herrnstein Smith in W. J. T. Mitchell's edited volume *On Narrative* (219–27, 255–57).

3. Compare this with Dannenberg's claim that "Genette's model is tied down to the concept of story; anachrony is thus conceived of as a narrative movement backward and forward along the single sliding scale of the past and the future of the story and not—as in an ontologically pluralistic approach—as a portal to different world versions" (50).

matters are intentionally confused, the chronological relations expressly concealed" (79). We also note the existence of circular narratives whose fabulas would thus be equally unnatural; they never end, even as the syuzhet connects the final words on the last page with those on the first, as the ending becomes a beginning. I will also point out that such works appear in popular culture and folk narratives in the form of the "shaggy dog story."

We have seen that many of Lorrie Moore's second-person stories mimic the form of the self-help manual and provide hypothetical sequences of possible events; there are, nevertheless, finite though variable indications of how much time elapses. The story proceeds as if the originally hypothetical events had in fact taken place, as possible future events become transformed into an incontrovertible past: this results in a "fuzzy" fabula. In works with contradictory sets of events, the fabula will necessarily include that contradiction. Concerning *A Midsummer Night's Dream*, its fabula will register that four days pass for the nobles in the city while—at the same time—two days pass for the lovers in the forest. In a more radical manner, contradictory narratives like Robbe-Grillet's *La Jalousie* (1957), Anna Kavan's *Ice* (1962), Robert Coover's "The Babysitter" (1969), and other novels of this type will never yield a single, consistent fabula. Robbe-Grillet, referring to the contradictory fabula in *La Jalousie*, stated: "It was absurd to propose that in the novel . . . there existed a clear and unambiguous order of events, one which was not that of the sentences of the book, as if I had diverted myself by mixing up a pre-established calendar the way one shuffles a deck of cards" (*New* 154). Emma Kafalenos observes that texts like Robbe-Grillet's *La Maison de rendez-vous* contain "multiple (fragmentary) *fabulas*, each of which shares common elements with at least one other fragmentary *fabula*" ("Toward" 396). The fabula is contradictory, and thus indeterminate. Concerning Coover's text, Hilary Dannenberg points out "the story's distortion of temporal sequentiality is so great that the reader is rendered incapable of even identifying the points of bifurcation" (*Coincidence* 216). An account like Peter Brooks's is clearly unhelpful before this kind of text: one cannot explore how the ending determines the events that lead up to it if there are multiple sets of events and divergent endings, as in Coover's narrative.

Many of the examples that I adduce elsewhere in this book employ multilinearity in one form or another, whether to determine the ending (Bradbury's "Composition"), the main parameters of the story (Castillo), or numerous narrative possibilities throughout the text (many hyperfictions); these works have multiple fabulas. Narratives with multiple versions that branch off from the same forking early in the narrative constitute a new kind of progression that is becoming increasingly prevalent in the novel and in film. The German film *Lola rennt* (1998), by Tom Tykwer, begins with the dilemma: Lola must obtain 100,000 marks in the next twenty minutes or her boyfriend will be killed. Lola starts to run. The film then provides three different versions of the same basic story, although in each case there is a slight alteration in a minor event, as the dodging of a hostile dog in a stairway produces three radically different scenarios. In the first version, Lola can't get the money, she runs to be with her boyfriend who is trying to rob a bank, and she is unintentionally shot dead by the police. In the next version, she robs a bank and gets the money to her boyfriend, but he is then accidentally hit by an ambulance and dies. In the last variation, Lola wins the money at roulette, her boyfriend recovers the money he had lost, and then the two walk happily off into the future.

The viewer is challenged to make sense out of this antimimetic sequence. One possible answer is that, according to the cultural logic that the latest version is the superior one, we may view the last one as the definitive or "real" story, the others being, as it were, "rough drafts" of the final, successful version. This view would also accord with the logic of comedy (it is hard to imagine the versions, in their current forms, being sequenced in a different order) and thus implies a kind of teleological progression of the different scenarios. As the narrator of *The French Lieutenant's Woman* described this situation, "I cannot give both versions at once, yet whichever is the second will seem, so strong is the tyranny of the last chapter, the final, the 'real' version" (318).

David Bordwell, in his study of forking-path films that present multiple possible outcomes following from the "base" narrative situation, insists that not all paths are equal: the last path taken both presupposes the rest and is the least hypothetical one ("Film" 96–101). He argues for the primacy of the last version and suggests that Lola seems somehow to learn from the previously presented possible futures (itself a wonderful unnatural device, since the self presented later cannot know the events that in another version lead to her death).[4] He states that "if something like a primacy effect establishes the first future as a benchmark, the 'recency effect' privileges the *final* future we see." To him, forking-path narratives "suggest the last future is the final draft, the one that *really* happened" ("Film" 100). But such a move concerning *Lola* is not entirely convincing, and there is little in the film to warrant these assumptions. In some multilinear stories, like Malcolm Bradbury's "Composition" and Robert Coover's "The Babysitter," the last dramatized possibility is arguably the most hypothetical and least likely outcome. In Krzysztof Kieślowski's film *Blind Chance* (1981), a kind of model for *Lola*, each of its three divergent

---

4. Bordwell notes, "Sometimes a film suggests that prior stories have taught the protagonist a lesson that can be applied to this one—thereby flouting any sense that parallel worlds are sealed off from one another" (99).

sequences is equally plausible—with the exception of the last version's explosive ending. In *Lola*, Manni's highly implausible reunion with the man who took his money is almost as unlikely as Lola's near-miraculous luck at roulette, itself seemingly abetted by Lola's preternatural scream just before the ball drops once again into exactly the right slot.

I suspect that Bordwell may be conflating a reality effect and audience satisfaction with the progression of the versions, which move from tragedy, to the absurd, to an essentially comic resolution. I resist that move, which ultimately tries to partially naturalize the sequence, and argue instead that Tykwer is palpably making his final version less realistic in order to comply with the general desire for a happy ending. I prefer to see the film as simply three possible narratives of a single set of events, unhierarchized and without *ontological* primacy being given to any one version.[5] In a series of paintings of the same object, we don't struggle to establish the primacy of one canvas and the consequent subordination of the others to it; all are equally variations of a scene—even if there is a meaningful sequencing of the variations. Perhaps more pertinently, as both Robyn Warhol ("Neonarrative" 229–30) and Tim Whalen have suggested, the film resembles a video game that is played several times; even as one gets better through practice, each playing is equally real, even though the game being played at the moment feels the most real of all.[6]

We also observe that even in cases in which each possible version produces a consistent and therefore mimetic narrative, we still find a text that violates the standard convention of purporting to narrate a fixed sequence of events that have already occurred. Each possible story is internally consistent; what is unnatural is that the course of events is not fixed. This practice thus violates the conventional retrospective nature of any story narrated in the past tense, in which an event is related after it has occurred, and the ending, which has already transpired, cannot be selected from among a list of options. Porter Abbott explains that narrative "is something that always *seems*" to come after the events it depicts; "to be a *re*-presentation" of them (*Cambridge* 36); it is the violation of this sense of the pastness of the narrative events that is foregrounded by multilinear fabulas.

As previously mentioned, there is one experimental technique that employs aspects of the discourse to negate or destroy the fabula; this is denarration. It appears prominently at the beginning of Robbe-Grillet's *In the Labyrinth*. First we learn that "outside it is raining [. . .] the wind blows between the bare black branches" (141). In the next sentence this setting is denarrated

---

5. From a rhetorical perspective, the existing sequencing is motivated by its producing a comic resolution, as I have already noted; I do not see that this affects the ontological status of any of versions.

6. See Kay Young for a discussion of additional problems with Bordwell's framework.

as we are informed instead that "outside the sun is shining: there is no tree, no bush to cast a shadow" (141). Finally, the definitive weather beyond the walls of the house is announced: "Outside it is snowing" (142). The external setting keeps being stated, negated, and re-created until snow is settled on. Denarration is foregrounded in Beckett's *Worstward Ho*, where a world is slowly and painstakingly constructed as a number of fictional possibilities are given and then immediately denied or revised to produce the most poetically bleak effect. "Say a body. Where none. No mind where none. That at least. A place. Where none. For the body. To be in. Move in. Out of. Back into. No. No out. No back. Only in" (7). A page later we get the following revision: "Say ground. No ground but say ground. So as to say pain. No mind and pain? . . . Say remains of mind where none to permit of pain" (8–9). Denarration here happens phrase by phrase, although what is left unchanged does then take on a minimal stability, if only a highly provisional one.

Shlomith Rimmon-Kenan states that "'story' designates the narrated events, abstracted from their disposition in the text [discourse], and reconstructed in their chronological order" (3). However, we cannot reconstruct any story when the discourse, as it unfolds, works to deny, negate, and erase the events recounted earlier. There is little recoverable fabula here at all, but rather a general, undifferentiated conglomerate of past events that may or may not have occurred. In the end, we have little more than the sequence in which the dubious events are presented or negated. We recall the words of Luc Herman and Bart Vervaeck cited in the introduction: "If it is impossible to reconstruct story events and to order them into a clear chronology, order in narrative texts cannot be assessed by using the structuralist method" (64). All of the narratives mentioned above extend far beyond the Russian formalists' fabula and syuzhet and Genette's category of order: unless both *histoire* and *récit* sequences are single and relatively fixed, one cannot establish the relation between them. Unnatural narrative theory offers a greatly expanded concept of fabula. Beyond the unilinear, retrievable fabula type, there are inherently unknowable fabulas; circular, recursive fabulas; those based on hypothetical, future events; internally contradictory fabulas; multilinear, forking-path fabulas; and those whose events have been denarrated.

The New Syuzhet

In recent years a number of authors have created innovative ways to construct syuzhets. One of these is the establishment of a new linearity in which authors deploy chronological sequencing in original ways, some of which can produce surprising results. Daniel Glattauer's novel *Gut gegen Nordwind* [*Love*

Virtually] is a transcription of a sequence of email messages between a man and a woman. The time of transmission can be calculated to the second that each email message was sent. This results in an intense attention to chronology as responses are emailed almost instantaneously or as one correspondent wonders in print why the other has not responded to the latest message. This practice updates, intensifies, and speeds up the kinds of interactions present in the eighteenth-century epistolary novel. One of the more intriguing manipulations of linearity occurs in William Gibson's electronic text, *Agrippa: Book of the Dead*. The text was constructed so that it would encrypt itself after its original viewing and thus become unreadable afterward. If anyone missed a key line, there would be no going back. The work thus uses a post-Gutenberg technology to approximate the occasional irretrievability of oral narration. This narrative, like life itself, goes only in one direction and cannot be rewound.

Others have played intriguingly with linearity; we see this in Eva Figes's 1981 novel, *Waking*. The narrative recounts the thoughts of a woman as she wakes; this narration depicts seven mornings, each separated by about a decade. Such a practice foregrounds the tenuous nature of individual identity over time, as well as residual personal characteristics that resist time's effacement. Other works that employ a comparable technique include Bernard Slade's *Same Time Next Year* (1975), a play about a man and a woman who are married to other people but who meet once a year for a night of love. This happens for twenty-four years; the play depicts several of their annual meetings. David Nicholls's *One Day* (2009) similarly narrates a single day each year, July 15, in the lives of a young man and a young woman from 1988 to 2007. This selective narration results in a very interesting kind of emplotment. Each episode of the narrative is highly "tellable" and creates considerable readerly interest. Typically, however, the resolution of a particular crisis is not disclosed until the next year's chapter, by which time the crisis may no longer have any traction. The consistent leap from one year to the next provides an unusual, episodic sort of reading experience in which we are repeatedly thrust in medias res as the narrative partially begins again. This effect is thematized in one of the character's comments: "How does it happen that you wake up one day, find yourself in your thirties and someone's mistress?" (220). By contrast, more enduring issues like the death of a beloved parent or persistent character traits continue to affect the protagonists year after year, providing a surprising sense of connection to otherwise wayward incidents as both central figures consciously try to impose a meaningful trajectory onto their lives. In these works, an unusually insistent linearity is played off against prominent gaps in the narration. These reveal how much backstory is, in fact, provided out of chronological order in so many seemingly linear nineteenth-century novels, and how much continuity of the periods represented is typically maintained in a traditional novel.

The latter part of the twentieth century and the first years of the twenty-first have seen a continuous development of the possibilities of the syuzhet. We may start by identifying some of the narratives that sequence their chapters in an antichronological order and thus move backward into the past as the reader moves forward in the text. Elizabeth Howard's *The Long View* (1956), a novel about the demise of a marriage, is composed of five parts that present the events of the years 1950, 1942, 1937, 1927, and 1926, respectively. The antichronological arrangement imbues the trajectory of events with a powerful sense of fatality. Similarly constructed works include C. H. Sisson's *Christopher Homm* (1955); Julia Alvarez' *How the García Girls Lost Their Accents* (1991); Sarah Waters's *The Night Watch* (2006); and, barring a couple of scenes, Harold Pinter's play about an adulterous affair, *Betrayal* (1978). In these works, each segment is set deeper into the past; at the level of the chapter or scene, the order of the syuzhet is thus the opposite of the order of the fabula, though within each scene the story unfolds in a linear manner, from past to present. This provides us with very different audience expectations, since we already know the ending to the story. Watching a performance of *Betrayal*, the audience keeps waiting to see the beginning of the story, wondering when it will reveal the crucial scene that is frequently remembered, what revelations will be divulged concerning the early events of the story, how the affair really began, and even "When will the playwright stop giving us backstory?" Seymour Chatman ("Backwards") and Per Krogh Hansen ("Backmasked") have published stimulating articles that discuss in depth the nature, effects, and reception of such texts, while Mieke Bal reveals an ancient (if brief) precedent for such strategies by pointing out that the opening passages of the *Iliad* narrate the development of the wrath of Achilles in a largely antichronological order (83–84).

Others have gone on to reconstruct the relation of fabula and syuzhet in other ways. Julia Alvarez' novel *In the Name of Salome* (2000), presents two narratives—a mother's and a daughter's—in alternating chapters. The mother's narrative is presented chronologically forward while the daughter's is presented in reverse chronological order. Michael Ondaatje uses a similar method to construct *Devisadero* (2007). Christopher Nolan's film *Memento* (2000) intersperses linear segments of a chronological narrative with a narrative whose segments are presented in reverse chronological sequence; the former are presented in black and white, the latter in color shots. The beginning of the film includes additional chronological play as a short sequence is run in reverse. One version of the DVD also offers the viewer the option of playing the entire film in a purely chronological sequence in which the syuzhet can be resequenced to reproduce the order of the fabula.

Tom Stoppard provides a number of creative deployments of his syuzhets; his play *Indian Ink* (1995) alternates two linear plotlines that are separated by several decades, and *Arcadia* (1993) does the same with stories that are nearly two hundred years apart in time but that take place in the identical physical space, an old English country house which Byron was rumored to have visited. His most playful syuzhet construction is no doubt *Artist Descending a Staircase* (1972), a ring composition in which each scene moves progressively further into the past until it reaches the middle of the syuzhet; then the play is presented in chronological segments that lead back into the narrative present as each temporally earlier scene is returned to and continued; the fabula is thus presented in the sequence 6, 5, 4, 3, 2, 1, 2, 3, 4, 5, 6. The sense of a compulsive narrative progression is made particularly powerful by the work's moving forward in time toward the resolution of the central mystery of the drama—and by the completion of the symmetrical pattern of temporal representation that moves progressively away from and then forward to the narrative present. A comparable but opposite trajectory informs David Mitchell's *The Cloud Atlas* (2004), a series of six nested narratives that extend progressively into the future and then return in reverse order to the previously represented time periods.

Still more elaborate is the sequencing of Jim Crace's novel *Being Dead* (1999), an account of the deaths of a husband and wife, both biologists, on a deserted beach. Three narrative strands are interwoven here into a strangely compelling totality: the linear narrative of the decomposition of the corpses in the days following the murders; the linear account of the first meeting of the two and the daily development of their relationship thirty years previously; and the account of the last day of their lives, told in an antichronological order that starts with their deaths and moves back in time, hour by hour. There are thus two chronological narratives, one covering different time periods and with different durations, and an antichronological narrative that intersects both.

Unlikely Syuzhets

In a typical work, the syuzhet is the narrative in the sequence that it appears in the text; it is usually co-extensive with its presentation, whether page by page or, in an oral narrative, word by word. Some ingenious authors, however, have played with this convention and offered a seemingly nonnarrative text from which a story is able to be derived. This strategy appears to have begun with Chekhov's short comedy, "The Harmfulness of Tobacco," in which a lecturer tries to speak on the subject but instead reveals the story of his unfortunate life. We find it in more extravagant form in Vladimir Nabokov's *Pale Fire* (1964), in which a 999-line poem and over two hundred pages of ostensible (and often wayward) commentary produce a narrative of a deluded critic's life and fantasies. Espen Aarseth has observed that it "can be read either unicursally, straight through, or multicursally, jumping between the comments and the poem." (8). A number of recent experimental works present an ostensibly nonnarrative text from which a compelling story can be derived; there is no doubt a greater range of such texts than is generally recognized. These forms are varied and include a dictionary, a catalogue of an art exhibition, and liner notes to a music disk: respectively, Milorad Pavić's *Dictionary of the Khazars: A Lexicon Novel* (1984) and Han Shaogong's *A Dictionary of Maqiao: A Novel* (1996); Stephen Millhauser's "Catalogue of the Exhibition: The Art of Edward Moorash" in *Little Kingdoms* (1993); and Christopher Miller's *Sudden Noises from Intimate Objects: A Novel in Liner Notes* (2002). Leanne Shapton creates the story of a failed love affair in the form of an illustrated auction catalogue in *Important Artifacts and Personal Property from the Collection of Lenore Doolan and Harold Morris* (2009).

In his story "Problems," John Updike employs the form of standard arithmetical test problems to produce a clever story. Thus, the third problem reads:

> *A* has four children. Two are in college, two attend private school. Annual college expenses amount to $6,300 each, those of private school to $4,700. *A*'s annual income is *n*. Three-seventh's (3/7) of *n* are taken by taxes, federal and state. One-third goes to *C*, who is having the driveway improved. Total educational expenses are equivalent to five-twentyfirsts (5/21) of *n*. The cost each week of a psychiatric session is $45, of a laundromat session, $1.10. For purposes of computation, consider these *A*'s only expenses.
>
> PROBLEM: How long can *A* go on like this? Round to the nearest week.
> (*Problems* 169–70)

Many other stories in the same collection use other unlikely media as inadvertent story receptacles.

Ron Carlson makes a story out of fictional front matter in his 2002 work "Disclaimer" (55–57). Alejandro Zambra's novel *Facsimil* [*Multiple Choice*, 2014] consists entirely of a series of multiple-choice tests. Other recent developments of this kind of presentation include Julie Schumacher's *Dear*

Committee Members (2014), an academic novel in the form of letters of recommendation, and Marisha Pessl's *Special Topics in Calamity Physics* (2006), which is loosely presented in the form of lectures for a college course and concludes with a final exam. Also noteworthy is Jennifer Egan's *A Visit from the Goon Squad* (2010), whose penultimate chapter is an extended PowerPoint presentation.

Syuzhets arranged in an alphabetical sequence include such varied works as Roland Barthes's book *Fragments d'un discours amoureux* (*A Lover's Discourse* 1977) and Michèle Roberts's "*Une Glossaire*/A Glossary" in her collection *During Mother's Absence* (1993). Xiaolu Guo's novel *A Concise Chinese-English Dictionary for Lovers* (2007) solves the problem of having a compelling plot run through the dramatically unpromising alphabetical syuzhet by arranging the book in the order in which key words were encountered by the protagonist during her visit to England; the first entries are "alien," "hostel," and "full English breakfast," while the work concludes with "fatalism," "race," and "departure." David Levithan's narrator reflects on the curious relation between the dictionary and lived experience in his novel *The Lover's Dictionary* (2012). Under the heading "Ineffable," we find "Trying to write about love is ultimately like trying to have a dictionary represent life. No matter how many words there are, there will never be enough" (120). The text temporally skips around quite a bit. Levithan is able to maintain narrative interest and provide a compelling plot by indicating that there was a significant break in the love relationship but not revealing until the end of the text (the entry for "Yesterday") whether the lovers were able to surmount it. Thus, the passage under "Dispel" reads: "It was the way you said, 'I have something to tell you.' I could feel the magic drain from the room" (74). Almost one hundred pages later we come to the heading "Quixotic," which portentously reads:

> Finally, I said, "It's over."
>
> You started to cry, and I quickly said, "No—I mean this part is over. We have to get to the next part."
>
> And you said, "I'm not sure we can." (165)

Rick Moody's "Primary Sources" (*Ring*) is an annotated list of the thirty books in the narrator's library that constitute a kind of autobiography; as we read more and more of the footnotes, we get more information about the narrator's life. Thus, the annotation to the first book, William Parker Abbé's *A Diary of Sketches*, begins: "Art instructor at St. Paul's School when I was there ('75–'79)" (231). J. G. Ballard's story "The Index" is a narrative in the form of the index to an autobiography. Ballard solves the problem of emplotment here by having the alphabetical order reproduce a largely linear temporality. Thus, the circumstances surrounding the birth of the protagonist of "The Index" (171–76) are revealed in an entry beginning with the letter "A" ("Avignon, birthplace of HRH, 9–13") while his final days are disclosed by the entries "Younghusband, Lord Chancellor" and "Zielinski, Bronislaw." Ballard has written another story that is composed solely of a heavily footnoted title, "Notes towards a Mental Breakdown," each word of which is annotated. There are still more extreme examples, such as the set of annotations to a text that has been erased in Jenny Boully's "The Body" (2003). As the second footnote states somewhat ominously, "It is not the story I know or the story that you tell me that matters; it is what I already know, what I don't want to hear you say. Let it exist this way, concealed" (437).

On the internet and in some performance pieces, lists are emerging as a medium of interest, especially unusual lists that can, insofar as they reveal an intended, connected sequence of events, disclose a potential narrative. There are several websites devoted to just such lists. Some of these have a strong narrative component that quickly becomes evident as the list begins to constitute a causally connected sequence of events. We find this in a piece by slam poet Big Poppa E (Eirik Ott) called "Receipt Found in the Parking Lot of the Super Walmart": "Anniversary Hallmark card. Flowers. Candles. Matches. Incense. . . . Block of white chocolate. Bottle of white wine. Barry White's Greatest Hits cd. . . . Honey. Box of condoms, 32 count, extra large . . . ." In a number of late modern and postmodern works, lists increasingly take on the form of a partial or protonarrative, as I discuss in an article on the subject.

Unusual Sequences

It is often said that narrative and its reception are sequential processes and that simultaneous events must therefore be presented and processed sequentially, not simultaneously. In works with multiple story lines, the fabula has to be presented in more than one discrete segment, as we see in most of Woolf's *To the Lighthouse*, since independent acts of perception or chains of events cannot be presented at the same time. We may refer to this as the "Meanwhile, back at the ranch . . ." principle. Genette comments that "Aristotle himself observes that one advantage of narrative over scenic representation is that it can treat several actions simultaneously," and, Genette adds, "But it must treat them successively" ("Boundaries" 7). This is, in fact, usually the case, but some experiments have provided multiple presentations of such events. Joyce Carol

Oates alters the physical layout of the standard printed page to create a "simultaneity effect" by using two parallel columns to disclose the thoughts of separate individuals at the same time in her story "The Turn of the Screw" (1971).[7] Harold Pinter uses two playing spaces on the same stage to indicate simultaneous events at two locations in his play "The Collection" (1961). Since the 1950s, film has used a split screen to achieve the same effect. In Roger Avary's *Rules of Attraction* (2002), the two characters come from disparate locations to meet at the end of the split-screen sequence as the two camera angles are fused together. Mike Figgis's splits his screen into four separate units that disclose simultaneous events in *Timecode* (2000). The audience thus helps choose some of the arrangement of the syuzhet.

The text of J. M. Coetzee's *Diary of a Bad Year* (2007) is, for the most part, divided into three segments on each page. The uppermost contains nonnarrative essays on an assortment of topics; the middle consists of a diary-like narrative that records the narrator's fascination with a young woman, Anya; and the final segment of the page contains Anya's narrative of their relationship and other matters. At several points the two linear narratives approach simultaneity, or at least different perspectives on the same events shortly after they occur. For much of the work the two narratives diverge as one moves ahead of the other in its disclosure of different periods of largely the same overall fabula. The reader typically starts processing the text left to right and top to bottom, but soon is tempted, usually irresistibly, to continue on with one or both of the narratives as their events become increasingly dramatic.

It is commonly believed and widely affirmed that the syuzhet of a work is always linear. In the words of Shlomith Rimmon-Kenan, "The disposition of elements in the text . . . is bound to be one-directional and irreversible, because language prescribes a linear figuration of signs and hence a linear presentation of information about things. We read letter after letter, word after word, sentence after sentence, chapter after chapter, and so on" (45). For the most part, she is correct: the syuzhet of a text is simply the sequence of pages you hold in your hand or experience in performance. However, as Jukka Tyrkkö has noted, this principle can be abrogated in classic novels; authors like Cervantes and Sterne "engaged readers by means of metanarratives giving instructions to skip certain 'irrelevant' chapters or to reread some previous ones" (279). Dave Eggers has recently extended this tradition in his note "Rules and Suggestions for Enjoyment of this Book," which precedes his narrative *A Heartbreaking Work of Staggering Genius* (2000). He suggests various

---

7. Brian McHale discusses other dual columned and superimposed narratives in *Postmodernist Fiction*, pp. 192–93.

pages and sections that an impatient reader may wish to ignore: "Many of you may want to skip much of the middle, namely pages 239–351, which concern the lives of people in their twenties, and those lives are very difficult to make interesting" (vii).

There is still greater freedom when the syuzhet is alterable. In some lexicon novels, like Richard Horn's *Encyclopedia* (1969), one may either follow the alphabetical sequence of entries or skip from one item to another that expands on it; for example, the entry "Bishop's Cope" concludes with an invitation to see the entries "Doom" and "Papageno" (21–22). An extreme example of a variable syuzhet is B. S. Johnson's "novel-in-a-box," *The Unfortunates* (1969), which is composed of individually bound chapters that may be read in any sequence (although one chapter is to be read first, and another last). Readers are informed that the sections appear in a random order; if they don't like the arrangement, they are invited to place the segments into a different sequence of their own choosing. The book, if one may call it that, describes the sensations and memories of a sports reporter who revisits the town where a close friend of his had died some time before. Each chapter primarily records one of two sets of events: poignant memories from the past or the meaningless events in the reporter's day. A few sections combine both temporal frameworks, but for the most part they situate themselves in one or the other period, each indicated by a different tense of narration—the past tense for the memories, and the present tense for the current day's account. What is interesting is that nearly all the chapters in the two sets can be situated within the earlier or later chronological sequence; there are no iterative accounts (e.g., "Year after year, we would . . .") and surprisingly little achrony, or temporally indeterminate events. Like a bound modernist novel, most of these segments can be placed within a normal fabula; the question that arises is: Why does Johnson forgo sequencing his syuzhet? The answer lies, I believe, in the irrelevance of any possible sequence to the grieving narrator. It does not matter where he situates the account of his lunch or where he places his memory of hitchhiking with his friend. The former event is utterly unimportant, and so is its placement; the latter event can appear anywhere, just as it will appear in a different temporal configuration when it is remembered again.

Drama also has interesting examples of unfixed or variable syuzhets. Charles Ludlam's *The Grand Tarot* (1969) contains twenty-two scenes. Before each performance of the play, tarot cards were dealt out to determine the sequence in which the scenes would be presented. Every performance was different and incorporated the play of chance into the presentation of events. Ludlam claimed that the piece was never the same twice. From our vantage point, we might say instead that the fabula was constant (all twenty-two scenes were always performed), though the syuzhet was always different. It is worth noting that this kind of production proved so difficult that Ludlam later established a fixed order of presentation for subsequent productions.

Milorad Pavić's *Landscape Painted with Tea* (1988) is a novel in the shape of a crossword puzzle that can be read either "Across," in the conventional sequence of numbered pages, or "Down," as different sequences narrating separate, largely independent story lines are suggested. The narrator provides an informative gloss that comments on this arrangement: "Why now introduce a new way of reading a book, instead of one that moves, like life, from beginning to end, from birth to death?" He concludes: "because any new way of reading that goes against the matrix of time, which pulls us toward death, is a futile but honest effort to resist this inexorability of one's fate, in literature at least, if not in reality" (185–86). A more sustained kind of leapfrog through a text appears in *Pale Fire*. In the work's index, we find an entry for "Word golf." We are then instructed to go to the entry "Lass." There we are told to look at "Mass," which directs us on to "Male," which then sends us back to "Word golf." The game is repeated for the entry "Crown Jewels" (306), as the reader is sent on to "Hiding Place" (307), "*Potaynik*" (311), "*Taynik*, Russ., secret place" (314), and then back to "Crown Jewels."

Other narrative genres may have unfixed syuzhets. Narrative paintings, in which several scenes of the life of an individual are depicted on a single canvas, can be read in several possible sequences. Graphic novels can also become unfixed temporally, as in the case of Chris Ware's *Jimmy Corrigan: The Smartest Kid on Earth*, where a page of images delineating some crucial backstory of the fabula can be read in different ways. As Thomas A. Bredehoft explains, "Ware's page-layout, which on one level enforces right-to-left reading, also demands a left-to-right reading of the same sequence of panels for a different narrative line" (878). Raphael Baroni, in his article on the subject, "(Un)natural," discusses this phenomenon at some length, arguing that such shifting reading paths are a conventional feature of comics. Hypertext fictions like Caitlin Fisher's *These Waves of Girls* are probably the most familiar narratives with an indeterminate syuzhet; these texts, however, often have a fixed, determinate fabula. It is interesting to note that in many hyperfictions, there is no way to know when the reader has read every unit of the text; the reader just keeps on clicking until the repetitions of the same segments become too common. This usually leaves some segments of the syuzhet unread.

Reconstructing the Physical Book

The adventures of the syuzhet continue in the physical layout of the material book. The traditional syuzhet is so entrenched that its contravention can be quite disconcerting, despite the fact that the dispersal of the paratext within the narrative proper is a practice that extends from Sterne's *Tristram Shandy* to Alasdair Gray's *Lanark* (1981), as noted in chapter 2. B. S. Johnson's *Albert Angelo* (1964) cheats the conventions of sequential pagination by placing literal holes in several pages that allow readers to glance ahead to suggestive portions of the syuzhet—for example, key words—that they will soon be encountering in a more fully contextualized format. This technique is partially borrowed by Jonathan Safran Foer in his volume *Tree of Codes* (2010). Katherine Hayles explains, "In Foer different complexities are created by the words that show through the die cut holes from one, two, or even three pages beyond, words that are read again as the page is turned, until they finally take their place on their own page" (229). Thus, Hayles observes, Foer has displaced the "zoom effect" from other media "to a material-semiotic mode that depends on the position of the holes."

Hélène Cixous' 1976 novel *Partie* goes much further. It is composed of two parts which are in reciprocal relation to each other. The book has two front covers, each of which is an inverted image of the other, and each of which is upside down in relation to the other. One can read the book from either beginning, following out the discourse of *Si,Je* and/or that of *Plusje*, which might be translated "If,I" and "I-more" (or "the More-I"). The text both depicts and creates fluctuating feminist subjectivity; the material form of the book is part of this project. Carol Shields's *Happenstance: Two Novels in One about a Marriage in Transition* (1981) is another book that can be read linearly from either direction. It narrates the story of a changing marriage from both the husband's and the wife's perspectives. The book has two front covers: one blue, the other pink; each part has thirty chapters. Due to an inverted binding, neither one has the place of being the first version or the last word; it all depends on how the reader holds the physical volume. Each narrative position literally stands the other on its head. This allows the author, incidentally, to dedicate the book to two different people, one on each side of the volume. There are no instructions for use, and the syuzhet can be constructed in a number of ways. A reader may read first one and then the other work in toto, or, since each covers the same time period from two perspectives in different locations, the reader may read a few chapters of one version and then turn the book upside down and read a few of what is literally the other side of the story.

Milorad Pavić has also written a novel in this form. *The Inner Side of the Wind, or The Novel of Hero and Leander* (1991) is a Janus-faced work that can be read in either direction. Though both texts are set in Belgrade, the stories are separated temporally by more than a century; Leander's takes place at the end of the eighteenth century, while Hero's is set in the 1920s. A key component of the work's plot is how the lovers, trapped in different centuries, can possibly meet. More recently (2006), Mark Z. Danielewski has produced a similar kind of text, *Only Revolutions*. As noted earlier, the book too has two covers, and both beginnings of the book have the copyright information and other prefatory material. Each side is narrated by a different character, and each page contains the other text in an upside-down version at the bottom of the page—which, of course, is the top of the page when read in the other direction. To describe this practice, we may repurpose an appropriately unusual word, one used to describe ancient systems of writing that move first left to right, then right to left, the way one plows a field: *boustrophedonic*.

Ali Smith creates a similar effect with a different publishing stratagem: her novel *How to Be Both* (2014) contains two parts, each occupying a different space and a different time period, late fifteenth-century Ferrara and contemporary Cambridge (UK). Half of the copies of the published book begin with the older half; the others invert this sequence. One's reading experience is typically determined by the text one chances to pick up at a bookstore or receive in the mail. There is no correct order of the two parts, although each sequencing produces a very different reading experience, depending on whether one begins with the life of the Italian Renaissance painter or the contemporary young woman who is looking at the painter's works. Starting with the sequence that more closely resembles the order of the fabula produces numerous mysteries that are clarified by the chronologically later text; starting with the historically later part, one receives a number of elements that are cunningly reconfigured in the text's other half. The former reading sequence may be the most satisfying; the latter the most easily comprehended. In either case, you only have a single opportunity to experience reading the book for the first time.

Some recent print narratives go beyond the confines of the book itself. Banana Yoshimoto's story "Newlywed" was serialized on posters aboard Japanese commuter trains from January to March 1991. The story, she noted, actually rode the rails around Tokyo. Multi-sited works are appearing with greater frequency; some books now include links to websites and other domains as the narrative's syuzhet is dispersed across several media. For example, in Elena Mauli Shapiro's novel *13, rue Thérèse*, readers are encouraged to use their smartphones to scan links to a website that contains additional elements of the work, including photos, maps, 3-D images, video clips, and other material. J. M. Abrams and Doug Dorst's *S* (2013) utilizes a greater number of transmedial and multimodal texts and sites, as Alison Gibbons has explored. Chris Ware's *Building Stories* (2013) comes in a large box; it contains fourteen differently sized, formatted, and bound items, including books, broadsheets, pamphlets, newspapers, flip books, comic strips, various scraps, and other self-designated "easily misplaced elements." Read together, in any sequence, they produce a single narrative with several interconnected strands. Most audacious no doubt is Shelley Jackson's "Ineradicable Stain," a 2,095-word story, each word of which is tattooed on the skin of a different person. It is a "mortal work of art" which exists solely on human flesh, present (for now) in small fragments on bodies all over the world. Once the tattooing is completed, the full text is planned to be disseminated only to those who already carry a part of it on their skin.

Together, these works should indicate that the physical sequencing of the actual text has become an important medium of artistic representation in its own right, in which dominant themes are creatively embodied, and that such unexpected and original syuzhet constructions are clearly worthy of sustained analysis.

Unfixed Texts, Changeable Stories

In some works, the way the reader arranges the text can alter the actual story. Texts like Queneau's 1961 "A Story as You Like It" have a forking-path structure that offers a number of possible outcomes, as the reader chooses a single path and thereby goes from the beginning to the end. Many hypertext narratives and some kinds of children's books in the "Choose Your Own Adventure" series function the same way. There is the "choose your own plot" kind of play in which the audience determines the events that will follow at several possible forkings of the action. In the scenario *The Theater Tree: A Combinatory Play* by Oulipo practitioners Paul Fournel and Jean-Pierre Énard, the audience is given the following situation: the king and queen argue; the king learns the queen has taken a lover, by whom she is pregnant; and the queen learns the king has a lost son. The spectators must decide whether the masked hero who just arrives is the king's son or the queen's lover (160). Several other such choices are offered to the audience, including the final fate of the principal characters. This type of work spans the entire spectrum of performance from avant garde opera (Michel Butor's libretto, *Votre Faust*) to popular dinner theater. They, too, have a multiple fabula with several possible variations.

Other strategies of literally rearranging the text are also possible. Marc Saporta's *Composition No. 1* is a collection of unbound, unnumbered pages that constitute a narrative. On the first page, the author invites the reader to take pages of his book and shuffle them as one might a deck of cards: "La lecture est prié de battre ces pages comme un jeu des cartes" (first printed page, unnumbered). The author claims that the resulting sequence determines the fate of the characters since, as he notes, it makes a considerable difference whether the protagonist met his mistress, Dagmar, before or after his marriage began. Thus, the author concludes, time and the order of events control a man's life more than the occurrence of the events themselves. Here, the fabula is arguably variable, and the syuzhet entirely so.[8]

The metaphor of the deck of cards is made literal in Robert Coover's story "Heart Suit" (2005), which is printed on thirteen oversized, glossy playing cards. The author states that the cards may be shuffled and read in any order, although the introductory card is to be read first and the Joker is to be read last. Each card begins with the continuation of a sentence that describes the adventures of an intruder, who is never named, and each card ends with a new sentence beginning with the name of an individual. Thus, the Five of Hearts card begins with the words, ". . . pent up with self-righteous anger, burst in upon the King of Hearts, who has fallen fast asleep on a kitchen maid, to complain that someone has penned a scurrilous accusation against him in the latrine." If the preceding card was the Deuce of Hearts, then the sequence identifies the intruder as the king's chaplain. If instead the previous card was the Eight of Hearts, then the intruder would have been the ambitious viceroy. The construction of the work (as well as the kingdom) indicates that this statement could be predicated of any of the male principals. This kind of variability of identities is particularly problematic when one reaches the Three of Hearts card, which begins, ". . . is the thief who actually stole the tarts," a statement that can be reasonably believed of any of the characters but proven of none, since the internal evidence is inconclusive—and, for that matter, the deck can always be shuffled again. The king decides to torture all the suspects, but the tactic fails: each of them confesses. The interchangeability of the figures in the drama is metafictionally indicated in the Eight of Hearts card: "The King feels lashed by uncertainty. Actions are known . . . but the actors are interchangeable, the perpetrators' varied and manifold motivations best understood as a collective one, a swarm of intent, from which can be snared only a faint glimmering of a general truth."

---

8. In a recent article, Courtney A. Pfall argues persuasively that the fabula of this text is in fact substantially fixed, even though the syuzhet is entirely variable. My own reading of the novel agrees with hers.

As has been noted previously, Ana Castillo's *The Mixquiahuala Letters* (1986) offers other possible ways of constructing a syuzhet. It is both a postmodern epistolary novel and an extension of a technique used by Julio Cortázar in *Rayuela* [*Hopscotch*, 1963]. The text itself consists of forty undated letters. As I noted in chapter 2, at the beginning of the novel the reader is warned not to read the book in the usual sequence, but rather to follow "one of the author's proposed options" (9); these are partial sequences of most of the letters designed, respectively, for the conformist, for the cynical, or for the quixotic personalities. Thus, the conformist is to begin with letters 2, 3, 6, 7, 9, 11, and 12, while the quixotic will read letters 2 through 10 and then skip to letter 12. The conformist is the only one who reads letters 39 and 40; only the cynic reads letter 38; and the first letter is intended only for the quixotic, and it is to be read after all the others. Each reading constructs a different syuzhet, and each yields a different story with a different resolution. It is also the case that simply reading all the letters in numerical sequence leads to an inconclusive, pointlessly (rather than productively) contradictory ending.

To situate the many original postmodern forms of sequencing identified above, we can revise and expand the standard concept of the syuzhet to include simultaneous fixed syuzhet sequences, in which textual material can be selected from different sources present at the same time (e.g., "The Turn of the Screw"); variable syuzhets, as in *The Unfortunates,* in which the story is presented in sequences that can be altered; multiple possible syuzhets in which the reader determines the selection and the sequence of the text (*The Mixquiahuala Letters*) and thereby helps determine the fabula; and excessive syuzhets which, due to their inaccessibility or to the fact that they are not expected to provide new, significant information, are unlikely to ever be fully accessed by even a dedicated reader (many extended hyperfictions). It should be noted that many of the strategies are directly related to the given narrative's specific themes; this relation shows how theoretical modeling can lead directly back to closer analysis of the narrative itself.

CHAPTER 7

Narrative Endings

Fixed, Unfixed, Illusory, and Unnatural

THE CONCEPT of endings has provoked considerable debate and generated a number of opposed positions; this may be due in part to the multiple different functions that endings perform. As Marianna Torgovnick observes, "An ending is the single place where an author most pressingly desires to make his points—whether those points are aesthetic, moral, social, political, epistemological, or even the determination not to make any point at all" (19). In what follows I will begin by providing an overview of a number of types of ending of mimetic texts, paying particular attention to fixed endings, the subject of so much earlier critical discussion and some misunderstanding as well. I will move from the fixed, to the less fixed, to the unfixed, and then to the unusual endings of unnatural narratives. I will conclude with some observations on some points concerning the aesthetics and the ideology of endings—questions that are often particularly prominent and especially pressing at the concluding point of a narrative.

Fixed Endings

Endings perform different functions, in part depending on the genre they belong to; there are also several ways in which an ending may be closed. A satisfying sense of an ending can be produced even when the major concerns of the characters are unresolved. Due to these ambiguities, I simply will refer to event sequences that seem to resolve major instabilities in the story as *fixed*. I use the term *fixed* rather than the more traditional *closed* because of the variety of meanings that have congealed around the latter concept and because of a growing skepticism about how closed a narrative can be. A fixed ending cuts through other distinctions: it may be carefully constructed or abruptly attached, like the deus ex machina; it may be ideologically imposed; and, as we will see, it may be mimetic or antimimetic.

The common assumption that runs through numerous critical and theoretical accounts over the past two and a half millennia is a general version of Aristotle's preference for endings like that of *Oedipus Rex*, "which itself naturally follows something else [. . .] but has nothing else after it" (94). John Dryden is more capacious: at the end of a play, "there you see all things settling again upon their first foundations; and, the obstacles which hindered the design or action of the play once removed, it ends with that resemblance of truth and nature, that the audience are satisfied with the conduct of it" (234). The poetics set forth by Bharata is similar, if more metaphorical. He advocates an organic development and conclusion which is to bring together the narrative "seeds" and objects of the play's different segments once "they have attained fruition" (384–85).

Many modern claims are either broader or more specific, even though they share the general tenor of the positions taken by earlier theorists who agree on fixed forms of ending. Tzvetan Todorov affirms that "the minimal complete plot consists in the passage from one equilibrium to another. An 'ideal' narrative begins with a stable situation which is disturbed by some power or force. There results a state of disequilibrium; by the action of a force directed in the opposite direction, the equilibrium is re-established" (111). Numerous other structuralist-oriented theorists have followed this general position. Perhaps the supplest account of fixed endings in this tradition has been formulated by Patrick Colm Hogan. He states that "the beginning and the ending are the points of transition between the unusual and the routine. Put differently, the beginning and ending are the points that immediately follow normalcy (in the case of the beginning) or precede it (in the case of the ending)" (*Affective* 76). The flexibility of this formulation is admirable, but the question remains whether we can in fact separate beginnings and endings so effectively, as I will discuss directly.

Peter Brooks makes one of the most sweeping claims for endings, asserting that "only the end can finally determine meaning. . . . The end writes the beginning and shapes the middle" (22).[1] This position is clearly an over-

---

1. Gerald Prince similarly notes the claim that "the end frequently determines the beginning at least as much as, if not more than, it is determined by it, since—from the beginning—the beginning is oriented by the idea of the end" (*Narratology* 158).

statement; D. A. Miller writes concerning the changed resolutions of *Great Expectations*: "From our perspective, the chief interest of these endings—the first forever parting Pip and Estella, the second forever joining them—lies in the sheer fact that they both were possible. For if either ending wholly regulated the narrative leading up to it, Dickens would simply have been *unable* to change the original without substantially revising the rest of his novel" (273–74). The same point might be made about the experimental narratives that I discuss below that have multiple endings.[2]

In his analysis of Brooks, James Phelan argues against such a dominant position for the ending, suggesting instead that beginnings, middles, and ends are mutually determinative (*Reading* 108–16, 130–31). He also objects that Brooks conflates the dynamics of plot with the dynamics of reading that plot (114–15). Susan Winnett argues that endings and beginnings are much more intertwined than is generally acknowledged in the kind of narrative theory argued for by Brooks; as opposed to his masculinist postulation that narrative reproduces the entirely end-driven arousal and significant discharge of the (male) sexual act, she convincingly points out that, concerning two female kinds of detumescence and discharge—birth and breastfeeding—"their ends (in both senses of the word) are, quite literally, beginning itself" ("Coming Unstrung" 143–44). It seems clear that Brooks's account is problematic at a number of different levels.[3]

There are several additional, conceptually larger, objections that can be raised at this point. First, the fixed ending may well be something of a narrative sleight of hand, providing the illusion of closure rather than the thing itself. We recall James's comment that "really, universally, relations stop nowhere, and the exquisite problem of the artist is eternally to draw, by a geometry of his own, the circle within which they will happily appear to do so" (171–72). E. M. Forster quipped, "If it was not for death and marriage, I do not know how the average novelist would conclude" (*Aspects* 95). But death and marriage do not end the thread of events, as divorce, probate, and child support amply illustrate. Forster also pointed out, in a lecture at the Working Men's College, that marriage, as a happy ending, was no longer the answer to the ending of a book: "We of today know that it is rather a beginning, and that the lovers enter upon life's real problems when those wedding bells are

---

2. See also Segal on the subject of alternative endings.

3. It should be clarified that Brooks does not explicitly argue for closed or fixed endings, although most of his examples come from such texts and his theory seems to be based primarily on the nineteenth-century realist novel. Furthermore, his few discussions of postmodern endings suggest they require a different analytical model: "Our most sophisticated literature understands endings to be artificial, arbitrary, minor rather than major chords, casual and textual rather than cosmic and definitive" (314).

silent" (cited in Beauman 190). Noting that a footnote following the final word of Laclos's *Les Liaisons dangereuses* suggests that the narrative might not be concluded, Armine Kotin Mortimer observes that "the possibility of a continuation of the work if it pleases . . . makes for endings with an open door, a raised foot, stepping stones—strategies that belie the claims of their beginnings and betray an underlying refusal of closure" ("Connecting" 217). In the case of Robert Louis Stevenson's *Kidnapped,* the author indicates that more of the story will follow, depending on "the public fancy"—that is, if the book's sales are vigorous enough (see Buckton).

Most significantly, as J. Hillis Miller astutely discloses, the unstoppable continuation of consequences is even true of Aristotle's tutor text:

> As for the end of the Oedipus, it is not really the end. It cannot be said that nothing follows causally from it. Oedipus is left at the end of the play uncertain about what Creon will do to him, whether or not he will allow him to go into exile. We know that something will follow next, as Creon consolidates his new power as king. Moreover, as the audience well knows, the events of this day are only an episode in the story that leads to Oedipus' own death and transfiguration at Colonus. (11)

Miller even argues that the play "is not a self-sufficient whole, but an arbitrarily excised segment of a larger action" (11). Though we may quarrel with Miller's affirmation of the arbitrariness of the ending, we may agree that in any story that is set within a social world, endings are nearly always partial, provisional, dubious, arbitrary, or forced—including those that can provide a distinctive sense of an ending for its audiences.

Not being entirely autonomous, stories may always be continued, either by the author, as the story of Stephen Dedalus, protagonist of *A Portrait of the Artist as a Young Man* (1916), is continued in *Ulysses* (1922); or Beaumarchais, who continued the story of *Le Barbier de Séville* (1775) in *Le Marriage de Figaro* (1781) and *La Mère coupable* (1792). At times, a different author will continue the story, as Ödön von Horváth does in *Figaro läßt sich scheiden* [*Figaro Gets a Divorce,* 1936]. An especially interesting case is that of Colley Cibber's *Love's Last Shift* (1696), a play that ended with a speedy reformation of the rakish hero into a responsible gentleman. But this improbable conversion was much too rapid to be credible, many felt. John Vanbrugh then wrote a sequel, *The Relapse* (1696), in which the protagonist reverts to his former character before experiencing a much more plausible transformation to his new, responsible state. The fact that Cibber approved of the extension of his story is demonstrated by the fact that the role of Lord Foppington was played onstage by Colley Cibber in both plays. Here, the physical body of the actor establishes an identity between the story worlds. In a comparable manner, the ultimately provisional nature of Jane Austen's well-wrought endings is testified to by many sequels, such as Samantha Whitman's *Ditching Mr. Darcy*, that have been written to extend Austen's stories beyond their original parameters.[4]

Orson Welles observed, "If you want a happy ending, that depends, of course, on where you stop your story" (*Big Brass Ring*, final line). At the end of chapter 2, I mentioned a number of authors who insisted on the arbitrary nature of beginnings; many, including James, Gide, Beckett, and Calvino, suggest that the same is true for endings. A comparable sentiment is articulated by Jack Burden, the narrator of Robert Penn Warren's *All the King's Men*: "I felt that a story was over, that what had been begun a long time back had been played out, that the lemon had been squeezed dry. But if anything is certain it is that no story is ever over, for the story which we think is over is only a chapter in a story which will not be over, and it isn't the game that is over, it is just an inning, and that game has a lot more than nine innings" (355). Closure thus often "seems less like the absence of the narratable than its strategic denial or expedient repression" as D. A. Miller states (267).

A fixed ending may always be illusory in any narrative that depicts a web of social relations. This is evident in the few works in which authors attempt to eliminate possible later consequences. At the end of Stendhal's *La Chartreuse de Parme*, Fabrice dies, his lover dies, her father dies, his small child dies, and his old lover dies. D. A. Miller observes that "in the *Chartreuse*, the love plot does not so much finish as it is finished off by death" (228–29); Miller is much too circumspect here—virtually all possible continuations are finished off by the many deaths. An even more definitive set of deaths concludes Conrad's *Victory* (1915), as the protagonist, Axel Heyst, his lover, and three criminals all wind up dead in the course of a few hours and Heyst's island home is set ablaze. Daniel Schwarz writes, "With its plethora of murders and suicides, the melodramatic climax . . . explodes the possibility of a meaningful conclusion" (78). The ending is almost comic in its attempts to provide a definitive closure that would defy any possible continuation.[5]

---

4. Even for a work like *Othello*, where all the principal characters are dead or about to be put to death, we could easily imagine a work called *The Further Adventures of Michael Cassio, and the True Story of What Happened to Othello*.

5. Additional discussion of this ending can be found in my article, "Negotiating Closure in *Victory* and Postcolonial Rewritings of *The Tempest*."

Inverted Syuzhets

As we have noted, a number of narratives, like Pinter's antichronological play *Betrayal*, present nearly all of its scenes in a reverse temporal order. The syuzhet of each of these works begin with their catastrophes; it ends with the disclosure of their origins. The conventional ending is here defamiliarized by being placed at the beginning. In the case of *Betrayal*, the end of the play's syuzhet discloses the rather arbitrary commencement of the affair dramatized in the rest of the work. Here, paradoxically, the enactment of the beginning of the story provides a very effective sense of closure. As noted in the previous chapter, a comparable effect is attained in Stoppard's *Artist Descending a Staircase*. Each scene moves progressively further into the past until it reaches the middle of the syuzhet; then the play is presented in chronological segments that lead back into the narrative present as each earlier scene is returned to and continued. The sense of an ending is provided both by the solution of the mystery and by the completion of the symmetrical pattern of temporal representation.

Loose Endings

At the opposite end of the spectrum from the fixed ending is the loose ending; it may seem minimally connected, adventitious, or arbitrary, even something of an afterthought. Ejner Jensen has pointed out that in many comedies, the center of interest is on the individual scenes taken together, rather than on a final scene that culminates and defines the preceding material. In such works, "to crown the end rather than to see it as a necessary and inevitable part of the total work is to . . . distort both the nature and function of Shakespeare's comedies" (21). The same is true of other episodic narratives, from picaresque novels to many classical Chinese dramas to Broadway revues and numerous works of popular culture. We saw in the case of Aristophanes' *Thesmophoriazusae* that the ending was so arbitrary that it seemed more a pretext for the quitting of the story than an actual solution to a problem. This can also be the case in extremely long works. Lynette Felber's study of the *roman fleuve* outlines the distinguishing features of novels that seem to have no end; it can be noted that while closure in Proust is quite definitive, in Dorothy Richardson's *Pilgrimage* it is fairly arbitrary and may have been imposed by her publisher. Robyn Warhol pushes still further as she contrasts the status and function of endings in two very different genres: "If romance novels require an ending, serial narratives actively resist coming to closure: formally speaking, [they] could have continued indefinitely" (*Having* 76). As Suzanne Keen comments, "The desire for a never-ending story may only be finally refused by writers' and readers' mortality" (77). These examples show the very different, in fact, at times, opposed functions of endings in different kinds of narratives, and thereby call for a much more flexible, nuanced, and genre-specific theory.

Covert Endings

There is a narrative equivalent of what Barbara Herrnstein Smith describes as "hidden closure," where "the poet will avoid the expressive qualities of strong closure while securing, in various ways, the reader's sense of the poem's integrity" (244). A full, fixed resolution may also be opposed for reasons of verisimilitude. As previously noted, Virginia Woolf praised the largely inconclusive endings of much Russian fiction, where the end might be simply "a note of interrogation or merely the information that they went on talking, as it is in Chekov. . . . Probably we have to read a great many stories before we feel, and the feeling is essential to our satisfaction, that we hold the parts together, and that Chekov is not merely rambling disconnectedly, but struck now this note, now that with intention, in order to complete his meaning" (*Common* 176). Like many modernists (and a few realists), she felt that a definitive ending that resolved all the major issues of the characters' lives was false, was, in fact, unrealistic. "We live in a world where nothing is concluded" she observes in "The Reader" (429).

At the same time, she indicates that some form or sense of closure may be useful. In *To the Lighthouse* (1927), she neither indicates any significant resolution of any of the central characters' problems nor informs us of the final fate of Lily's finished painting. Nevertheless, a strong sense of ending is provided: as we noted, Lily completes her painting at the same time that the trip to the lighthouse is finally concluded, which takes place as Mr. Ramsay finishes reading a book in the boat, as Woolf playfully enhances the end of our reading by having us experience the cessation it depicts. The work's story is left open even as the text's discourse, thematic elements, and architectural symmetries produce a feeling of closure; though we don't know how the novel's central issues and events will be concluded, we do know that the work is complete. This is true of many modernist works, including Joyce's *Ulysses*. Phelan's distinction between completeness and closure—completeness addresses the resolution of instabilities; closure concerns matters set in motion whose endpoints signal the endpoint of the narrative—is very helpful in articulating how many covert endings work (*Reading* 17–20; see also Richter 6–9). In some cases, such as the word *yes* which famously concludes *Ulysses* and whose letters repeat in inverted order part of the novel's first word, *stately*, we may say that there is a closure in the discourse, but not in the events of the story.

Absent Endings

Moving beyond loose endings, we come to narratives that will not or cannot conclude, as the works build toward resolutions that are deliberately withheld or that cannot be written. I have argued that Joyce provides a marvelous pseudo-ending to "The Dead," a strategy that foreshadows his notorious refusal to narrate any resolution to the major plot elements at the end of *Ulysses*. Woolf's *Between the Acts* (1939) appears to cease in medias res as a struggle between two of the book's protagonists is about to occur: "Before they slept, they must fight" (219), we are told. Melba Cuddy-Keane has observed that the novel ends "on the brink of beginnings projected beyond narrative time, perhaps even beyond the language or discourse which has constituted the textual world. . . . In *Between the Acts*, the closing lines recast the entire narrative as prologue to the text about to play: 'Then the curtain rose. They spoke,' (219)" (177). Noël Carroll has further clarified that a narrative history that ends with the present normally is not supposed to have any closure. Woolf's novel is set just after the beginning of the World War II, when its outcome was uncertain; it is thus especially appropriate that the ending of the novel, like the contemporary English history it represents, is unwritten. We see something comparable at the end of Conrad's *Nostromo* (1904) where, despite the fact that the fates of many of the main characters are fairly conclusively settled, it is clear that many of the other characters will be plunged into a new cycle of struggle and violence as labor trouble is brewing and a new war is being planned. As one of those characters observes, "There is no peace and no rest in the development of material interests [. . . .] The time approaches when all that the [silver mine] stands for shall weigh as heavily upon the people as the barbarism, cruelty, and misrule of a few years back" (511). The modernist refusals to provide closed endings testify to the inherently fabricated nature of a definitive ending to a complex series of intersecting events.

This kind of refusal of resolution is a strategy common in postcolonial fiction, quite prominently in the final scene of Aimé Cesaire's *Une Tempête* (1969), which leaves his Prospero and Caliban in medias res, locked in battle for control of the island. It would appear that lives that are so imbricated within contemporary events will not attain any sense of closure until the political struggles that surround them have progressed further or come to a pause. Nadine Gordimer's *The Late Bourgeois World* (1966) concludes with the protagonist about to make a decision to either assist or ignore the Black Nationalist resistance in South Africa under apartheid. This ending, like Woolf's and Cesaire's, gestures out to the political situation it represents; all South Africans had to come to a decision about this situation.

Looking into other works that end with the central concerns of the text blatantly unresolved, we note other reasons for the refusal of an ending. At the end of *Changing Places,* David Lodge briefly discusses endings and quotes the metafictional comment at the end of Jane Austen's *Northanger Abbey* in which her narrator observes that readers "will see in the tell-tale compression of pages before them, that we are hastening together toward perfect felicity" (540). Lodge, however, refuses to disclose the final fate of protagonist Morris Zapp, who, seated in an airplane high above the Atlantic, is literally left in midair as the narrative ceases. This humorous play with conventional narrative expectations is more intense in postmodern experiments like Thomas Pynchon's *The Crying of Lot 49* (1967), in which the resolution to the narrative is provocatively withheld. Hugh S. Manon uses the term *truncation* to denote works like John Sayle's film *Limbo* (1999) or the final episode of the HBO series *The Sopranos* (2007) in which the narrative abruptly ceases. Such refusals to provide an ending are done, Manon states, to "smash the tidy smugness of the Hollywood ending in an act of pure defiance" (25). Other authors may invoke personal reasons to refuse to conclude, as in Serge Doubrovsky's autofiction, *Le Livre brisé* (1989), in whose pages the author's wife figures prominently. Before he was able to write the final chapter, his wife died. Her death "broke apart the design of composition established at the outset and pursued in the first three quarters of the book"; afterward, "no ending seemed possible," Armine Kotin Mortimer explains ("Connecting" 224). Instead, Doubrovsky concluded the unfinished book simply by reproducing a poem by Victor Hugo mourning his daughter's death.

Hyperfiction has given us a new possible kind of ending. In many such works, there is no map or other means to indicate which textons are left to be accessed. One can, that is, never know whether one has finished reading all of the text. Michael Joyce explains his theory and practice in the unit "work in progress" in *afternoon, a story*: "Closure is, as in any fiction, a suspect quality, although here it is made manifest. When the story no longer progresses, or when it cycles, or when you tire of the paths, the experience of reading ends" (see J. Yellowlees Douglas). We can conclude our account of mimetic endings by affirming that the theorists who set forth accounts of fixed endings frequently overstate their case. While it is largely true that some traditional genres like classical tragedy or the nineteenth-century realist novel do aspire to such fixed conclusions, there are several other narrative forms that ignore, resist, or cannot have such endings.

Unnatural Endings

In addition to the various kinds of mimetic endings I have examined above, there is also a world of antimimetic or unnatural endings; interestingly, they may either refuse closure or provide a powerful sense of an ending. These include the circular narrative, like Nabokov's "The Circle," discussed in previous chapters; its ending always returns to and departs from its point of origin—which is also its conclusion and which never ceases, as the ending is infinitely repeated and infinitely eluded. There are also denarrated endings that negate themselves and present instead another equally possible ending, as in John Fowles's *The French Lieutenant's Woman*.[6]

Many works have parodic endings that problematize or destroy any mimetic pretense of the narrative representation. Peter Rabinowitz observes that the conventional ending can be undermined both by overthrowing it and "by following it in such an ostentatious way that it looks absurd. . . . Farce is particularly apt to use this mode" (*Before* 167). Happy endings are particularly susceptible to such explodings. Henry James notes satirically that the typical popular ending concludes with "a distribution at the last of prizes, pensions, husbands, wives, babies, millions, appended paragraphs, and cheerful remarks" (32). Too much closure can prove to be destabilizing—the gratuitous fifth marriage at the end of *Measure for Measure* is certainly a synecdoche of the arbitrary nature of every such conclusion. *The Importance of Being Earnest* satirizes the entire tradition of comic resolutions since Menander invented New Comedy, as the lost child is found, lovers are reunited, a missing manuscript is restored, three marriages are now about to take place, and the true, fortunate name of the protagonist is revealed. Likewise, the preposterous series of revelations and couplings at the end of *Cymbeline*, Joe Orton's *What the Butler Saw*, and Stoppard's *Travesties* ruthlessly parody the classical impulse toward anagnoresis enshrined by Aristotle and observed by so many playwrights; they subvert the effect of the resolution these devices are normally intended to create.

---

6. Phelan, however, attempts to show how the different endings together form an appropriate conclusion to the novel (*Reading* 101–2).

Two other types of unnatural ending may be identified: forking-path endings and metafictional fusions. Forking-path narratives are those whose different branches produce two or more incompatible endings. David Bordwell has noted that such works stretch back to O. Henry's "Roads of Destiny" (1909), which narrates three different possible fates for the protagonist after he has a spat with his beloved; each ending depends on which road he (literally) takes. Narratives with multiple fabulas, each with a different ending, also present the same issues. In a text like Castillo's *The Mixquiahuala Letters,* the ending depends on which textual sequence was selected by the reader—and there are very different resolutions prepared for the conformist, the cynic, and the quixotic reader.[7] The same is true of hyperfictions that offer multiple incompatible endings. B. S. Johnson has composed a story, "Broad Thoughts from Home" (1973), in which the reader is explicitly offered numerous possible endings to choose from (see Dannenberg 61–62).

Malcolm Bradbury's "Composition" (1976) tells the story of a new teaching assistant at a Midwestern university during the Vietnam War. At a party with his students after classes have ended, some extremely compromising photos of him are taken. The students who took the pictures then request he give a passing grade to another student who did not do the coursework. He knows that if the pictures get circulated, he is certain to lose his position. The earlier sections of the work are numbered 1 through 4; the final section offers three different resolutions, designated 5A, 5B, and 5C. In the first option, the instructor quietly raises the grade and saves his job. In the second, he corrects the grammar of the letter, sends it back to the blackmailers, and defiantly turns in the deserved failing grade. In the third, he agrees with the student that the grading system is silly, that all words are inadequate, and what matters most in life is love. He therefore destroys the grade sheet and abandons his academic position in order to devote himself fully to life and love. The text offers no indication of which of these possibilities will be (or has been) actualized; each option has a certain plausibility. There are a number of ways to interpret the multiple endings. I suspect that we may best regard this as a demonstration of the difficulty of determining in advance how a character (or person) will actually act in a given situation; it also demonstrates the radically different consequences that can follow from a single event. In any case, it reveals that "you have to write your own ending" (141), as the instructor is informed by one of the other characters.

---

7. It is worth noting that many texts with multiple fabulas nevertheless have a fixed beginning and a single ending, such as Johnson's *The Unfortunates* or Coover's "Heart Suite."

Metafictional Fusions

In Felipe Alfau's story "A Character" (1936), a figure escapes from the pages of a work of fiction and enters the human world. He meets and falls in love with a real woman, but their romance is doomed. At the end of the story, the character is returned to the fictional storyworld. This kind of scenario, which harks back to the dialogue between a suicidal character and his author in Miguel de Unamuno's *Niebla* (*Mist*, 1909), can be found in many other works in Spanish. Brian McHale notes that Gabriel García Marquez' *Cien años de soledad* [*One Hundred Years of Solitude*, 1967)] ends as its protagonist, Aureliano Buendia, "reads the gypsy Melquíades's prophetic narrative of the destiny of the Buendías down to the very page on which the moment of his reading of this page is itself prefigured" (*Postmodernist* 123); at this point, the manuscript and its reader are instantaneously destroyed, and the narrative comes to an end.

Mexican novelist David Toscana's *El Ultimo lector* [*The Last Reader*, 2009] also utilizes this general stratagem. The work recounts the story of Lucio, a librarian in a small town in northern Mexico where no one reads books. He receives numerous volumes, but before putting any out on his shelves, he reads them to see whether they are original works or poor quality volumes filled with narrative clichés. His evaluations are both aesthetic and ideological: he hates novels in which "the murderer is always caught and age doesn't matter as long as there is will; in those, the characters act out of conviction even though the writer does it for money." In such works, "the tubercular is cured and the alcoholic redeemed, and the writer receives prizes" (144). Nowadays, "artistry is lost" and "we are left only with noisy, cheap movie endings" (176). He throws these pathetic books into an adjacent room to be devoured by cockroaches. For him, it is much preferable that "a man should end up under a pile of snow or earth, bleeding to death in a cell, thrown out of a pickup truck or off a bridge, in a well or septic tank, entangled in the roots of a tree. . . . That is the only worthy ending for a novel or a life" (176).

His own life is quite troubled. The town is dying, he has no income since the government suspended his salary, he cannot recover from the grief he feels over the death of his wife, and the body of a dead girl has been found at the bottom of a well on his son's property. As the story progresses, he ever more insistently views events in the world from the perspective of the well-written novels he has allowed to remain on the library's shelves. Finally, he opens a new box of books and cuts out several words from their pages until he is able to spell out the narrative of his dead wife, one that has never appeared in any story. She then materializes, and he tries to fix her features and habits in his memory, since he knows that she will not stay long: "There will be no way of avoiding the tragic fate assigned her by its author" (188). He also knows that "he too has to succumb at any moment, ashamed, with a knife twisted under his sternum; knows that a city writer, an idiot [. . .], must cut him down to nothing in a novel fit for hell and cockroaches." In the book's last sentence, he states that he will be buried "in the sands of the sea or the desert every time somebody opens to the last page of *The Last Reader*" (188). The fiction he has read and the self that is fading now merge in the pages that readers hold in their hands. Such metafictional transformations provide a strong sense of closure and at the same time affirm the fundamental fictionality of the narrative. They utterly elude traditional strategies of concluding. By extension, they may also point to the constructed nature of all personal and political narratives and invite a healthy skepticism toward predictable, ostensibly nonfictional fabrications.

Unnatural Endings in Performance

A metadramatic reversal of fortunes may come at the request of a character. In John Gay's *The Beggar's Opera,* as Macheath is about to be hanged, an actor complains onstage to the author of the play, "Friend, this is a downright deep tragedy. The catastrophe is manifestly wrong, for an opera must end happily" (158). The beggar then gives up his goal of "strict poetical justice" and changes the ending by giving Macheath a reprieve in order to comply "with the taste of the town" (158). A more recent example appears in Marc Forster's film *Stranger than Fiction* (2006): the novelist, after conversing with a character in the flesh, takes pity on the same character, whose death she is composing; she decides to rewrite the narrative so that, at its end, he may live.[8]

After the ending of *A Midsummer Night's Dream*, Robin Goodfellow, still in character, metadramatically addresses the audience: "If we shadows have offended / Think but this and all is mended." Speeches like this indicate that not all plays end once the final scene is over; sometimes, there are elements of the performance that extend beyond the representation of events. There are several other plays whose performance stretches past the end of the story. At the end of many Elizabethan and Jacobean masques, the spectators are invited to join the characters in a dance that both concludes the story and extends

---

8. For additional discussion of endings in drama, see my essay, "Endings in Drama and Performance," some sections of which I have repurposed for this chapter.

the performance. A more recent example of this practice appears in Amiri Baraka's black revolutionary play *Slave Ship*, where the audience is invited to join the actors dancing onstage and then participate in insurrectionary activity outside the theater.

In Bertolt Brecht's *Der gute Mensch von Sezuan* [*The Good Person of Szechwan*, 1941], a group of deities visit the city to see whether any good people can be found. Despite witnessing the considerable harshness, exploitation, and difficult moral tradeoffs essential for survival, the gods finally ascend back to heaven in a pink cloud. They do not offer to help the inhabitants because they insistently deny that there are any problems, and the deus ex machina trope is made literal in the production (see Pfister 97). The play's central dilemma remains, however: moral injunctions are often incompatible with human survival. The characters are left without any resolution of their problems. In an epilogue, the audience is invited to reflect on the play's inconclusive ending and is implicitly urged to change the society that engenders such contradictions. Here, the performance moves outward from the world of the play to the world of the audience:

> It is for you to find a way, my friends,
> To help good men arrive at happy ends.
> You write the happy ending to the play!
> There must, there must, there's got to be a way! (113)[9]

One of the most inventive endings in modern drama—and one that has no precise equivalent in narrative fiction—is found in Caryl Churchill's *Cloud Nine*. This play has two acts between which the characters age twenty-five years. In each part the same characters are played by different actors, thus enabling one figure, Betty, to literally embrace her former self in front of almost all the other characters at the play's end, and thus provide a powerful sense of closure to a series of actions and events that otherwise remain substantially inconclusive.

---

9. The lines in the German original read:

> Der einzige Ausweg wär aus diesem Ungemach:
> Sie selber dächten auf der Stelle nach
> Auf welche Weis' dem guten Menschen man
> Zu einem guten Ende helfen kann.
> Verehrtes Publikum, los, such dir selbst den Schluß!
> Es muß ein guter da sein, muß, muß, muß! (279)

The Endings of Contradictory Narratives

Some readers of this book may wonder about the endings of stories that have numerous contradictory sets of events, like Robbe-Grillet's *La Jalousie* or Coover's "The Babysitter." Curiously, in these texts we often find an effect which is the opposite of that of the multiple incompatible endings discussed earlier. The works with multiple endings generally take a fairly mimetic story and give it two or more plausible endings. In contradictory narratives, we find a different strategy, as most of the works conclude with a sense of tranquil ordinariness as the instabilities that generate narrative vanish. In the final episode of *Jealousy*, all is calm, the workmen are gone, the visiting planter leaves promptly and does not act like a potential seducer, there are no cries of animals in the jungle, and the emotionally charged centipede stain has largely vanished, leaving only a barely visible trace. There is no reason for any jealousy; all is well. In one ending of Coover's story, the parents return home and all is well; in the more catastrophic ending, the mother lies in bed with a neighbor, bored, as they prepare to watch the late movie together. As described above, in the last sections of Kate Atkinson's *Life after Life*, the first death of the infant protagonist is rewritten so that the girl is saved by her mother, and her brother is also allowed to return home from the war, alive. Internally contradictory stories would appear to lend themselves particularly well to placid endings that restore the harmony that has been disrupted so outrageously throughout the text.

Aesthetics

Aesthetic flaws are especially prominent at the point where the author tries to wrap up the story. Aristotle pointed out that numerous endings are disappointing, noting that many develop the plot well but resolve it badly (103). Several centuries later, Lessing would complain about plays in which a perfectly healthy character appears to "die of the fifth act" (10). And Toscana's protagonist bemoans that "we are left only with noisy, cheap movie endings" (176). To begin to achieve the kind of ending so many have desired, two separate trajectories need to be merged. It is necessary to fuse the chain of events, governed by the work's canon of probability, onto the traditional generic pattern that dictates a satisfying closure.[10] The more realistic the work, the more

---

10. Marie-Laure Ryan refers to this opposition as one between the plot devised by the author and that devised by the characters ("Cheap" 56). I'm not sure this formulation gets to the main issues involved.

unsatisfying an improbable resolution. Most "cheap plot tricks," as Marie-Laure Ryan calls them, are built around unlikely coincidences. This is why the deus ex machina ending is still despised long after Aristotle first denounced it.

Peter Rabinowitz articulates a general metarule that "leads us to expect balance in a text, to expect that somehow the ending will be prefigured by the beginning" (*Before* 161) and notes that if "readers expect the initial point of view to return at the end of the text (as in a musical ABA structure), authors can fulfill that expectation to create a sense of closure" (126). The balance referred to here can also include architectural symmetries as the narrative recapitulates various aspects of its beginning. This can and often does produce an aesthetic effect. Here, too, aesthetic pleasure is frequently created by the seamless fusion of independent organizing systems, such as the conventions of a genre and the demands of verisimilitude. This effect is also produced by symmetrical relations and overarching patterns, such as what E. M. Forster (*Aspects* 149–70) called the "hour-glass shape" of the inverted final roles of the protagonists of James's *The Ambassadors* or the extremely consequential train station scenes at the beginning and end of *Anna Karenina*.[11] These can be especially resonant when deftly interwoven with probabilistic developments in realist works, though they also provide an aesthetic effect when the patterns violate realist requirements, such as the otherwise unmotivated reversal of the positions of Stott and Law in Pinter's *The Basement* or the geometrical shapes of many of the antimimetic works of Robbe-Grillet.

Value and Ideology

The endings of many narratives illustrate or valorize particular ways of thinking or acting. This is the design of a parable, moral story, most allegories, and many satires: social values are often built into endings. Aristotle maintained that a tragic ending was superior to all others, but noted that many playwrights ignore this fact and instead cater to the weakness of the spectators. This principle has been frequently reiterated during the past 150 years. Nietzsche famously denounced individuals and societies too weak to endure tragedy: "Broadly speaking, a preference *for questionable or terrifying things* is a symptom of *strength*; while a taste for the *pretty and dainty* belongs to the weak and delicate. *Pleasure* in tragedy characterizes *strong* ages and natures" (450). In "Happy Endings," Margaret Atwood suggests that the only true ending is that the protagonists die, and she warns: "Don't be deluded by any

---

11. See also Phelan's work on this subject in *Experiencing*, pp. 133–48.

other endings, they're all fake, either deliberately fake, with malicious intent to deceive, or just motivated by excessive optimism [or] sentimentality" (55). All other endings are lies. This seems to be the general sensibility behind the unwittingly satirical comment by Miss Prism in *The Importance of being Earnest*: when asked how her lost novel concluded, she replied, "The good ended happily and the bad unhappily. That is what fiction means!" (26). This sentiment, like Nietzsche's and Atwood's, unites ethical issues with a critique of the verisimilitude of the happy ending.

It is certainly the case that authors have held out for more tragic endings against publishers or producers who wanted a sunnier conclusion; Ibsen was furious when he learned that the ending of *A Doll's House* had been transformed for its German premier. Conrad expressed contempt for his editor's suggestion that he provide a happy ending to "Freya of the Seven Isles" to improve its chances of being published in *Century Magazine*: "As to faking a 'sunny' ending to my story I would see all the American Magazines and all the american [sic] editors damned in heaps before lifting my pen to the task" (*Collected* 469). The suppression of a tragic ending has famously happened to many Hollywood films. For example, Alfred Hitchcock's *Suspicion* (1941), based on Francis Iles's novel, *Before the Fact* (1938), was originally a story of a woman who gradually realized that her husband was murdering her. RKO studios, not wishing the images of their stars, Cary Grant and Joan Fontaine, to be associated with such events, succeeded in getting the ending altered so that it would become a romantic comedy. Until recently, tragedy was almost entirely, if unofficially, banned on network television.

It is also the case that too merciless an ending can destroy the tragic effect and make the work seem to promote a nihilistic or fatalistic view. Conrad may be guilty of this in "Because of the Dollars" (1914). Paula Vogel's play *Hot 'n' Throbbing* (1994) is about a woman who flees an abusive husband and starts a new life. Then, at the end of the play, the husband enters her house and strangles her with his belt. Many audience members find this ending unendurable. Aristotle appears to be correct: a good person who is without a tragic flaw and who suffers is not tragic and this situation does not make for good drama. Issues of narrative ethics—ethics concerning characters, genres, or the relation between them—are often especially resonant in endings.

It is also the case that a number of politically radical authors have created original kinds of endings in the service of their ideological positions. This is especially prominent in works employing carnivalesque strategies, which have enabled political satire since the time of Aristophanes (see Toker, *Ethics*). Totalitarian regimes demand compliance with national myths and look askance at ambiguous or open endings. Stalin insisted on literature that produced optimism. In 1938, the Hays commission, charged with censoring US films, refused to allow the depiction of criminals' lives unless the character in the film was punished for the crimes he was shown to have committed (see Belknap 133–34). However, one cannot go much beyond these general tendencies. For many years it was postulated that an open, inconclusive ending was more socially progressive than a fixed, closed conclusion, but it is now widely accepted that no narrative form or technique has any inherent ideological valence—especially now that open endings have become rather conventional, at least in literary fiction (see Richardson, "Linearity"). As Alison Booth has written in the introduction to her anthology of essays on the endings of nineteenth-century narratives, "We do not find a clear correlation between disruption of formal convention and radical departure from social convention" (9). The politics can be powerfully present, but it can take a variety of different shapes.

Masculinist societies insist on a very limited range of possible options for female protagonists, as a number of feminist scholars have documented (see, for example, Rachel Blau duPlessis's *Writing beyond the Ending*). Feminist theorists have examined the ways female novelists have eluded society's master narratives, in particular, the ubiquitous "marriage plot" which leads so many writers to provide only a limited range of possible endings for their female protagonists: marriage, death, madness, or painful isolation. They also note that female authors who stray from this trajectory have historically been accused of violating probability, as Nancy K. Miller has shown. Other similar social plots have historically produced comparable conclusions, such as the frequent deaths of homosexual characters at the end of works by heterosexual authors, the ultimately sacrificial status of many working-class or minority characters in white bourgeois fiction and film (what we might call the "Gunga Din effect"), and the invariable deaths of women who have been raped in traditional Bollywood films. The desperate measures that some writers take to achieve such an ideologically closed ending are evident in D. H. Lawrence's "The Fox" (1921), a story about two unmarried women living together on a farm in the countryside. Lawrence cannot seem to allow this to be a successful union and concludes the work by having a tree fall on and kill the weaker of the two women. Most improbably, she ignores a shouted warning and stands still while the tree is falling; it strikes her at just the point on her body that will cause her quick death. She dies, and the imagined threat to heterosexual unions is removed. Such texts often pass largely unnoticed by many readers, while those that elude such expected developments can be powerfully affecting.

In a self-reflexive moment in Mart Crowley's *The Boys in the Band*, one character states: "It's not always like it happens in plays, not all faggots bump themselves off at the end of the story" (81). The cultural script alluded to here creates a situation where a traditional happy ending can be repurposed for a progressive political agenda. At the end of Jeanette Winterson's story "The Poetics of Sex" (1993), the reader is prepared for a tragic separation to isolate the text's extraordinary lesbian lovers. Suddenly, a different, favorable end appears that provides a harmonious conclusion. Here, to write beyond the traditional ending is, paradoxically, to reproduce that very ending with a difference. In his epilogue to *Lolita*, Nabokov noted that the central situation of the book was one of only three that were completely taboo for American publishers in the 1950s, the others being "a Negro-White marriage which is a complete and glorious success resulting in lots of children and grandchildren; and the total atheist who lives a happy and useful life, and dies in his sleep at the age of 106" (316). It is noteworthy that a definitive closure with a happy resolution was an essential component of these forbidden fictions. Winterson's amorous and experimental text with the scandalously placid ending could certainly be added to this list and could not have been published in America at that time.

In some cases a narrative seems to be getting out of control and moving toward forbidden territory. In such cases a kind of ideological closure cuts off the flow of dangerous events; sometimes, this seems to be done with a wink to the audience. We see this at work in many venues such as the end of the medieval morality play *Youth*; the conclusion of Molière's *Tartuffe* (1664); and the ending of Bankim Chandra Chatterjee's novel *Anandamath* (1882) in which it seems to be deliberately employed to elude British colonial censors. In addition, attention should be drawn to the work of Russell Reising who, examining major works of American literature in several genres, argues that the formal imperative to conclude a work often clashes with the unresolvable ideological tensions that generated its central events. Verisimilitude is thus brought into collision with a genre's demands for closure.

We conclude that stories do not end naturally, that virtually all endings are arbitrary to some degree, and that the narrative they purport to resolve can always be extended further. As Louis O. Mink has observed: "Stories are not lived but told. Life has no beginnings, middles, or ends" (557). I do agree that a plausible, apparently conclusive ending that flows directly from the antecedent events is highly desirable for some genres in some periods, like tragedy, classical comedy, and realistic eighteenth-, mid-nineteenth, and early twentieth-century fiction; that is, works like *Tom Jones, Emma, Madame Bovary,* and *Anna Karenina* but excluding novelists like Sterne, Woolf, Rushdie, and authors of serial fiction (at least until its final installment). It is also the case that in some genres a conclusive ending is not possible (histories that stretch into the present and some of the fictions that are modeled on them). In other forms and periods, fixed endings are not particularly desired. Modernist narratives often favor a diptych ending in which the problems driving the events remain unresolved while the text provides a feeling of completion. The ending of the story is best viewed not as part of a binary opposition of open or closed, fixed or unfixed, but rather as part of a spectrum ranging from the fairly fixed through the hidden to the lax to the unwritten. Endings in hyperfiction provide additional options for ending, offering both multiple and possibly unaccessed denouements. We also note the peculiarities of the endings of unnatural narratives; they elude the conventional in a variety of ways. The most obvious are the rules governing real-life experience: the endings we see in these narratives can happen only in fiction. Parodic and circular endings return to their points of origin, though no originary equilibrium is restored in a traditional manner. The same can be said of the unusually serene endings of narratives with contradictory story lines.

As Marianna Torgovnick has suggested (108–9), an abrupt shift in setting or narrative pace, as at the end of Flaubert's *L'Éducation sentimentale* (1869), can produce a sense of closure. This is also true of an abrupt break with the type of narration, focalization, narrative style, or any other salient aspect of the narrative. In many of the unnatural endings discussed above, we see a similar move being made, although here it is the ontological frame that is being exploded; this is especially evident in metafictional and metadramatic conclusions. We have, once again, a vigorous sense of closure despite the unnatural passage leading up to such conclusions. In such cases, a fixed ending proves to be more resilient than many might expect, and it often seems to be employed in order to better frame the more sustained violations of traditional narrative orders elsewhere in the text. At the same time, the virtues of the fixed ending appear to be overstated, and alternative forms of ending undertheorized. As was discussed at some length in the previous chapter, we need to modify and expand the concept of the fabula in order to allow us to include fabulas with different kinds of unnatural endings. In addition, we need to attend to the performative aspect of enacted narratives and be able to include the moments where the story cannot be contained by its "natural" limits but rather bursts beyond its frame and into its performance.

CONCLUSION

Narrative Theory and the Poetics of Story and Plot

THE CONCEPTION of narrative that has animated this book is a dialectical one: constantly changing, evolving, playful, and recursive—cannibalizing adjacent discursive forms and interjecting itself into new formats. Narrating events is a dynamic activity that feeds off and alters itself; it builds on and strays from its earlier forms, negates and transforms existing genres and conventions, and creates new patterns and organizations. To represent fictional narratives accurately, we need a supple, flexible conceptual framework and correspondingly malleable models. Specifically, I argue for a dual, dialectical model that incorporates both mimetic narratives and the antimimetic narratives that partially negate them.

This book has stressed the distinctive nature of narrative fiction and has repeatedly documented antimimetic strategies in narrative that cannot be contained within a merely mimetic theory of narrative. I have titled this book *A Poetics of Plot for the Twenty-First Century: Theorizing Unruly Narratives* and have drawn many of my most compelling examples from postmodern and contemporary fiction since it is this narrative practice that is finally forcing the hand of narratology and insisting that its many distinctive—and distinctively fictional—achievements be acknowledged and theorized. And, of course, many of these practices do not begin with postmodernism but extend back to Aristophanes and Lucian, Rabelais and Cervantes, Denis Diderot and Oscar Wilde, Lewis Carroll and Gilbert and Sullivan.

I wish to emphasize that the point of this book is not simply to add some new categories to our concepts of narrative—though to be sure, many postmodern and contemporary strategies require some substantial additions to the existing narratological toolbox. More importantly, I hope to help alter a concept of narrative that is too deeply (and erroneously) rooted in a strict mimetic conception of narrative fiction. As noted throughout this book, narratologists often employ categorical formulations that may be plausible when applied to mimetic works but are simply false when unnatural narratives are taken into consideration.[1] These formulations serve to perpetuate the long-standing mimetic bias of narratology. Why would we want to limit ourselves to Genette's categories of temporality when there are so many other compelling ones to include? And why call them an account of narrative temporality when they are solely an account of the temporality of nonfictional and mimetic narratives?

It is evident that any theory of story, plot, and adjacent areas that is able to embrace the new worlds of postmodern narratives will have to be expansive. It will need a capacious, effective definition of narrative in order to accurately locate its boundaries and more accurately comprehend the work of daring writers who have played on one side or the other of those frontiers. I have been able to adjust and extend the most flexible existing definition, centered on causal connection, rather than formulate a new one. Nevertheless, since narrative is a highly pliable entity and numerous authors cannot resist exploring, extending, or transgressing those boundaries, I have also posited the complementary concept of the "quasi narrative" to designate a work that plays on those borders.

An expansive approach to narrative explores the ways that creative authors challenge, massage, or reconfigure the act of beginning—in the story, the text, and the antetext. Beginnings and endings turn out to be surprisingly arbitrary points in a narrative; they are always capable of being extended into the past or the future by additional narrative material. Beginnings can also carry much greater weight than is often suspected. Concerning plot, the model presented here calls for a generous conception of plot that is able to embrace a wide range of types of emplotment, in particular the unnatural kinds that feature parody, forking-path narratives, and contradictory events. It also calls for a more nuanced approach to both episodic and nonprobabilistic plots, along with a revaluation of classic conceptions of plot. Plot and tellability are much more historically variable than is often recognized; additional theoretical analysis would be beneficial for seemingly plotless works and other nar-

---

1. I critique a number of such statements in *Unnatural Narrative* (28–47).

ratives that challenge the standard parameters of plot. I have tried to indicate the range of non-plot-based strategies of ordering a text and show how these strategies can complement, parallel, impede, or contest the movement of plot proper in a narrative.

Concerning temporality, many recent texts require broader analytical categories that allow us to include references to historical time, construction of the time of reception, and the main varieties of unnatural or impossible temporal constructions, particularly the antimimetic categories of circular, antinomic, hypothetical, multiple, and contradictory. Many of these techniques, it turns out, also appear in a variety of narratives from several periods. Antimimetic temporal formations have major implications for story construction and invite a parallel expansion of our model of fabula to embrace the full range of postmodern practices, including multilinear, circular, multiple, contradictory, and denarrated fabulas. Similarly, the notion of syuzhet can now be expanded to include simultaneous, fixed syuzhet sequences ("The Turn of the Screw"); variable syuzhets, as in *The Unfortunates*; and multiple possible fixed syuzhets (*The Mixquiahuala Letters*). Contemporary narratives ask for a more comprehensive overview of endings that can incorporate the diversity of ending practices—fixed and unfixed, obvious and hidden, mimetic and antimimetic, narrated and enacted—and that gives appropriate attention to the multiple uses of endings in unnatural narratives. Above all, we need to recognize more fully the typically provisional, arbitrary, or ephemeral nature of endings.

Finally, we may directly address the question that many readers have raised concerning antimimetic fiction: why do writers insist on making works like these? There are several good answers to this query. Above all, creative writers like to innovate, and rather than do the same thing the same way over and over, they are repeatedly impelled to "make it new." Thus, they push plot into new directions, permutations, and transformations, going beyond what has been done before or, at times, beyond what has ever been conceived. It is an imaginative challenge that many writers cannot resist. Antimimetic practices may also be effectively used to contest typical, official, standard, or old-fashioned narrative practices and the sensibility they cater to. They attempt to undermine cultural and social master narratives in a most irreverent way; we see this especially in some of the more extreme texts from the 1960s and '70s. It is no coincidence that many writers with radical politics prefer to employ radical narrative constructions; even though there is no inherent connection between the two, there is often a psychological association between them.

Interestingly, mimetic reasons can also be employed to explain many experimental features, as authors reject conventional strategies of representation in order to more accurately reproduce their subject matter. If life is not shaped like a typical novel, then new forms need to be developed to attempt to represent it more accurately. This is essentially Woolf's argument for most of her innovative narrative forms. As Woolf also shows, although rather more indirectly, experimental narrative structures can point to the conventional and therefore dubious patterns that nonfictional narratives often assume. It can also be argued that postmodern existence is best modeled with a postmodern form; the older narrative strategies are no longer entirely adequate to convincingly depict contemporary experience. This opposition is the subject of Grace Paley's playful story, "A Conversation with My Father," in which the daughter insists on the freedom of open endings, abrupt character transformations, and unlimited narrative possibilities, against her father's insistence on the deterministic worldview he finds in nineteenth-century novels. She has always despised a traditional "plot, the absolute line between two points"; she feels instead that "everyone, real or invented, deserves the open destiny of life" (261–62).

There are a number of cognitive studies that attempt to explain the psychological value of the kind of mental operation provoked by extreme and unnatural narratives. Gilles Fauconnier and Mark Turner write that "people pretend, imitate, lie, fantasize, deceive, delude, consider alternatives, simulate, make models, and propose hypotheses. Our species has an extraordinary ability to operate mentally on the unreal, and this ability depends on our capacity for advanced conceptual integration" (37). More specifically, Reuven Tsur has identified what he suggests may be the psychological mechanism for processing discourse that eludes referential boundaries. In humans' response to poetry, adaptive devices are turned to an aesthetic end; in an unpredictable environment, readers of poetry find pleasure in the reassertion that their adaptive devices, when disrupted, function properly. Cognitive sociologist Paul DiMaggio similarly argues that difficult texts provoke what he calls "deliberative cognition," a natural cognitive ability that involves overriding "programmed modes of thought to think critically and reflexively." Such texts arouse a degree of heightened attention that arises when "existing schemata fail to account adequately for new stimuli" (271–72)" (see also Abbott, *Real* 5).[2] Engaging with unnatural narratives is good for your mind. I hope to see more research on the cognitive processing of unnatural narratives.

There may also be prominent aesthetic reasons for innovative narrative configurations, as authors deform or re-form their plots and progressions in order to better embody a dominant theme or trope. From Shakespeare to Vir-

---

2. Abbott expertly discusses this position at the beginning of his book. I borrow from his description of it above.

ginia Woolf, we see authors distort real-world laws in order to create thematically apposite aesthetic patterns, thereby showcasing, as it were, art's triumph over nature. We see this quite transparently in Robbe-Grillet's "La Chambre secrète," in which Newtonian space and time and the law of noncontradiction are violated to produce a narrative temporality in the form of a spiral. And finally, we can point to the Loki Principle and its often irresistible impulse to transgress the boundaries that others have established and, always in vain, attempted to enforce.

WORKS CITED

Aarseth, Espen. *Cybertext: Perspectives on Ergodic Literature*. Johns Hopkins UP, 1997.

Abbott, H. Porter. *The Cambridge Introduction to Narrative*. 2nd ed., Cambridge UP, 2008.

———. "Law, Agency, and Unnarratable Events." *Michigan State Law Review*, 2009, pp. 1–12.

———. *Real Mysteries: Narrative and the Unknowable*. Ohio State UP, 2014.

———. "What Do We Mean When We Say 'Narrative Literature?' Looking for Answers across Disciplinary Borders." *Style*, vol. 34, no. 1, 2001, pp. 260–73.

Abel, Elizabeth. "Narrative Structure(s) and Female Development: The Case of *Mrs. Dalloway*." *Virginia Woolf: A Collection of Critical Essays*. Edited by Margaret Homans, Prentice Hall, 1993.

Abish, Walter. *Alphabetical Africa*. New Directions, 1974.

Adams, Hazard. "Critical Constitution of the Literary Text: The Example of *Ulysses*." *New Literary History*, vol. 17, 1986, pp. 595–619.

———, editor. *Critical Theory since Plato*. Harcourt Brace Jovanovich, 1971.

Aichinger, Ilse. "Life Story in Retrospect." Translated by J. C. Alldridge. *Ilse Aichinger*, by J. C. Alldridge, Dufour, 1969.

———. *Werke*. Vol. 1. *Der Gefesselte. Erzählungen*, Fischer Verlag, 1991.

Alber, Jan, and Rüdiger Heinze, editors. *Unnatural Narratives – Unnatural Narratology*. de Gruyter, 2011.

Alber, Jan, and Brian Richardson, editors. *Unnatural Narratology: Extensions, Revisions, and Challenges*. Ohio State UP, forthcoming 2020.

Amis, Martin. *Time's Arrow*. Random House, 1992.

Aristophanes. *Four Plays by Aristophanes*. Translated by William Arrowsmith, New American Library, 1984.

Aristotle. "Poetics," *The Norton Anthology of Theory and Criticism*. 2nd ed. Edited by Vincent B. Leitch, Norton, 2010, pp. 88–15.

Atkinson, Kate. *Life after Life*. Little, Brown/Hachette, 2013.

Atwood, Margaret. "Happy Endings." *Good Bones and Simple Murders*, Doubleday, 2001, pp. 50–56.

Austen, Jane. *The Complete Novels of Jane Austen,* Vol. 2. Random House, 1950.

Auster, Paul. *The New York Trilogy.* Penguin, 1990.

Baker, Nicholson. *The Mezzanine.* Grove, 1988.

Bakhtin, Mikhail. *The Dialogical Imagination.* Translated by Caryl Emerson and Michael Holquist, U of Texas P, 1981.

Bal, Mieke. *Narratology: Introduction to the Study of Narrative.* 3rd ed., U of Toronto P, 2009.

Ballard, J. G. "The Index." *War Fever.* Farrar, Straus and Giroux, 1990, pp. 171–76.

———. "Notes towards a Mental Breakdown." *War Fever,* Farrar, Straus and Giroux, 1990, pp. 161–70.

Bancroft, Corinne. "The Braided Narrative," *Narrative* vol. 26, no. 3, 2018, pp. 262–81.

Baroni, Raphael. "Tellability." *Living Handbook.* Edited by Hühn, et al., Hamburg, lhn.uni-hamburg.de/article/tellability.

———. *Le tension narrative.* Seuil, 2007.

———. "(Un)natural Temporalities in Graphic Narratives." *Unnatural Narratology: Extensions, Revisions, and Challenges.* Edited by Alber and Richardson, Ohio State UP, forthcoming 2020.

Baroni, Raphael, and Françoise Revaz, editors. *Narrative Sequence in Contemporary Narratology.* Ohio State UP, 2016.

Barret, J. K., "Vacant Time in the *Faerie Queene.*" *ELH,* vol. 88, no. 1, 2014, pp. 1–28.

Barthes, Roland. *Image-Music-Text.* Translated by Stephen Heath, Hill and Wang, 1977.

———. "Introduction to the Structural Study of Narrative." *Image-Music-Text.* Translated by Stephen Heath, Hill and Wang, 1977, pp. 79–124.

Beauman, Nicola. *Morgan: A Biography of E. M. Forster.* Hodder and Stoughton, 1993.

Beckett, Samuel. *Collected Shorter Plays.* Grove, 1984.

———. *Endgame* and *Act without Words.* Grove, 1958.

———. *How It Is.* Grove, 1964.

———. *Molloy.* Les Éditions de Minuit, 1951.

———. "Ping." *The Complete Short Prose, 1929–1989,* Grove, 1995, pp. 193–96.

———. *Three Novels:* Molloy, Malone Dies, The Unnamable. Grove, 1965.

———. *Worstward Ho.* Grove, 1983.

Belknap, Robert L. *Plots.* Columbia UP, 2016.

Bharata. *Natyashastra.* Vol. 2. Translated by Manomohan Ghosh, Asiatic Society, Bibliotheca Indica, no. 272, 1961.

Black, Alethea. "You, On a Good Day." *One Story* #163, Maribeth Batcha, 2012.

Bode, Christoph, and Rainer Dietrich. *Future Narratives: Theory, Politics, and Media-Historical Moment.* de Gruyter, 2013.

Bordwell, David. "Film Futures." *SubStance,* vol. 31, no. 1, 2002, pp. 88–104.

Bordwell, David, and Kristin Thompson. *Film Art.* 3rd ed., McGraw-Hill, 1990.

Borges, Jorge Luis. *Collected Fictions.* Translated by Andrew Hurley, Penguin, 1998.

Boswell, James. *The Life of Samuel Johnson.* Penguin, 2008.

Boully, Jenny. "The Body." *The Next American Essay*. Edited by John D'Agata, Graywolf, 2003, pp. 435–66.

Bowen, Zack. "Joyce and the Epiphany Concept: A New Approach." *Journal of Modern Literature*, vol. 9, no. 1, 1981–82, pp. 103–14.

Boyle, T. Coraghessan. "The Extinction Tales." *Descent of Man*, Penguin, 1990, pp. 99–108.

Bradbury, Malcolm. 1976. "Composition." *Who Do You Think You Are? Stories and Parodies*, Penguin, 1993, pp. 119–46.

Brecht, Bertolt. *Two Plays*: The Good Woman of Setzuan *and* The Caucasian Chalk Circle. Translated by Eric Bentley. New American Library, 1983.

———. *Werke*. Vol. 6, Aufbau and Suhrkamp, 1988.

Bredehoft, Thomas A. "Comics Architecture, Multidimensionality, and Time: Chris Ware's *Jimmy Corrigan: The Smartest Kid on Earth*." *Modern Fiction Studies*, vol. 52, no. 4, 2006, pp. 869–90.

Bremond, Claude. "The Logic of Narrative Possibilities." *New Literary History*, vol. 11, 1980, pp. 387–411.

Brooks, Peter. *Reading for the Plot: Design and Intention in Narrative*. Random, 1984.

Brown, Marshall. "Plan vs. Plot: Chapter Symmetries and the Mission of Form." *Stanford Literature Review*, vol. 4, pp. 103–36.

Brown, Susan Sutliff. "The Mystery of the *Fuga per Canonem* Solved." *Joycean Unions: Post-Millennial Essays from East to West*. Edited by R. Brandon Kershner and Tekla Mecsnóber, Rodopi, 2013, pp. 173–94.

Buckton, Oliver. "'Mr. Betwixt-and-Between': The Politics of Narrative Indeterminacy in Stevenson's *Kidnapped* and *David Balfour*." *Narrative Beginnings*. Edited by Richardson, U of Nebraska P, 2008, pp. 228–45.

Burton, Stacy. "Rereading Faulkner: Authority, Criticism, and *The Sound and the Fury*." *Modern Philology*, vol. 98, 2001, pp. 604–28.

Byron, George Gordon, Lord. *The Poetical Works of Byron*. Houghton Mifflin, 1975.

———. *Selected Prose*. Edited by Peter Gunn, Penguin, 1972.

Calvino, Italo. *If on a winter's night a traveler*. Translated by William Weaver, Harcourt Brace Jovanovich, 1981.

Carrard, Philippe. "September 1939." *Narrative Beginnings*. Edited by Richardson, U of Nebraska P, 2008, pp. 63–78.

———. "Telling the Game: Baseball as an AP Report." *Journal of Narrative Theory*, vol. 18, no. 1, 1988, pp. 47–60.

———. "What If Pizarro Had Not Found Potatoes in Peru: Historigraphic Discourse and Counterfactuality." 2014 Conference of the International Society for the Study of Narrative, Cambridge MA, academia.edu.

Carroll, Noël. "Narrative Closure." *Philosophical Studies*, vol. 35, 2007, pp. 1–15.

———. "On the Narrative Connection." *New Perspectives on Narrative Perspective*. Edited by Willie van Peer and Seymour Chatman, SUNY UP, 2001, pp. 21–41.

Castillo, Ana. *The Mixquiahuala Letters*. Doubleday, 1992.

Chatman, Seymour. "Backwards." *Narrative*, vol. 17, no. 1, 2009, pp. 31–55.

———. *Story and Discourse: Narrative Structure in Fiction and Film*. Cornell UP, 1978.

Cheng, Vincent. *Joyce, Race, and Empire*. Cambridge UP, 1995.

Chiang, Ted. *Stories of Your Life and Others*. Random House, 2016.

Cohn, Dorrit. *The Distinction of Fiction*. Johns Hopkins UP, 1999.

Conrad, Joseph. *Collected Letters of Joseph Conrad*. Edited by Frederick Karl and Laurence Davies, Cambridge UP, 1983.

———. *Lord Jim*. Doubleday, Doran, 1921.

———. *Nostromo: A Tale of the Seaboard*. Doubleday, Doran, 1921.

Coover, Robert. "The Babysitter." *Pricksongs and Descants*, Penguin, 1970, pp. 206–39.

———. "Heart Suite." Narrative playing cards affixed in sleeve of *A Child Again*, McSweeney's, 2005.

Corneille, Pierre. "Of the Three Unities of Action, Time, and Place." *Critical Theory*. Edited by Adams, Harcourt Brace Jovanovich, 1971, pp. 219–26.

Corngold, Stanley, editor. "In the Circle of 'The Judgement.'" *Kafka's Selected Stories*. Translated by Stanley Corngold, Norton, pp. 221–34.

Crace, Jim. *Being Dead*. Farrar, Straus and Giroux, 1999.

Crowley, Mart. *Three Plays by Mart Crowley*. Alyson, 1996.

Cuddy-Keane, Melba. "Inside and Outside the Covers: Beginnings, Endings, and Woolf's Non-Coercive Ethical Texts." *Woolfian Boundaries*. Edited by Anna Burrells, et al., Clemson U Digital P, 2007, pp. 171–80.

Culler, Jonathan. "Fabula and Sjuzhet in the Analysis of Narrative: Some American Discussions." *Poetics Today*, vol. 1, no. 3, 1980, pp. 27–37.

Curry, Mark. *Postmodern Narrative Theory*. 2nd ed. New York: Palgrave Macmillan, 2011.

Dannenberg, Hilary P. *Coincidence and Counterfactuality: Plotting Space and Time in Narrative Fiction*. U of Nebraska P, 2008. 435–39.

———. "Plot." *Routledge Encyclopedia*. Edited by Herman, et al., Routledge, 2005, pp. 435–39.

Davenport, Guy. *Da Vinci's Bicycle*. New Directions, 1979.

DelConte, Matt. "Why *You* Can't Speak: Second Person Narration, Voice, and a New Model for Understanding Narrative." *Style*, vol. 37, no. 2, 2003, pp. 204–19.

DeLillo, Don. *Cosmopolis*. Scribner, 2004.

———. *White Noise*. Penguin, 1985.

Del Lungo, Andrea. "Pour une poétique de l'incipit." *Poétique*, vol. 94, 1993, pp. 131–52.

Dick, Philip K. *The Eye of the Sybil and Other Classic Stories*. Kensington, 1992.

Dickens, Charles. *Bleak House*. Norton, 1977.

DiMaggio, Paul. "Culture and Cognition." *Annual Review of Sociology*, vol. 23, 1997, pp. 263–85.

Dixon, Stephen. *Phone Rings*. Melville House, 2005.

Douglas, J. Yellowlees. "'How Do I Stop This Thing?': Closure and Indeterminacy in Interactive Narratives," *Hyper/Text/Theory*. Edited by George P. Landow, Johns Hopkins UP, 1994, pp. 159–88.

Douglas, Mary. *Thinking in Circles: An Essay on Ring Composition*. Yale UP, 2007.

Dryden, John. "An Essay of Dramatic Poesie." *Critical Theory*. Edited by Adams, Harcourt Brace Jovanovich, 1971, pp. 228–57.

Dubois, Jean-Paul. *Vie Française*. Translated by Linda Coverdale, Random, 2009.

Eggers, Dave. *A Heartbreaking Work of Staggering Genius*. Simon & Schuster, 2000.

Elam, Diane. "Postmodern Romance." *Postmodernism across the Ages*. Edited by Bill Readings and Bennet Schaber, Syracuse UP, 1993, pp. 216–31.

Eliot, George. *Daniel Deronda*. Blackwood 1878. Reprint Harper Brothers, 1960.

Eliot, T. S. 1932. *Essays on Elizabethan Drama*. Harcourt Brace and World, 1960.

Ellmann, Richard. *James Joyce*. Rev. ed., Oxford UP, 1982.

Ermarth, Elizabeth Deeds. *Sequel to History: Postmodernism and the Crisis of Representational Time*. Princeton UP, 1992.

Erpenbeck, Jenny. *The End of Days [Aller Tage Abend]*. Translated by Susan Bernofsky, New Directions, 2014.

Faas, Ekbert. *Tragedy and After: Euripides, Shakespeare, Goethe*. McGill-Queen's UP, 1986.

Fauconnier, Gilles, and Mark Turner. *The Way We Think: Conceptual Blending and the World's Hidden Complexities*. Basic Books, 2003.

Federman, Raymond. *Double or Nothing*. Swallow, 1971.

Felber, Lynette. *Gender and Genre in Novels without End: The British* Roman-Fleuve. U of Florida P, 1995.

Fernandez, Macedonio. *The Museum of Eterna's Novel (The First Good Novel)*. Translated by Margaret Schwartz. Open Letter, 2010.

Fielding, Henry. *Tom Jones*. 2nd ed., Norton, 1995.

Fiore, Robert L. *Lazarillo de Tormes*. Twayne, 1984.

Fisher, Caitlin. *These Waves of Girls,* yorku.ca/caitlin/waves.

Fludernik, Monika. "'Ithaca'—An Essay in Non-Narrativity." *International Perspectives on James Joyce*. Edited by Gottlieb Gaiser, Whitsun, 1986, pp. 88–105.

———. "Mediacy, Mediation, and Focalization: The Squaring of Terminological Circles." *Postclassical Narratology: Approaches and Analyses*. Edited by Jan Alber and Monika Fludernik, Ohio State UP, 2010, pp. 105–33.

———. *Towards a 'Natural' Narratology*. Routledge, 1996.

Foer, Jonathan Safran. *Incredibly Loud and Extremely Close*. Houghton Mifflin, 2005.

Ford, Ford Madox. 1905. *The Soul of London: A Survey of a Modern City*. Haskell House, 1972.

Forster, E. M. 1927. *Aspects of the Novel*. Harcourt, 1927.

———. Lecture, *Working Men's College Journal*, vol. 10, Jan.–Feb. 1907, pp. 9–10.

Fournel, Paul, and Jean-Pierre Énard. "The Theater Tree: A Combinatory Play," *Oulipo: A Primer of Potential Literature*. Translated and edited by Warren F. Motte Jr., U of Nebraska P, 1986, pp. 159–62.

Fowles, John. *The French Lieutenant's Woman*. Signet, 1970.

Frow, John. "The Literary Frame." *Narrative Dynamics*. Edited by Richardson, Ohio State UP, 2002, pp. 333–38.

Gallagher, Catherine. "Formalism and Time." *Modern Language Quarterly*, vol. 61, no. 1, 2000, pp. 229–51.

———. "Undoing." *Time and the Literary*. Edited by Karen Newman, Jay Clayton, and Marianne Hirsch, Routledge, 2002, pp. 11–29.

Garcha, Amanpal. *From Sketch to Novel: The Development of Victorian Fiction.* Cambridge UP, 2009.

Gay, John. *The Beggar's Opera. The Beggar's Opera and Other Eighteenth Century Plays.* Edited by John Hampden, Dutton, 1975.

Genette, Gérard. "The Boundaries of Narrative." *New Literary History,* vol. 8, 1976, pp. 1–13.

———. *Discours du récit.* Translated by Jane E. Lewin, Cornell UP, 1980.

———. *Narrative Discourse: An Essay in Method.* Translated by Jane E. Lewin, Cornell UP, 1980.

———. "Order, Duration, and Frequency." *Narrative Dynamics.* Edited by Richardson, Ohio State UP, 2002, pp. 25–34.

Geronimo. *Geronimo: His Own Story.* Edited by S. M. Barrett. Ballantine, 1971.

Gibbons, Alison. "Reading *S.* across Media: Transmedial Storyworlds, Multimodal Fiction, and Real Readers." *Narrative* vol. 25, no. 3, 2017, pp. 321–41.

Gibson, William. *Agrippa: Book of the Dead,* agrippa.english.ucsb.edu.

Gide, André. *The Counterfeiters.* Translated by Dorothy Bussy, Random, 1973.

Gioia, Ted. "The Rise of the Fragmented Novel." *Fractious Fiction,* fractiousfiction.com/rise_of _the_fragmented_novel.

Glattauer, Daniel. *Love Virtually.* Translated by Katharina Bielenberg and Jamie Bulloch, Silver Oak, 2007.

Gontarski, S. E. "Introduction: The Conjuring of Something Out of Nothing: Samuel Beckett's 'Closed Space' Novels." *Nohow On:* Company, Ill Seen Ill Said, Worstward Ho, by Samuel Beckett, Grove, vii–xxvii.

Goodhart, Sandor. "Oedipus and Laius' Many Murderers." *Diacritics,* vol. 7, 1978, pp. 55–71.

Goodman, Nelson. "The Telling and the Told." *On Narrative.* Edited by Mitchell, U of Chicago P, 1981, pp. 255–57.

Gray, Alasdair. *Lanark: A Life in Four Books.* Harvest, 1996.

Guo, Xiaolu. *A Concise Chinese-English Dictionary for Lovers.* Anchor, 2008.

Handler, Daniel. *Watch Your Mouth.* Ecco, 2002.

Hansen, Per Krogh. "Backmasked Messages: On the *Fabula* Construction in Episodically Reversed Narratives." *Unnatural Narratives –Unnatural Narratology.* Edited by Alber and Heinze, de Gruyter, 2011, pp. 162–85.

Hardy, Thomas. *The Return of the Native.* Norton, 2006.

Harshav [Hrushovski], Benjamin. *Segmentation and Motivation in the Text Continuum of Literary Prose: The First Episode of* War and Peace. Papers on Poetics and Semiotics No. 5, Tel Aviv University, 1976. Reprinted in *Poetics Today* 9.3, 1988, pp. 635–66.

Hawkes, John. "An Interview" *Wisconsin Studies in Contemporary Literature,* vol. 6, 1965, pp. 141–55.

Hawthorn, Jeremy. "Life Sentences: Linearity and Its Discontents in Joseph Conrad's *An Outcast of the Islands.*" *Joseph Conrad: Voice, Sequence, History, Genre.* Edited by Jakob Lothe, et al., Ohio State UP, 2008, pp. 83–99.

Hawthorne, Nathaniel. *The Scarlet Letter.* Norton, 1961.

Hayles, N. Katherine. "Combining Close and Distant Reading: Jonathan Safran Foer's *Tree of Codes* and the Aesthetic of Bookishness." *PMLA,* 2013, pp. 226–31.

Hayman, David. *Re-Forming the Narrative: Toward a Mechanics of Modernist Fiction*. Cornell UP, 1987.

Heinze, Rüdiger. "The Whirligig of Time: Toward a Poetics of Unnatural Temporality." *A Poetics of Unnatural Narrative*. Edited by Jan Alber, Henrik Slov Nielsen, and Brian Richardson, Ohio State UP, 2013, pp. 31–44.

Heise, Ursula. *Chronoschisms: Time, Narrative, and Postmodernism*. Cambridge UP, 1997.

Hejinian, Lyn. *The Language of Inquiry*, U of California P, 2000.

——. *My Life*. Green Integer, 2004.

Herman, David. *Basic Elements of Narrative*. Wiley-Blackwell, 2009.

——. "Limits of Order: Toward a Theory of Polychronic Narrative." *Narrative*, vol. 6, 1998, pp. 72–95.

——. *Story Logic*. U of Nebraska P, 2004.

Herman, David, Manfred Jahn, and Marie-Laurie Ryan, editors. *Routledge Encyclopedia of Narrative Theory*. Routledge, 2005.

Herman, David, James Phelan, Peter J. Rabinowitz, Brian Richardson, and Robyn Warhol. *Narrative Theory: Core Concepts and Critical Debates*. Ohio State UP, 2012.

Herman, Luc, and Bart Vervaeck. *Handbook of Narrative Analysis*. U of Nebraska P, 2005.

Hermann. Martin. "Hollywood Goes Computer Game: Narrative Remediation in the Time-Loop Quests *Groundhog Day* and *12:01*." *Unnatural Narratives – Unnatural Narratology*. Edited by Alber and Heinze, de Gruyter, 2011, pp. 145–61.

Higdon, David Leon. *Time and English Fiction*. Rowman and Littlefield, 1977.

Hogan, Patrick Colm. *Affective Narratology: The Emotional Structure of Stories*. U of Nebraska P, 2011.

——. "Stories, Wars, and Emotions: The Absoluteness of Narrative Beginnings." *Narrative Beginnings*. Edited by Richardson, U of Nebraska P, 2008, pp. 44–62.

Horace. "Ars Poetica." *The Norton Anthology of Theory and Criticism*. 2nd ed., Norton, 2010, pp. 122–33.

Horn, Richard. *Encyclopedia: A Novel*. Grove, 1969.

Hühn, Peter. "The Eventfulness of Non-Events." *Narrative Sequence*. Edited by Baroni and Revaz, Ohio State UP, 2016, pp. 37–50.

Hühn, Peter, et al., editors. *The Living Handbook of Narratology*. Hamburg UP, lhn.uni-hamburg.de/.

Hutcheon, Linda. *A Poetics of Postmodernism: History, Theory, Fiction*. Routledge, 1988.

Hyvärinen, Matti. "Prototypes, Genres, and Concepts: Travelling with Narratives." *Narrative Works*, vol. 2, no. 1, 2012, pp. 10–32.

Irving, Dan. "Eighteen Hours of Salmon: On the Narrativity of Slow TV." *Frontiers of Narrative Studies*, vol. 3, no. 2, 2017, pp. 238–55.

Jackson, Shelley. "Ineradicable Stain," ineradicablestain.com/skin-faqs.html.

Jahn, Manfred. "Narrative Voice and Agency in Drama: Aspects of a Narratology of Drama." *New Literary History*, vol. 32, no. 3, 2001, pp. 659–80.

James, Henry. *Henry James: Theory of Fiction*. Edited by James E. Miller, U of Nebraska P, 1972.

Jensen, Ejner. *Shakespeare and the Ends of Comedy*. Indiana UP, 1991.

Johnson, B. S. *The Unfortunates*. New Directions, 2009.

Joyce, James. "The Dead." *Dubliners*, Viking, 1961, pp. 175–224.

——. *Ulysses: The Corrected Text*. Edited by Hans Walter Gabler, Random House, 1986.

Joyce, Michael. *afternoon, a story*. Hypertext, Eastgate Systems, Inc., 1990.

Kafalenos, Emma. *Narrative Causalities*. Ohio State UP, 2006.

——. "Toward a Typology of Indeterminacy in Postmodern Narrative." *Comparative Literature*, vol. 44, 1992, pp. 380–408.

Keen, Suzanne. *Narrative Form*. 2nd ed., Palgrave, 2015.

Kellman, Stephen. "Grand Openings and Plain: On the Poetics of Opening Lines." *Sub-Stance*, vol. 17, 1977, pp. 139–47.

Kenner, Hugh. *Ulysses*. 2nd ed., Johns Hopkins UP, 1987.

Keymer, Tom. "Reading Time in Serial Fiction before Dickens." *Yearbook of English Studies*, vol. 30, 2000, pp. 34–45.

Kieślowski, Krzysztof. *Blind Chance* [film]. 1987.

Killeen, Terence. *Ulysses Unbound*. 3rd ed., U of Florida P, 2014.

Konstantinou Lee. "Xu Bing's Big Village." Forthcoming.

Korte, Barbara. *Techniken der Schlußgebung im Roman: Eine Untersuchung englisch- und deutschsprachiger Romane*. Peter Lang, 1985.

Kozloff, Sarah. *Invisible Storytellers: Voice-Over Narration in American Fiction and Film*. U of California P, 1988.

Laccetti, Jessica. "Where to Begin? Multiple Narrative Paths in Web Fiction." *Narrative Beginnings*. Edited by Richardson, U of Nebraska P, 2008, pp. 179–90.

Lambrou, Marina. "*La La Land*: Counterfactuality, Disnarration and the Forked (Motorway) Path." *Rethinking Language, Text and Context: Interdisciplinary Research in Stylistics in Honour of Michael Toolan*. Edited by R. Page, B. Busse, and N. Nørgaard, Routledge, 2019.

LaSalle, Peter. *Tell Borges if You See Him: Tales of Contemporary Somnambulism*. U of Georgia P, 2007.

Leander, Niels Buch. *The Sense of a Beginning: Theory of the Literary Opening*. Museum Tusculanum Press, 2018.

Lee, Hermione. *Virginia Woolf*. Random, 1999.

Leitch, Thomas B. *What Stories Are: Narrative Theory and Interpretation*. Pennsylvania State UP, 1986.

Lessing, Gotthold Ephraim. *Hamburg Dramaturgy*. Translated by Helen Zimmern, Reprint, Dover, 1962.

Letzler, David. *The Cruft of Fiction: Mega-Novels and the Science of Paying Attention*. U of Nebraska P, 2017.

Levin, Richard. *The Multiple Plot in English Renaissance Drama*. U of Chicago P, 1971.

Levine, Caroline. *The Serious Pleasures of Suspense: Victorian Realism and Narrative Doubt*. U of Virginia P, 2003.

Levine, Caroline, and Mario Ortiz-Robles, editors. *Narrative Middles: Navigating the Nineteenth-Century British Novel*. Ohio State UP, 2011.

Levithan, David. *The Lover's Dictionary: A Novel*. Picador, 2007.

Lispector, Clarice. "The Fifth Story." *The Foreign Legion*. Translated by Giovanni Pontiero, New Directions, 1992, pp. 75–77.

Manon, Hugh S. "Resolution, Truncation, Glitch." *Cinematic Cuts: Theorizing Film Endings*. Edited by Sheila Kunkle, SUNY Press, 2016, pp. 19–38.

Markson, David. *This Is Not a Novel*. Counterpoint, 2001.

Martin, Timothy. "*Ulysses* as a Whole." *A Collideorscape of Joyce*. Edited by Ruth Frehner and Ursula Zeller, Lilliput, 1998, pp. 202–14.

Martin, Wallace. *Recent Theories of Narrative*. Cornell UP, 1986.

Mathews, Harry. "Country Cooking from Central France: Roast Boned Rolled Stuffed Shoulder of Lamb (*Farcie double*)." *The Way Home: Selected Longer Prose*, Atlas, 1999, pp. 9–25.

Matz, Jesse. "*Maurice* in Time." *Style*, vol. 34, 2000, pp. 188–211.

McHale, Brian. *Constructing Postmodernism*. London: Routledge, 1992.

———. *Postmodernist Fiction*. Methuen, 1987.

———. "Weak Narrativity: The Case of Avant-Garde Narrative Poetry." *Narrative*, vol. 9, 2001, pp. 161–67.

McInerney, Jay. *Bright Lights, Big City*. Random, 1984.

Mendilow, A. A. *Time and the Novel*. Humanities Press, 1965.

Michener, James A. *Hawaii*. Fawcett Crest, 1959.

Miller, D. A. *Narrative and Its Discontents: Problems of Closure in the Traditional Novel*. Princeton UP, 1981.

Miller, J. Hillis, *Reading Narrative*. U of Oklahoma P, 1998.

Mink, Louis O. "History and Fiction as Modes of Comprehension." *New Literary History*, vol. 1, 1970, pp. 541–58.

Mitchell, W. J. T., editor. *On Narrative*. U of Chicago P, 1981.

Moody, Rick. *The Ring of Brightest Angels around Heaven: A Novella and Stories*. Little, Brown, 1994.

Moore, Lorrie. *Self-Help*. Reprint, Random House, 2007.

Moraru, Christian. *Memorious Discourse: Reprise and Representation in Postmodernism*. Farleigh Dickinson UP, 2005, pp. 40–53.

Morhange, Jean-Louis. "Incipit Narratifs." *Poetique*, vol. 104, 1995, pp. 387–410.

Mortimer, Armine Kotine "Connecting Links: Beginnings and Endings." *Narrative Beginnings*. Edited by Richardson, U of Nebraska P, 2008, pp. 213–27.

———. "Romantic Fever: The Second Story as Illegitimate Daughter in Wharton's 'Roman Fever.'" *Narrative*, vol. 6, no. 2, 1998, pp. 188–98.

Nabokov, Vladimir. *The Annotated Lolita*. Edited by Alfred Appel Jr., McGraw-Hill, 1970.

———. "The Circle." *The Stories of Vladimir Nabokov*, Random House, 1995, pp. 375–84.

———. *Look at the Harlequins!* McGraw-Hill, 1974.

———. *Nikolai Gogol*. New Directions, 1961.

———. *Pale Fire*. Putnam, 1980.

Narayan, Gaura. "Lost Beginnings in Salman Rushdie's *Midnight's Children*." *Narrative Beginnings*. Edited by Richardson, U of Nebraska P, 2008, pp. 37–48.

Nelson, Roy Jay. *Causality and Narrative in French Fiction from Zola to Robbe-Grillet.* Ohio State UP, 1990.

Nichols, David. *One Day.* Random House, 2010.

Nietzsche, Friedrich. *Will to Power.* Translated by Walter Kaufmann, Random House, 1968.

Nuttall, A. D. *Openings: Narrative Beginnings from the Epic to the Novel.* Oxford UP, 1992.

O'Donnell, Thomas D. "Thematic Generation in Robbe-Grillet's *Projet pour une révolution à New York.*" *Twentieth Century French Fiction: Essays for Germaine Brée.* Edited by George Stambolian, 1975, Rutgers UP, 184–97.

Onega, Susana, and José Angel García Landa. *Narratology: An Introduction.* Pearson, 1996.

O'Neill, Patrick. *The Fictions of Discourse: Reading Narrative Theory.* U of Toronto P, 1994.

Orr, Leonard. *Problems and Poetics of the Nonaristotelian Novel.* Bucknell UP, 1991.

Ott, Eirik R. "Receipt Found in Parking Lot of the Super Walmart." *Greatest Hits: Poems to Read out Loud,* Sanctum Sanctorum, 2007, p. 45.

Oz, Amos. *The Story Begins: Essays on Literature.* Translated by Maggie Bar-Tura, Harcourt Brace, 1999.

Paley, Grace. "A Conversation with My Father." *Enormous Changes at the Last Minute,* Farrar, Strauss and Giroux, 1974.

Pavić, Milorad. *Landscape Painted with Tea.* Translated by Christina Pribićević-Zorić, Random, 1990.

Peake, C. H. 1967. *James Joyce: The Citizen and the Artist.* Stanford UP, 1977.

Pearson, John H. "The Politics of Framing in the Late Nineteenth Century." *Mosaic,* vol. 23, 1990, pp. 15–30.

Peterson, R. G. "Critical Calculations: Measure and Symmetry in Literature." *PMLA,* vol. 91, 1976, pp. 367–75.

Pettersson, Bo. "What Happens When Nothing Happens? Interpreting Narrative Technique in the Plotless Novels of Nicholson Baker." *Narrative Interrupted: The Plotless, the Disturbing and the Trivial in Literature.* Edited by Markku Lehtimäki, et al., de Gruyter, 2012, pp. 42–56.

Pfall, Courtney A. "Shuffling the *Sjuzhet* in Marc Saporta's *Composition No. 1.*" *Critique: A Journal of Contemporary Fiction,* vol. 56, no. 3, 2015, pp. 330–43.

Pfister, Manfred. *Theory and Analysis of Drama.* Translated by John Halliday, Cambridge UP, 1991.

Phelan, James. "Authors, Resources, Audiences: Toward a Rhetorical Poetics of Narrative." *Style,* vol. 52, no. 1–2, 2018, pp. 1–34.

———. "The Beginning of *Beloved*: A Rhetorical Approach." *Narrative Beginnings.* Edited by Richardson, U of Nebraska P, 2008, pp. 195–212.

———. *Experiencing Fiction: Judgments. Progressions, and the Rhetorical Theory of Narrative.* Ohio State UP, 2007.

———. *Living to Tell about It: A Rhetoric and Ethics of Character Narration.* Cornell UP, 2005.

———. "Present Tense Narration, Mimesis, the Narrative Norm, and the Positioning of the Reader in *Waiting for the Barbarians.*" *Understanding Narrative.* Edited by James Phelan and Peter Rabinowitz, Ohio State UP, 1994, pp. 222–45.

———. "Privileged Authorial Disclosure about Events: Wolff's 'Bullet in the Brain' and O'Hara's 'Appearances.'" *Narrative Sequence.* Edited by Baroni and Revaz, Ohio State UP, 2016, pp.51–70.

———. *Reading People, Reading Plots: Character, Progression, and the Interpretation of Narrative.* U of Chicago P, 1989.

Phelan, James, and Peter J. Rabinowitz, editors. *A Companion to Narrative Theory*, Blackwell, 2005.

Phillips, Caryl. *Crossing the River.* Random House, 1993.

Pier, John, and José Ángel García Landa, editors. *Theorizing Narrativity.* de Gruyter, 2008, pp. 277–306.

Prince, Gerald. *Dictionary of Narratology.* 2nd ed., U of Nebraska P, 2003.

———. "The Disnarrated." *Style,* vol. 22, 1988, pp. 1–8.

———. "Narrativehood, Narrativeness, Narrativity, Narratibility." *Theorizing Narrativity.* Edited by Pier and García Landa, de Gruyter, 2008, pp. 19–28.

———. "Narrativity." *Routledge Encyclopedia.* Edited by Herman, et al., Routledge, 2005, pp. 387–88.

———. *Narratology: The Form and Functioning of Narrative.* Mouton, 1982.

Prose, Francine. "Review of *Life after Life* by Kate Atkinson." *New York Times,* 26 April 2013, p. BR 15.

Punday, Daniel. "UI Time and the Digital Event." *The Edinburgh Companion to Contemporary Narrative Theories.* Edited by Zara Dinnen and Robyn Warhol, Edinburgh UP, 2018, pp. 202–12.

Queneau, Raymond. *The Bark Tree.* Translated by Barbara Wright, New Directions, 1971.

———. "A Story as You Like It." Translated by Warren F. Motte Jr., thing.de/projekte/7:9%23/queneau_1.html.

Rabinowitz, Peter J. *Before Reading: Narrative Conventions and the Politics of Interpretation.* Cornell UP, 1987.

———. "'They Shoot Tigers, Don't They?': Path and Counterpoint in *The Long Goodbye*." *Companion.* Edited by Phelan and Rabinowitz, Blackwell, 2005, pp. 181–91.

Rader, Ralph. 1973. "Defoe, Richardson, Joyce, and the Concept of Form in the Novel." *Fact, Fiction, and Form: Selected Essays,* Ohio State UP, 2011, pp. 172–99.

Reising, Russell. *Loose Ends: Closure and Crisis in the American Social Text.* Duke UP, 1996.

Ricardou, Jean. "Naissance d'une fiction." *Nouveau roman: hier, aujourd'hui.* Vol. 2. *Practiques.* Edited by Jean Ricardou and Françoise van Rossum-Guyon, 10 18 Press, 1972, pp. 379–92.

———. *La Prise de Constantinople.* Minuit, 1965.

———. *Problèmes du nouveau roman.* Seuil, 1967.

Richardson, Brian. "Causality in *Molloy*: Philosophic Theme, Narrative Transgression, and Metafictional Paradox." *Style,* vol. 26, 1992, pp. 66–78.

———. "Endings in Drama and Performance: A Theoretical Model." *Current Trends in Narratology.* Edited by Greta Olson, de Gruyter, 2011, pp. 181–99.

———. "Genre, Transgression, and the Struggle for (Self) Representation in U.S. Ethnic Drama." *The Journal of American Drama and Theatre,* vol. 9, 1996, pp. 1–18.

———. "Linearity and Its Discontents: Rethinking Narrative Form and Ideological Valence." *College English,* vol. 62, 2000, pp. 685–95.

———. "Modern Fiction, the Poetics of Lists, and the Boundaries of Narrative," *Style,* vol. 50, 2016, pp. 327–41.

———. "Nabokov's Experiments and the Question of Fictionality." *Storyworlds*, vol. 3, 2011, pp. 73–92.

———, editor. *Narrative Beginnings: Theories and Practices*. U of Nebraska P, 2009.

———, editor. *Narrative Dynamics: Essays on Time, Plot, Closure, and Frames*. Ohio State UP, 2002.

———. "Negotiating Closure in *Victory* and Postcolonial Rewritings of *The Tempest*." *Conradiana*, 39.2-3, forthcoming.

———. "'Time Is Out of Joint': Narrative Models and the Temporality of the Drama." *Poetics Today*, vol. 8, 1987, pp. 299–309.

———. *Unnatural Narrative: Theory, History, and Practice*. Ohio State UP, 2015.

———. *Unnatural Voices: Extreme Narration in Modern and Contemporary Fiction*. Ohio State UP, 2006.

———. "Voice and Narration in Postmodern Drama." *New Literary History*, vol. 32, 2001, pp. 681–94.

———. "Words Made Flesh: Imagery as Causality in the Drama." *Within the Dramatic Spectrum*. Edited by Karelisa Hartigan, UP of America, 1986, pp. 160–67.

Richardson, Dorothy. *Journey to Paradise: Short Stories and Autobiographical Sketches*. Virago, 1989.

Richter, David. *Fable's End: Completeness and Closure in Rhetorical Fiction*. U of Chicago P, 1974.

Ricoeur, Paul. "Narrative Time." *On Narrative*. Edited by Mitchell, U of Chicago P, 1981, pp. 165–86.

———. *Time and Narrative*. Vol. 2. Translated by Kathleen McGlaughlin and David Pellauer, U of Chicago P, 1985.

Rimmon-Kenan, Shlomith. *Narrative Fiction: Contemporary Poetics*. Methuen, 1983.

Robbe-Grillet, Alain. "Le Chambre secrète" [The Secret Room]. *Snapshots*. Translated by Bruce Morrissette, Grove, 1968, pp. 63–72.

———. *For a New Novel*. Translated by Richard Howard, Grove, 1965.

———. "Order and Disorder in Film and Fiction." *Critical Inquiry*, vol. 4, 1977, pp. 1–20.

———. *Two Novels by Alain Robbe-Grillet:* Jealousy *and* In the Labyrinth. Translated by Richard Howard, Grove, 1965.

Robinson, Mark C. *The Other American Drama*. Johns Hopkins UP, 1997.

Robinson, Michael. *The Long Sonata of the Dead: A Study of Samuel Beckett*. Grove, 1969.

Rohy, Valerie. *Lost Causes: Narrative, Etiology, and Queer Theory*. Oxford UP, 2015.

Romagnolo, Catherine. *Opening Acts: Narrative Beginnings in Twentieth-Century Feminist Fiction*. U of Nebraska P, 2015.

Ronen, Ruth. "Description, Narrative and Representation." *Narrative*, vol. 5, no. 3, 1997, pp. 274–86.

———. *Possible Worlds and Narrative Theory*. Cambridge UP, 1994.

Rossholm, Göran. "Narrative as Story Representation." *Disputable Core Concepts of Narratology*. Edited by Göran Rossholm and Christer Johansson, Peter Lang, 2012, pp. 183–200.

Rushdie, Salman. *Midnight's Children*. Random, 1991.

Ryan, Marie-Laure. *Avatars of Story*. U of Minnesota P, 2006.

———. "Cheap Plot Tricks, Plot Holes, and Narrative Design." *Narrative,* vol. 17, no. 1, 2009, pp. 56–74.

———. "Narrative." *Routledge Encyclopedia.* Edited by Herman, et al., Routledge, 2005, pp. 344–48.

———. *Narrative as Virtual Reality: Immersion and Interactivity in Literature and Electronic Media.* Johns Hopkins UP, 2003.

———. *Possible Worlds, Artificial Intelligence, and Narrative Theory.* Indiana UP, 1991.

———. "Tellability." *Routledge Encyclopedia.* Edited by Herman, et al., Routledge, 2005, pp. 589–91.

———. "Temporal Paradoxes in Narrative." *Style,* vol. 43, no. 2, 2009, pp. 142–64.

———. "Sequence, Linearity, Spatiality, or: Why Be Afraid of Fixed Order?" *Narrative Sequence.* Edited by Baroni and Revaz, Ohio State UP, 2016, pp. 176–94.

Ryding, William R. *Structure in Medieval Narrative.* Mouton, 1971.

Sacks, Sheldon. *Fiction and the Shape of Belief.* U of California P, 1964.

Said, Edward. *Beginnings: Intention and Method.* Columbia UP, 1985.

Saporta, Marc. *Composition No. 1.* Translated by Richard Howard, Simon & Schuster, 1963.

Sartre, Jean-Paul. *La nausée.* Gallimard, 1938.

———. *Nausea.* Translated by Lloyd Alexander. New Directions, 1964.

Schechner, Richard. "There's Lots of Time in *Godot.*" *Aspects of Time.* Edited by C. S. Patrides, U of Toronto P, 1976, pp. 217–24.

Schmid, Wolf. *Narratology: An Introduction.* de Gruyter, 2010.

Schwarz, Daniel R. *Conrad: The Later Fiction.* Macmillan, 1982.

See, Sam. "Fast Books Read Slow: The Shapes of Speed in *Manhattan Transfer* and *The Sun Also Rises.*" *Journal of Narrative Theory,* vol. 38, no. 3, 2008, pp. 342–77.

Segal, Eyal. "Ending Twice Over (or More): Alternate Endings in Narrative." *Narrative Sequence.* Edited by Baroni and Revaz, Ohio State UP, 2016.

Shakespeare, William. *The Complete Works.* 5th ed. Edited by David Bevington, Pearson Longman, 2004.

Shen, Dan. *Style and Rhetoric of Short Narrative Fiction: Covert Progressions behind Overt Plots.* Routledge, 2014.

Sherzer, Dina. *Representation in Contemporary French Fiction.* U of Nebraska P, 1986.

Shields, David. "Life Story." *Remote: Reflections on Life in the Shadow of Celebrity,* U of Wisconsin P, 2003, pp. 15–17.

Shklovsky, Viktor. "The Novel as Parody: Sterne's *Tristram Shandy.*" *Theory of Prose.* Translated by Benjamin Sher, Dalkey Archive Press, 1990, pp. 147–70.

———. "The Relationship between Devices of Plot Construction and General Devices of Style." *Theory of Prose.* Translated by Benjamin Sher, Dalkey Archive Press, 1990, pp. 15–51.

Singal, R. L. *Aristotle and Bharata: A Comparative Study of Their Theories of Drama.* Vishveshvaranand Vedic Research Institute Press, 1977.

Smith, Ali. *How to Be Both.* Pantheon, 2014.

Smith, Barbara Herrnstein. *Poetic Closure: A Study of How Poems End.* U of Chicago P, 1968.

Sommer, Roy. "Unnatural Fallacy? The Logic of Unnatural Narrative Theory." *Style*, vol. 50, no. 4, 2016, pp. 405–9.

———. "The (Un)Natural Response: Reading Walter Abish's *Alphabetical Africa*." *Unnatural Narratology: Extensions, Revisions, and Challenges*. Edited by Alber and Richardson, Ohio State UP, forthcoming 2020.

Stein, Gertrude. 1922. *Geography and Plays*. U of Wisconsin P, 1993.

———. *Lectures in America*, Beacon, 1993.

Stein, Nancy L., and Margaret Policastro. "The Concept of a Story: A Comparison between Children's and Teachers' Viewpoints." *Learning and Comprehension of Text*. Edited by Heinz Mandel, et al., Erlbaum, 1984, pp. 113–55.

Sternberg, Meir. *Expositional Modes and Temporal Ordering in Fiction*. Johns Hopkins UP, 1978.

———. "Narrativity: From Objectivist to Functional Paradigm." *Poetics Today*, vol. 31, no. 3, 2010, pp. 507–659.

———. "Reconceptualizing Narratology: Arguments for a Functionalist and Constructivist Approach to Narrative." *Enthymema*, vol. 4, 2011, pp. 35–50.

———. "Telling in Time II: Chronology, Teleology, Narrativity." *Poetics Today*, vol. 13, no. 3, 1992, pp. 463–541.

Sterritt, David. *The Films of Jean-Luc Godard: Seeing the Invisible*. Cambridge UP, 1999.

Sue, Eugène. *Les Mystères de Paris* [*The Mysteries of Paris*]. 1842–43. Translated by Carolyn Betensky, foreword by Peter Brooks, pp. xiii–xv. Penguin, 2015.

Sutherland, John. "Clarissa's Invisible Taxi." *Can Jane Eyre Be Happy? More Puzzles in Classic Fiction*. Oxford UP, 1997, pp. 215–24.

———. *How to Read a Novel: A User's Guide*. St. Martin's, 2006.

Tammi, Pekka. "Against Narrative ('A Boring Story')." *Partial Answers*, vol. 4, no. 2, 2006, pp. 19–40.

Todorov, Tzvetan. *Introduction to Poetics*. Translated by Richard Howard, U of Minnesota P, 1981.

Toker, Leona. *Nabokov: The Mystery of Literary Structures*. Cornell UP, 1989.

———. *Towards an Ethics of Form in Fiction*. Ohio State UP, 2010.

Tomashevsky, Boris. "Thematics." *Russian Formalist Criticism: Four Essays*. Edited and translated by Lee T. Lemon and Marion J. Reis, U of Nebraska P, 1965, pp. 61–95.

Torgovnick, Marianna. *Closure in the Novel*. Princeton UP, 1981.

Toscana, David. *The Last Reader* [*El Ultimo lector*]. Translated by Asa Zatz, Texas Tech UP, 2009.

Tykwer, Tom. *Lola rennt* [film]. 1998.

Tyrkkö, Jukka. "'Kaleidoscope' Novels and the Act of Reading." *Theorizing Narrativity*. Edited by Pier and García Landa, de Gruyter, 2008, pp. 277–306.

Updike, John. *Problems and Other Stories*. Knopf, 1979.

Vishakhadatta. *Rakshasa's Ring*. *Three Sanskrit Plays*. Edited and translated by Michael Coulson, Penguin, 1981, pp. 171–294.

von Contzen, Eva. "'Both Close and Distant': Experiments of Form and the Medieval in Contemporary Literature." *Frontiers of Narrative Study*, vol. 3, no. 2, 2017, pp. 289–303.

Walsh, Richard. *The Rhetoric of Fictionality: Narrative Theory and the Idea of Fiction*. Ohio State UP, 2007.

Ware, Chris. *Building Stories*. 2nd ed., Pantheon, 2012.

Warhol, Robyn. *Having a Good Cry: Effeminate Feelings and Pop Culture Forms*. Ohio State UP, 2003.

———. "Neonarrative; or How to Render the Unnaratable in Realist Fiction and Contemporary Film." *Companion*. Edited by Phelan and Rabinowitz, Blackwell, 2005, pp. 220–31.

Warren, Robert Penn. *All the King's Men*. Harcourt Brace, 1949.

Welles, Orson with Oja Koder. *The Big Brass Ring: An Original Screenplay*. Santa Theresa Press, 1987.

Whalen, Tim. "Run Lola Run." *Film Quarterly*, vol. 53, no. 3, 2000, pp. 33–40.

White, Hayden. "The Value of Narrativity in the Representation of Reality." *On Narrative*. Edited by Mitchell, U of Chicago P, 1981, pp. 1–23.

Wilde, Oscar. *The Importance of Being Earnest*. Norton, 2006.

Wilson, R. Rawdon. "Time." *The Spenser Encyclopedia*. Edited by A. C. Hamilton, U of Toronto P, 1990.

Winnett, Susan. "Coming Unstrung: Women, Men, Narrative, and Principles of Pleasure." *Narrative Dynamics*. Edited by Richardson, Ohio State UP, 2002, pp. 138–58.

Winterson, Jeanette. "The Poetics of Sex." *Granta*, vol. 43, 1993, pp. 309–20.

Wolf, Werner. "Defamiliarized Initial Framings in Fiction." *Framing Borders in Literature and Other Media*. Edited by Werner Wolf and Walter Bernhart, Rodopi, 2006.

Wolff, Tobias. *Our Story Begins: New and Selected Stories*. Knopf, 2008.

Woolf, Virginia. *Between the Acts*. 1941. Harcourt, 1970.

———. *The Common Reader: First Series*. Harcourt, 1983.

———. *Night and Day*. 1919. Harcourt, 1977.

———. *Orlando: A Biography*. 1928. Harcourt, 1973.

———. "The Reader." Brenda R. Silver, "'Anon' and 'The Reader': Virginia Woolf's Last Essays." *Twentieth Century Literature*, vol. 25, 1979, pp. 356–441.

———. *To the Lighthouse*. 1925. Harcourt, 1989.

———. *Women and Writing*. Harcourt, 1980, pp. 188–91.

Xue, Can. *Blue Light in the Sky and Other Stories*. Translated by Karen Gernant and Chen Zeping. New Directions, 2006.

Yacobi, Tamar. "Time Denatured into Meaning: New Worlds and Renewed Themes in the Poetry of Dan Pagis." *Style*, vol. 22, 1988, 93–115.

Young, Kay. "'That Fabric of Times': A Response to David Bordwell's 'Film Futures.'" *Sub-Stance*, vol. 97, no. 31.1, 2002, pp. 115–18.

INDEX

Aarseth, Espen, 137
Abbott, H. Porter, 20, 21n11, 32, 33–34, 53, 58, 82, 106, 132, 172
Abel, Elizabeth, 80
Abish, Walter, *Alphabetical Africa*, 92
Abrams, J. M. and Doug Dorst, *S*, 145
Adams, Hazard, 95
Aeschylus, *Libation Bearers*, 59
aesthetic effects and orderings, 97, 163–64
Aichinger, Ilse, "Spiegelgeschichte," 105–6
Alfau, Felipe, "A Character," 160
Alvarez, Julia, 135
Amis, Martin, *Time's Arrow*, 106–7
antetext, authorial, 48–51
antetext, institutional, 52–53
antimimetic narrative and strategies, 2–5, 23–24, 48, 50–51, 53–56, 69–77, 90–94, 103–12, 114–16, 122–23, 129–33, 158–63, 171–72
Aristophanes, 165; *The Frogs*, 71–72; *The Peace*, 125; *Thesmophoriazusae*, 59, 70, 154
Aristotle, 14, 39, 46, 57, 59–62, 116, 139, 150, 152, 163, 164, 165
Armah, Ayi Kwei, *Two Thousand Seasons*, 31
Atkinson, Kate, *Life after Life*, 73–77, 163
Atwood, Margaret, "Happy Endings," 164–65

Austen, Jane, *Emma*, 63; *Northanger Abbey*, 120, 157; *Pride and Prejudice*, 153
Auster, Paul, *City of Glass*, 115
Avary, Roger, *Rules of Attraction*, 140

Baker, Nicholson, *The Mezzanine*, 69
Bakhtin, Mikhail, 71, 111, 124–25
Bal, Mieke, 17, 19n8, 45, 115, 129–30, 135
Ballard, J. G., "The Index," 138–39; "Notes towards a Mental Breakdown," 139
Bancroft, Corinne, 66
Baraka, Amiri, "Slave Ship," 31, 161
Baroni, Raphael, 7, 78, 118n15, 142
Barret, J. K., 111
Barth, John, "Frame-Tale," 104
Barthes, Roland, 6, 15, 47, 92, 138
Beaumarchais, Pierre, 152
Beckett, Samuel, 38, 53–54, 57, 96, 119, 153; *Endgame*, 53, 72–73; *Fizzles*, 53–54; *How It Is*, 64; "Lessness," 95; *Malone Dies*, 55; *Molloy*, 29, 54–56, 112; *Murphy*, 46; "Ping," 22–23, 69; "Play," 48, 104; *The Unnamable*, 56; *Waiting for Godot*, 35; *Worstward Ho*, 53, 133
beginnings, 37–58; of authorial antetext, 48–51; of fabula, 44–48; of institutional antetext, 51–53; of syuzhet, 43–44;
Belknap, Robert L., 166

Bell, Vanessa, 52
Beowulf, 87
Bharata, 40, 59–60, 150
Bierce, Ambrose, "An Occurrence at Owl Creek Bridge," 114
Big Poppa E, "Receipt Found in the Parking Lot of the Super Walmart," 139
Bing, Xu, *Book from the Ground,* 15
Black, Alethea, "You, On a Good Day," 35
Bode, Christoph, 119n17
Bollywood films, 166
book, reconfiguration of physical, 143–45
Booth, Alison, 166
Bordwell, David, 131–32, 159
Bordwell, David and Kristin Thompson, 17–18
Borges, Jorge Luis, "The Garden of Forking Paths," 104; "The Secret Miracle," 111; "Tlön, Uqbar, Orbis Tertius," 92
Bouilly, Jenny, "The Body," 139
Boyle, T. Coraghessan, "The Extinction Tales," 30
Bradbury, Malcolm, "Composition," 130, 131, 159
Brecht, Bertolt, *Der gute Mensch von Sezuan,* 162
Bredehoft, Thomas, A, 142
Brooke-Rose, Christine, *Amalgamemnon,* 117–18
Brooks, Peter, 6–7, 47, 60–62, 78, 81, 103–3, 128, 130, 150–51
Brown, Marshall, 88n2
Buckton, Oliver, 152
Burgess, Anthony, *Earthly Powers,* 101
Burton, Stacy, 51
Butor, Michel, *Mobile,* 92; *Votre Faust,* 145
Byron, George Gordon, Lord, 117; *Cain,* 112

Calderón de la Barca, Pedro, *El gran teatro del mundo,* 111
Calvino, Italo, 153; *If on a winter's night a traveler,* 29, 39, 57; "t zero," 115

Camus, Albert, *L'Etranger,* 37
Carpentier, Alejo, *Concierto barroco,* 110; *El siglo de las luces,* 90n4; "Viaje a la semilla," 105
Carrard, Philippe, 35, 57, 127
Carroll, Noël, 18, 156
Carter, Angela, *Nights at the Circus,* 109; *The Passion of New Eve,* 105
Castillo, Ana, *The Mixquiahuala Letters,* 44, 130, 147, 159
causality, inverted, 106, 118
Cervantes, Miguel de, *Don Quixote,* 63, 140
Cesaire, Aimé, *Une Têmpete,* 156–57
Chanson de Roland, 87
Chatman, Seymour, 47, 61–62, 106–7, 113, 135
Chatterjee, Bankim Chandra, *Anandamath,* 167
Chaudhuri, Amit, *Afternoon Raag,* 88
Chekhov, Anton, 79, 80; "The Harmfulness of Tobacco," 137
Chiang, Ted, "The Story of Your Life," 118–19
chronicle, 33
Churchill, Caryl, *Cloud Nine,* 111, 162; "Heart's Desire," 93
Cibber, Colley, *Love's Last Shift,* 152–53
Cixous, Hélène, *Partie,* 142
Coetzee, J. M., *Dairy of a Bad Year,* 140; *Waiting for the Barbarians,* 117
Cohn, Dorrit, 18, 100, 117
Coleridge, Samuel Taylor, 63
Conrad, Joseph, 79; "Because of the Dollars," 165; "Freya of the Seven Isles," 165; *Lord Jim,* 79; "Malay trilogy," 58; *Nostromo,* 44, 49–50, 51, 156; *Victory,* 153
Coover, Robert, "The Babysitter," 20, 97, 130, 131, 163; "Heart Suite," 146
Corneille, Pierre, 115
Corngold, Stanley, 91
Cortázar, Julio, *Hopscotch,* 104, 147
Crace, Jim, *Being Dead,* 108, 136
Cross, Amanda. *See* Heilbrun, Caroline
Crowley, Mart, *The Boys in the Band,* 166–67

Cuddy-Keane, Melba, 42, 124, 156
Culler, Jonathan, 129
Cusk, Rachel, 62–63

Danielewski, Mark Z., *The Familiar*, 116; *Only Revolutions*, 144
Dannenberg, Hilary, 7, 60n1, 81n10, 121, 129n3, 130, 159
Dante Alighieri, *Purgatorio*, 91
Davenport, Guy, "The Haile Selassie Funeral Train," 101
Del Lungo, Andrea, 42–43
DelConte, Matt, 108
DeLillo, Don, *Cosmopolis*, 118; *White Noise*, 81
denarration, 56, 73, 132–33
Dick, Philip K., "A Little Something for Us Tempunauts," 105; *The Man in the High Castle*, 101
Dickens, Charles, *Bleak House*, 65–66; "A Christmas Carol," 102; *Great Expectations*, 151
Dickey, George, 27
DiMaggio, Paul, 172
disnarration (Prince), 34–35
Dixon, Stephen, *Phone Rings*, 93–94
Doubrovsky, Serge, *Le Livre brisé*, 157
Douglas, Mary, 87
Dryden, John, 65, 150
Dubois, Jean-Paul, *Vie Française*, 100
DuPlessis, Rachel Blau, 166

Egan, Jennifer, "Black Box," 15; *A Visit from the Goon Squad*, 29, 63, 138
Eggers, Dave, *A Heartbreaking Work of Staggering Genius*, 140–41
Elam, Diane, 103
Eliot, George, *Daniel Deronda*, 66; *Middlemarch*, 66
Eliot, T. S., 68
Ellmann, Richard, 96
endings, 6, 105, 149–68; absent, 156–58; aesthetic of, 163–64; antimimetic, 158–62;

ethics and ideology of, 164–67; fixed, 149–53; loose, 154–56
Ermarth, Elizabeth Deeds, 99
ethics, narrative, 164–65
Euripides, 57, 70; *Orestes*, 59
events, eventfulness, 33–34

Faas, Ekbert, 40
fabula, 44–48, 100, 103–12, 126–33, 145–47; contradictory, 73–77, 93–94, 108–10, 130, 163; linear, 133–35; antichronological, 135
Fauconnier, Gilles and Mark Turner, 172
Faulkner, William, *Sartoris*, 52; *The Sound and the Fury*, 51; *The Wild Palms*, 30
Federman, Raymond, *Double or Nothing*, 38
Felber, Lynette, 116
feminism and feminist narrative theory, 6, 166
Fernandez, Macedonio, *The Museum of Eterna's Novel*, 39
Fielding, Henry, *Tom Jones*, 63, 120
Figgis, Mike, *Timecode*, 140
Fiore, Robert, 62
Fisher, Caitlin, *These Waves of Girls*, 142
Flaubert, Gustave, *L'Education sentimentale*, 127
Fludernik, Monika, 15–16, 86, 128–29
Foer, Jonathan Safran, *Extremely Loud and Incredibly Close*, 107–8; *Tree of Codes*, 143
Ford, Ford Madox, 17
Forster, E. M., 61–62, 80, 86, 151–52, 164
Forster, Marc, *Stranger than Fiction*, 161
Fournel, Paul and Jean-Pierre Énard, *The Theater Tree*, 145
Fowles, John, *The French Lieutenant's Woman*, 25, 109, 131, 158
Freytag, Gustav, 78
Frow, John, 53
Fuentes, Carlos, *La Muerta de Artemio Cruz*, 118

Gallagher, Catherine, 116

Garcha, Amanpal, 33
García Landa, José Angel, 18
Garcia Marquez, Gabriel, *Cien años de soledad*, 160
Garrett, Peter, 66
Gay, John, *The Beggar's Opera*, 161
Genette, Gérard, 4, 16, 25, 28, 49, 52, 99–100, 103, 113, 117, 119, 128, 139, 170
Geronimo, 46
Gibbons, Alison, 145
Gide, André, 153; *The Counterfeiters*, 57; *La Symphonie pastorale (The Pastoral Symphony)*, 88
Gioia, Ted, 64
Godard, Jean-Luc, 3
Goethe, Johann Wolfgang von, *Faust*, 40; "Novelle," 89
Gogol, Nikolai, *Dead Souls*, 91
Goodhart, Sandor, 45n4
Goodman, Nelson, 129n2
Gordimer, Nadine, *The Late Bourgeois World*, 157
Gray, Alasdair, *Lanark*, 39, 52, 143
Groff, Lauren, *Fates and Furies*, 64
Grossman, Richard, *Breeze Avenue*, 116
Guo, Xiaolu, *A Concise Chinese-English Dictionary for Lovers*, 138

Handler, Daniel, *Watch Your Mouth*, 39
Hansen, Per Krogh, 135
Hardy, Thomas, *The Mayor of Casterbridge*, 101; *The Return of the Native*, 50–51
Hawthorn, Jeremy, 58
Hawthorne, Nathaniel, *The Scarlet Letter*, 51
Hayles, N. Katherine, 143
Hays Commission, 166
Hazzard, Shirley, *The Transit of Venus*, 64
Heilbrun, Caroline, 49
Heinze, Rüdiger, 118
Heise, Ursula, 109
Hejinian, Lyn, 95

Henry, O., "Roads of Destiny," 159
Herman, David, 32, 118, 119
Herman, Luc and Bart Vervaeck, 4, 133
Higdon, David Leon, 125n21
Hitchcock, Alfred, *Suspicion*, 165
Hogan, Patrick Colm, 7, 57, 150
Homer, 71; *Iliad*, 40; *Odyssey*, 55, 62, 85
Horace, 39–40
Horn, Richard, *Encyclopedia*, 141
Horváth, Ödön von, *Figaro läßt sich scheiden*, 152
Howard, Elizabeth, *The Long View*, 135
Hühn, Peter, 34
Hyder, Qurratulain, *River of Fire*, 31
hyperfiction, 44, 50, 130, 142, 145, 157, 159, 168
Hyvärinen, Matti, 19n8

Ibsen, *A Doll's House*, 165
ideological aspects of narrative, 6, 36, 37, 85, 96, 160, 164–67
institutional theory of art, 27

Jackson, Shelley, *Ineradicable Stain*, 145
Jahn, Manfred, 14
James, Henry, 57, 151, 153, 158; *The Ambassadors*, 41, 44, 86
Jensen, Ejner, 62, 154
Johnson, B. S., *Albert Angelo*, 143; "Broad Thoughts from Home," 159; *The Unfortunates*, 141
Johnson, James Weldon, *Autobiography of an Ex-Colored Man*, 49
Johnson, Samuel, 79; *Rasselas*, 85
Jones, Spike and Charlie Kaufman, *Adaptation*, 46
Jonson, Ben, 3, 66, 68; *The Alchemist*, 63; "A Vision of Delight," 111n10; *Volpone*, 91
Josipovici, Gabriel, "Mobius the Stripper," 104
Joyce, James, "The Dead," 44–47, 66–68, 86–87; *Dubliners*, 30; *Finnegans Wake*, 48, 96, 104; *Portrait of the Artist as a Young Man*, 152; *Ulysses*, 49, 52, 55, 83–96, 152

Joyce, Michael, *afternoon: a story*, 44, 157

Kafalenos, Emma, 90n4, 130
Kafka, Franz, 70, 91; "A Little Woman," 33; "A Country Doctor," 70
Kalidasa, *Shakuntala*, 40
Kavan, Anna, *Ice*, 93
Kaymer, Tom, 102
Keen, Suzanne, 155
Kellman, Stephen, 41–42
Kenner, Hugh, 85
Kieślowski, Krzysztof, *Blind Chance*, 131–32
Killeen, Terrence, 84
Konstantinou, Lee, 15
Kraus, Nicole, *The History of Love*, 66
Kundera, Milan, *Slowness*, 110
Kurosawa, Akira, *Rashomon*, 103

Laccetti, Jessica, 44
Laclos, Pierre Choderlos de, *Les Liaisons dangereuses*, 152
Lambrou, Marina, 76
Langbauer, Laurie, 116
LaSalle, Peter, "Where We Last Saw Time," 110
Lawrence, D. H., "The Fox," 166
Lazarillo de Tormes, 62
Leach, Mark, *Marienbad My Love*, 116
Leander, Niels Buch, 42
Lee, Hermione, 38, 52
Leitch, Thomas B., 15
Lessing, Gotthold Ephraim, 163
Letzler, David, 116
Levine, Caroline, 7
Levithan, David, *The Lover's Dictionary*, 138
Lispector, Clarice, "The Fifth Story," 31
Lodge, David, *Changing Places*, 157
Loki Principle, 3–4, 32–33, 51, 69–70, 103–4, 173
Longus, *Daphnis and Chloe*, 89

Lucian, *A True Story*, 71
Ludlum, Charles, *The Grand Tarot*, 141–42

Mahabharata, 39
Mann, Heinrich, "Drei-Minuten-Roman," 114
Mann, Thomas, *Der Tod in Venedig*, 88
Manon, Hugh S., 157
Mansfield, Katherine, "Bliss," 64
Markson, David, *This is Not a Novel*, 25–29
Marlowe, Christopher, *Doctor Faustus*, 114
Martin, Timothy, 84
Martin, Wallace, 17
Matz, Jesse, 119n19
McEwan, Ian, *The Child in Time*, 111
McHale, Brian, 39, 68, 80–81, 104, 160
McInerney, Jay, *Bright Lights, Big City*, 81
Melville, Herman, *Moby Dick*, 32
Mendilow, A. A., 125n21
methodology, 8–9
Michener, James A., *Hawaii*, 46
Miller, D. A., 34, 60, 151, 153
Miller, J. Hillis, 7, 42, 57, 82, 152
Miller, Nancy K., 166
Milton, John, *Paradise Lost*, 41, 74
mimetic bias of narrative theory, 4, 128, 170
mimetic narrative and strategies, 2–5
Mink, Louis, O., 167
Mitchell, David, *Cloud Atlas*, 29, 136
modernism and modernist poetics, 5, 31, 35–36, 47, 66–69, 79–80, 82, 103, 120, 128, 155–56, 168
Molière [Jean-Baptiste Poquelin, known as], *Tartuffe*, 167
Moody, Rick, "The Grid," 118; "Primary Sources," 138
Moore, Alan and Dave Higgins, *Watchman*, 118n15
Moore, Lorrie, "How," 108, 118n16, 130
Morhange, Jean-Louis, 43n3
Morrison, Toni, *Jazz*, 88

Mortimer, Armine Kotin, 64, 152, 157

Müller, Günther, 102

Nabokov, 51, 91; *Ada*, 39; "The Circle," 48, 104, 158; *The Gift*, 104; *Lolita*, 115, 167; *Look at the Harlequins!*, 49; *Pale Fire*, 137, 142

narrative, definition of, 13–29; as act of narration, 14–15; causal definition, 17–19, 25, 28–29, 96; literary narrative, 21; Genette's definition, 16, 25, 28; prototype account of, 19–21; reception theory of, 15–16, 25, 28; rhetorical theory of, 17–18, 25, 28; temporal definition of, 17–18, 25, 28

narrative, single vs. multiple, 29–31

narrative vs. nonnarrative texts, 32–33

Nelles, William, 15–16

Nelson, Roy J., 62

Nietzsche, Friedrich, 164

Nolan, Christopher, *Memento*, 135–36

non-events, 34

non-plot-based narrative progressions, 83–98; aesthetic ordering, 86–89; alphabetical ordering, 92; event generation, 89–92; rhetorical ordering, 85–86; serial ordering, 93–94

Nuttall, A. D., 42

Oates, Joyce Carol, "The Turn of the Screw," 140

O'Brien, Flann, *At Swim-Two-Birds*, 38–39

O'Donnell, Thomas, 90

Oedipus story, 57–58, 152

Ondaatje, Michael, *Devisadero*, 135

Onega, Susan, 18

O'Neill, Patrick, 128

Orton, Joe, *What the Butler Saw*, 158

Oz, Amos, 46

Pagis, Dan, 107

Paley, Grace, "A Conversation with My Father," 172

Pavić, Milorad, *Dictionary of the Khazars*, 137; *The Inner Side of the Wind*, 144; *Landscape Painted with Tea*, 141

Peake, C. H., 85–86

Perkins, Maxwell, 52

Peterson, R. G., 88n2

Pettersson, Bo, 68–69

Pfall, Courtney, A., 146n8

Pfister, Manfred, 72

Phelan, James, 6–7, 17–18, 22, 25, 28, 32, 41, 42–43, 47, 114, 117, 151, 155–56, 164n11

Phelan, James and Peter Rabinowitz, 78

Phillips, Caryl, *Crossing the River*, 30

Pinget, Robert, *Passacaille*, 109–10

Pinter, Harold, *The Basement*, 86, 164; *Betrayal*, 105, 154; *The Collection*, 140

plot, 6–7, 59–78, 81–82; carnivalesque, 70–73; classic account of, 7–8, 63–64; contradictory, 73–77; fabula, contradictory; double and multiple, 65–66; episodic, 62–63; non-probabilistic kinds of, 69–77; oneiric, 70. *See also* non-plot-based narrative progressions

portrait, literary, 33

postmodernism, 1–2, 5, 54, 69, 80–82, 99–103, 109, 160–61

Prince, Gerald, 17, 25, 34–35, 46, 150

Propp, Vladimir, 40

Prose, Francine, 73–74

Proust, Marcel, *À la recherche du temps perdu*, 117, 128, 154

Punday, Daniel, 120–21

Pynchon, Thomas, *The Crying of Lot 49*, 157

quasi-narrative texts, 21–29

Queneau, Raymond, *Le Chiendent*, 104, 114; "A Story as You Like It," 145

Rabinowitz, Peter, 112, 158, 164

Rader, Ralph, 83n1

Ramis, Harold, *Groundhog Day*, 105

reader, reading, 64, 67–76, 116, 120–21, 122, 124, 144, 155

realism. *See* mimetic narrative

Reed, Ishmael, *Flight to Canada*, 110; *Mumbo Jumbo*, 51

Reising, Russell, 167

Ricardou, Jean, 90, 97; *La Prise de Constantinople*, 91

Richardson, Brian, works on narrative theory, x–xi

Richardson, Dorothy, 80; *Pilgrimage*, 154

Richter, David, 156

Ricoeur, Paul, 60, 99, 102n3, 104n5

Rimmon-Kenan, Shlomith, 17, 18–19, 133, 140

ring structures, 87, 136

Robbe-Grillet, Alain, 33, 93, 103; "La Chambre secrète, 23–24, 173; *Dans le labyrinthe*, 89–90, 132–33; *La Jalousie*, 93, 97, 109, 130; *La Maison de rendez-vous*, 109, 129, 130; *Project pour une revolution en New York (Project for a Revolution in New York)*, 90; *Topologie d'une cité fantôme*, 109n9

Robinson, Mark C., 22

Rohy, Valerie, 49

Romagnolo, Catherine, 43, 47

Ronen, Ruth, 33, 109, 129

Rossholm, Göran, 18

Roth, Joseph, *Radetzkymarsch*, 63

Rushdie, Salman, 39; *Midnight's Children*, 91–92, 101, 102, 112, 113–14; *Two Years, Eight Months, and Twenty-Eight Nights*, 105

Ryan, Marie-Laure, 15n1, 19–20, 33, 74–75, 78, 79, 80, 121, 163–64

Ryding, William W., 87

Sacks, Sheldon, 85

Said, Edward, 41

Saporta, Marc, *Composition No. 1*, 44, 146

Sartre, Jean-Paul, *La Nausée*, 58

Sayles, John, *Limbo*

Schmid, Wolf, 19n6, 19n8, 34, 78

Schwarz, Daniel, 153

See, Sam, 120

Segal, Eyal, 151n2

Shakespeare, William, 62, 78; *Cymbeline*, 158; *Hamlet*, 115; *Henry IV, Part 1*, 66; *King Lear*, 29; *Macbeth*, 115; *Measure for Measure*, 158; *A Midsummer Night's Dream*, 111, 115, 130, 161; *Much Ado about Nothing*, 63; *Othello*, 153n4; *A Winter's Tale*, 3–4

Shaogong, Hao, *A Dictionary of Maqiao*, 137

Shapiro, Elena Mauli, *13, rue Thérèse*, 144–45

Shields, Carol, *Happenstance*, 143

Shen, Dan, 64n2

Sherzer, Dina, 92, 93, 95

Shields, David, "Life Story," 24–25

Shklovsky, Viktor, 82, 87, 99, 124

Simon, Claude, *Les Corps conducteurs*, 110; *Triptych*, 90n4

Singal, R. L., 60

sjužet. *See* syuzhet

sketch, 33

Smith, Ali, *How to Be Both*, 19, 30, 66, 144

Smith, Barbara Herrnstein, 129n2, 155

Sommer, Roy, 92

Sophocles, *Oedipus Rex*, 57, 63

Sopranos, The, 157

Spenser, Edmund, *The Faerie Queen*, 111

Stein, Gertrude, "What Happened: A Play," 22

Stein, Nancy and Margaret Policastro, 40

Stendhal, *La Chartreuse de Parme*, 153

Sternberg, Meir, 15–16, 40–41, 44, 61, 120, 121, 128

Sterne, Laurence, *Tristram Shandy*, 37–38, 41, 51, 82, 91, 102, 127–28, 140

Stevenson, Robert Louis, 152

Stoppard, Tom, 136, *Artist Descending a Staircase*, 87, 136, 154; *Travesties*, 158

story. *See* fabula

story grammar, 5–6

Strindberg, August, *Ghost Sonata*, 88

structuralism, 5–6, 40, 60, 150; mimetic presuppositions of, 4

Sue, Eugène, 102–3

Sutherland, John, 49

syuzhet, 43–44, 100, 127–29, 133–47; multiple, 145–47; unusual, 136–39; variable, 139–47

Tammi, Pekka, 15–16, 21
tellability, 78–81
Terence, *Adelphi*, 65; *Andria*, 115
Thomas, D. H., *The White Hotel*, 118
time, narrative, 99–125; antimimetic, 103–16; duration, 113–16, 122; frequency and pseudofrequency, 103, 122; future tense narratives, 117–19; historical, 100–101, 121–22; length, 116; of reception, 102–3, 123; of writing, 102; order, 103–12, 122–23; pace, 120–21, 124; present tense narratives, 117
Todorov, Tzvetan, 33, 40, 84, 150
Toker, Leona, 104n6, 165
Tolstoy, Leo, *Anna Karenina*, 86, 164; *War and Peace*, 100
Tomashevsky, Boris, 18, 47
Torgovnick, Marianna, 149, 168
Toscana, David, *El Ultimo lector*, 160–61, 163
Tsur, Reuven, 172
Tykwer, Tom, *Lola Rennt*, 97, 131–32
Tyrkkö, Jukka, 140

Unamuno, Miguel de, *Niebla*, 160
unnarrated events, 34–36
unnatural narrative. *See* antimimetic narrative and strategies
Updike, John, "Problems," 137

Valéry, Paul, 31
Vanbrugh, John, *The Relapse*, 152–53
Vishakadhatta, *Rakshasa's Ring*, 50
Vogel, Paula, *Hot 'n' Throbbing*, 165

Wallace, David Foster, "Wiggle Room," 115
Walsh, Richard, 128
Ward, Jesmyn, *Salvage the Bones*, 101
Ware, Chris, *Building Stories*, 145; *Jimmy Corrigan, The Smartest Kid on Earth*, 142
Warhol, Robyn, 35–36, 116, 132, 154–55
Warren, Robert Penn, *All the King's Men*, 153
Welles, Orson, *Big Brass Ring*, 153
Wells, H. G., *The Time Machine*, 112
Whalen, Tim, 132
White, Hayden, 33
Whitman, Samantha, *Ditching Mr. Darcy*, 153
Wilde, Oscar, *The Importance of Being Earnest*, 71, 158, 165; *The Picture of Dorian Gray*, 53
Wilson, R. Rawdon, 111
Winnett, Susan, 78, 151
Winterson, Jeanette, "The Poetics of Sex," 167
Wolfe, Thomas, 52
Wolff, Tobias, "Bullet in the Brain," 114
Woolf, Virginia, 52, 80, 155, 172; *Between the Acts*, 156; "The Mark on the Wall," 100; *Mrs. Dalloway*, 37, 38, 66; *Night and Day*, 53; *Orlando*, 110–11, 114; *To the Lighthouse*, 38, 121–24, 155
Wordsworth, William, *The Prelude*, 41

Xue, Can, "The Lure of the Sea," 70

Yacobi, Tamar, 107
Yoshimoto, Banana, "Newlywed," 144

THEORY AND INTERPRETATION OF NARRATIVE
JAMES PHELAN, PETER J. RABINOWITZ, AND KATRA BYRAM, SERIES EDITORS

Because the series editors believe that the most significant work in narrative studies today contributes both to our knowledge of specific narratives and to our understanding of narrative in general, studies in the series typically offer interpretations of individual narratives and address significant theoretical issues underlying those interpretations. The series does not privilege one critical perspective but is open to work from any strong theoretical position.

A Poetics of Plot for the Twenty-First Century: Theorizing Unruly Narratives by Brian Richardson

Playing at Narratology: Digital Media as Narrative Theory by Daniel Punday

Making Conversation in Modernist Fiction by Elizabeth Alsop

Narratology and Ideology: Negotiating Context, Form, and Theory in Postcolonial Narratives edited by Divya Dwivedi, Henrik Skov Nielsen, and Richard Walsh

Novelization: From Film to Novel by Jan Baetens

Reading Conrad by J. Hillis Miller, edited by John G. Peters and Jakob Lothe

Narrative, Race, and Ethnicity in the United States edited by James J. Donahue, Jennifer Ann Ho, and Shaun Morgan

Somebody Telling Somebody Else: A Rhetorical Poetics of Narrative by James Phelan

Media of Serial Narrative edited by Frank Kelleter

Suture and Narrative: Deep Intersubjectivity in Fiction and Film by George Butte

The Writer in the Well: On Misreading and Rewriting Literature by Gary Weissman

Narrating Space / Spatializing Narrative: Where Narrative Theory and Geography Meet by Marie-Laure Ryan, Kenneth Foote, and Maoz Azaryahu

Narrative Sequence in Contemporary Narratology edited by Raphaël Baroni and Françoise Revaz

The Submerged Plot and the Mother's Pleasure from Jane Austen to Arundhati Roy by Kelly A. Marsh

Narrative Theory Unbound: Queer and Feminist Interventions edited by Robyn Warhol and Susan S. Lanser

Unnatural Narrative: Theory, History, and Practice by Brian Richardson

Ethics and the Dynamic Observer Narrator: Reckoning with Past and Present in German Literature by Katra A. Byram

Narrative Paths: African Travel in Modern Fiction and Nonfiction by Kai Mikkonen

The Reader as Peeping Tom: Nonreciprocal Gazing in Narrative Fiction and Film by Jeremy Hawthorn

Thomas Hardy's Brains: Psychology, Neurology, and Hardy's Imagination by Suzanne Keen

The Return of the Omniscient Narrator: Authorship and Authority in Twenty-First Century Fiction by Paul Dawson

Feminist Narrative Ethics: Tacit Persuasion in Modernist Form by Katherine Saunders Nash

Real Mysteries: Narrative and the Unknowable by H. Porter Abbott

A Poetics of Unnatural Narrative edited by Jan Alber, Henrik Skov Nielsen, and Brian Richardson

Narrative Discourse: Authors and Narrators in Literature, Film, and Art by Patrick Colm Hogan

An Aesthetics of Narrative Performance: Transnational Theater, Literature, and Film in Contemporary Germany by Claudia Breger

Literary Identification from Charlotte Brontë to Tsitsi Dangarembga by Laura Green

Narrative Theory: Core Concepts and Critical Debates by David Herman, James Phelan and Peter J. Rabinowitz, Brian Richardson, and Robyn Warhol

After Testimony: The Ethics and Aesthetics of Holocaust Narrative for the Future edited by Jakob Lothe, Susan Rubin Suleiman, and James Phelan

The Vitality of Allegory: Figural Narrative in Modern and Contemporary Fiction by Gary Johnson

Narrative Middles: Navigating the Nineteenth-Century British Novel edited by Caroline Levine and Mario Ortiz-Robles

Fact, Fiction, and Form: Selected Essays by Ralph W. Rader, edited by James Phelan and David H. Richter.

The Real, the True, and the Told: Postmodern Historical Narrative and the Ethics of Representation by Eric L. Berlatsky

Franz Kafka: Narration, Rhetoric, and Reading edited by Jakob Lothe, Beatrice Sandberg, and Ronald Speirs

Social Minds in the Novel by Alan Palmer

Narrative Structures and the Language of the Self by Matthew Clark

Imagining Minds: The Neuro-Aesthetics of Austen, Eliot, and Hardy by Kay Young

Postclassical Narratology: Approaches and Analyses edited by Jan Alber and Monika Fludernik

Techniques for Living: Fiction and Theory in the Work of Christine Brooke-Rose by Karen R. Lawrence

Towards the Ethics of Form in Fiction: Narratives of Cultural Remission by Leona Toker

Tabloid, Inc.: Crimes, Newspapers, Narratives by V. Penelope Pelizzon and Nancy M. West

Narrative Means, Lyric Ends: Temporality in the Nineteenth-Century British Long Poem by Monique R. Morgan

Understanding Nationalism: On Narrative, Cognitive Science, and Identity by Patrick Colm Hogan

Joseph Conrad: Voice, Sequence, History, Genre edited by Jakob Lothe, Jeremy Hawthorn, James Phelan

The Rhetoric of Fictionality: Narrative Theory and the Idea of Fiction by Richard Walsh

Experiencing Fiction: Judgments, Progressions, and the Rhetorical Theory of Narrative by James Phelan

Unnatural Voices: Extreme Narration in Modern and Contemporary Fiction by Brian Richardson

Narrative Causalities by Emma Kafalenos

Why We Read Fiction: Theory of Mind and the Novel by Lisa Zunshine

I Know That You Know That I Know: Narrating Subjects from Moll Flanders *to* Marnie by George Butte

Bloodscripts: Writing the Violent Subject by Elana Gomel

Surprised by Shame: Dostoevsky's Liars and Narrative Exposure by Deborah A. Martinsen

Having a Good Cry: Effeminate Feelings and Pop-Culture Forms by Robyn R. Warhol

Politics, Persuasion, and Pragmatism: A Rhetoric of Feminist Utopian Fiction by Ellen Peel

Telling Tales: Gender and Narrative Form in Victorian Literature and Culture by Elizabeth Langland

Narrative Dynamics: Essays on Time, Plot, Closure, and Frames edited by Brian Richardson

Breaking the Frame: Metalepsis and the Construction of the Subject by Debra Malina

Invisible Author: Last Essays by Christine Brooke-Rose

Ordinary Pleasures: Couples, Conversation, and Comedy by Kay Young

Narratologies: New Perspectives on Narrative Analysis edited by David Herman

Before Reading: Narrative Conventions and the Politics of Interpretation by Peter J. Rabinowitz

Matters of Fact: Reading Nonfiction over the Edge by Daniel W. Lehman

The Progress of Romance: Literary Historiography and the Gothic Novel by David H. Richter

A Glance Beyond Doubt: Narration, Representation, Subjectivity by Shlomith Rimmon-Kenan

Narrative as Rhetoric: Technique, Audiences, Ethics, Ideology by James Phelan

Misreading Jane Eyre: *A Postformalist Paradigm* by Jerome Beaty

Psychological Politics of the American Dream: The Commodification of Subjectivity in Twentieth-Century American Literature by Lois Tyson

Understanding Narrative edited by James Phelan and Peter J. Rabinowitz

Framing Anna Karenina: Tolstoy, the Woman Question, and the Victorian Novel by Amy Mandelker

Gendered Interventions: Narrative Discourse in the Victorian Novel by Robyn R. Warhol

Reading People, Reading Plots: Character, Progression, and the Interpretation of Narrative by James Phelan

www.ingramcontent.com/pod-product-compliance
Lightning Source LLC
Chambersburg PA
CBHW020332240426
43665CB00043B/442